Brief Histories of Almost Anything

This book was edited by Chris Brazier, and the responsibility for any updating of the histories that was required rests with him. But the book was based on an original idea by former *New Internationalist* co-editor Richard Swift, who contributed nine of the histories featured here.

NI co-editors past and present who wrote histories contained here are (in descending order of the number of contributions): David Ransom, Richard Swift, Chris Brazier, Vanessa Baird, Dinyar Godrej, Nikki van der Gaag, Anouk Ride, Sue Shaw, Jess Worth, Wayne Ellwood, Adam Ma'anit, Chris Richards, Troth Wells, Katharine Ainger and Peter Stalker. The work of two guests is also featured: Ziauddin Sardar on Islam and Rana Mitter on China.

Illustrations inside this book
Chocolate:	Ato de Graft-Johnson
Apple:	Clive Offley
Ethics:	Anne Cakebread
Development:	Polyp
Feminism:	Angela Martin
Architecture:	Hector Cattolica
Islam:	Zafar Malik
Work:	Steve Weston
Cities:	Michael Terry
Debt:	Hector Cattolica
Food:	Clive Offley
Money:	Hector Cattolica
Health:	Hector Cattolica
Green Ideas:	Jeff Douwes
Landmines:	Eric Jones
Taxation:	Clive Offley
Slavery:	Alan Hughes
Amazon:	Clive Offley
Bretton Woods:	Gail Geltner

Brief *of Almost* Histories *Anything* ^

50 savvy slices of our global past

Edited by
Chris Brazier

New Internationalist

Brief Histories of Almost Anything
First published in 2008 by
New Internationalist™ Publications Ltd
55 Rectory Road
Oxford OX4 1BW, UK
www.newint.org
New Internationalist is a registered trade mark.

Front cover illustration by Joanna Szachowska/Three in a Box

© New Internationalist 2008

Designed by Andrew Kokotka

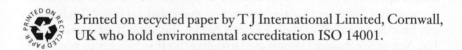 Printed on recycled paper by T J International Limited, Cornwall, UK who hold environmental accreditation ISO 14001.

British Library Cataloguing-in-Publication Data.
A catalogue for this book is available from the British Library.

Library of Congress Cataloguing-in-Publication Data.
A catalogue for this book is available from the Library of Congress.

ISBN 978-1-906523-00-8

Foreword

*B*rief Histories of Almost Anything. You'll note that we stopped short of claiming that you could find in here 'Histories of Almost Everything' – it would have been a good marketing pitch but there would have been more than a touch of hubris about it. In a sense, though, the 50 histories contained in this book should cover almost everything of note, given that they are developed and updated from more than a decade's worth of material created by a magazine that certainly aims to cover all the issues that matter most in the world. Not, perhaps, the history of fashion, or of *haute cuisine* – though you will find in here the story of Blue Jeans, together with histories of Chocolate, Bananas and the Apple.

As this suggests, these histories are an eclectic bunch, ranging from Cities: a History of Ideas to Migration: a Journey through Time, from Key Moments of Islamic Civilization to The Story of Money, from Pan-Africanism to Reproduction, Contraception and Control. But all of them have an 'alternative' tilt that reflects the *New Internationalist* magazine's general skepticism about the way the world currently works.

They are also concise – designed to be easily digestible, each of them is broken up into even shorter chunks with snappy subtitles, a world away from the academic volumes that their authors – many and various **NI** editors – will have had to read in their research before distilling their ideas down. The *New Internationalist* always used to market itself as 'quicker to read than a book', as a kind of instant primer to global issues, and here, in your hand, is the book that might save you the trouble of reading 50 other books.

The book is replete with challenging ideas. It contains, for example, probably the most concise summary of the history of ethical philosophy that has ever appeared in print. It has an account of how political thinking about development (and on the Left in general) has changed over the last four decades, using the *New Internationalist* magazine as a window on the world. It has introductions to the key movements in architecture and two sections on history itself that show how it is often misinterpreted or even hijacked for political ends.

There are many common strands interweaving through the patchwork made up by these histories. It is somewhat disturbing, for example, to note how often we have been required to return to the subject of slavery, with something of the horrified fascination that the Nazi Holocaust has consistently provoked in the collective mind of the late 20th and early 21st centuries – it crops up unavoidably in the histories of sugar and migration, of Africa and Latin America, as well as in its own dedicated chapter.

Brief Histories... is also global in its scope. There is a section offering a spread of regional histories, but in general each of the individual histories is as internationalist as the magazine that spawned them. This is something we are all going to have get used to – seeing the world as a whole, for which we all have responsibility. We are all too easily locked off in our national, cultural boxes – with, these days, even digital TV channels dedicated to particular interests so that we can engage even less with a diverse, difficult reality – yet the world is now interconnected in all kinds of ways that would not have been thought possible even a single generation ago.

We may deplore the way globalization is exporting Western consumerist culture to every corner of the world but the interconnectedness affords all kinds of opportunities to resistance movements, too. There is a fascination in this book with the ways in which people have fought back against oppression through the ages, setting examples that continue to inspire us today. There is a whole section dedicated to various histories of resistance, including a panoply of heroes who pursued their goals through nonviolence. If human history is frustrating it is because of its apparent inability to avoid repeating its mistakes; here the motivation is rather different, to seek to learn from past attempts at resistance so as to discover how to proceed in challenging injustice in the present and the future. Thus if we understand how and why child labor was banished from Western industrial societies generations ago we might grasp how best to eliminate it in the Majority World today. And is there any way of emulating the campaign to defuse the demon of landmines, which mushroomed incredibly swiftly from people's movement to global convention?

One of the things I found most extraordinary about researching the history of the 20th century – both for the magazine and for the subsequent book *The No-Nonsense Guide to World History* – was the readiness with which establishment commentators elided and ignored the contributions of protest movements in shaping the world we now accept as our own, from the women campaigning so forlornly for the vote in 1900 to the Africans meeting in the same year to advance the then-ludicrous idea that they might govern themselves. In the kinds of histories of resistance outlined here – from popular defiance of corporate power to the irresistible rise of Green awareness – are doubtless to be found the ideas that will be accepted as self-evident pillars of civilization a century from now.

Chris Brazier

Contents

A bunch of fives

From big ideas to ridiculous wars – the 20th century in lists of five.

5 martyrs

Amilcar Cabral Inspirational revolutionary from Guinea-Bissau, assassinated just before independence in 1973.

Yitzhak Katzenelson Poet and friend of the Halutz Underground resistance to the Nazis in the Warsaw Ghetto, murdered in Auschwitz in 1944.

Rosa Luxemburg Socialist who led the abortive German Revolution and was murdered by paramilitaries in 1918.

Chico Mendes Union activist among Amazon indigenous people and rubber tappers, murdered by landed interests in 1988.

Fernando Pereira Photographer killed when French secret-service agents blew up the Greenpeace ship *Rainbow Warrior* in 1985.

5 unfulfilled national dreams

Kurdistan Occupied by Turkey, Iraq, Iran and Syria.
Tibet Occupied by China since 1950.
West Papua Occupied by Indonesia since 1963.
Palestine Occupied by Israel since 1948.
Western Sahara Occupied by Morocco since 1975.

5 fulfilled national dreams

Israel Created in 1948.
Vietnam Reunited after the US War in 1975.
Namibia Liberated from apartheid South Africa in 1990.
The Baltic states Estonia, Latvia and Lithuania, liberated from the Soviet Union in 1991.
Eritrea Liberated from Ethiopia in 1993.

5 resistance quotes

'The life of a single human being is worth a million times more than all the property of the richest man on earth.'
Ernesto 'Che' Guevara, Latin American revolutionary
'Washing one's hands of the conflict between the powerful and the powerless means to side with the powerful, not to be neutral.'
Paulo Freire, Brazilian educator
'When the white man came we had the land and they had the Bible. They taught us to pray with our eyes closed and when we opened them, they had the land and we had the Bible.'
Jomo Kenyatta, who led Kenya to independence
'There are very few jobs that actually require a penis or a vagina. All other jobs should be open to everybody.'
Florynce R Kennedy, US civil-rights activist
'It is better to die on your feet than live on your knees.'
Emiliano Zapata, Mexican revolutionary

5 nonviolent direct actions

Suffragette chainings Women campaigning for the vote in Edwardian Britain chained themselves to railings outside places of power.
The Salt March Gandhi's 380-kilometer mass march to the sea to make salt in protest at the salt monopoly of the British colonial government in India, 1930.
Mothers of the Disappeared In Argentina, Chile and then in Turkey, mothers of people murdered by repressive regimes demonstrated on the same day every week for years.
Peace marches All over the world in the 1980s, the sheer numbers of anti-nuclear demonstrators made a difference.
Greenpeace voyages From the Arctic to the Pacific, small boats have sailed into the teeth of the Dragon.

5 big ideas that did big damage

Fascism The first new political philosophy of the 20th century – and the worst.
Nuclear energy From Hiroshima to Chernobyl, it has a lot to answer for.
Mega-dams Still being built, despite all the environmental evidence.
Structural adjustment It may be simplistic, schoolchild economics, but that hasn't stopped Washington imposing it on most of the Majority World.
'Ethnic cleansing' Actually the most small-minded, savage idea, which has afflicted Armenians, Jews, Bosnians and Rwandans, to name but four.

5 big ideas whose day will come

Sustainability Green economics and new patterns of living.

Debt jubilee If only to look after its own long-term interest, the West must soon lift the debt noose from the necks of the poor.

A UN independent of the US There may ultimately be no UN otherwise.

Tobin Tax The tax on foreign-exchange transactions that would transform the global economy.

United States of Africa Common interests and self-defense.

5 dangerous corporations

Newscorp Rupert Murdoch's vehicle for world domination.

Nestlé Still guilty of pushing artificial babymilk to Majority World mothers after all these years.

Monsanto The cutting edge in genetic mutilation of food.

Philip Morris Its tobacco still causes disease but it is now spreading its tentacles into food.

Global Climate Coalition A club of transnationals which works to stall action on global warming; its board members include Chevron, Chrysler, Exxon, Ford, General Motors, Mobil and Texaco.

5 ridiculous wars

Boer War Where Churchill made his name and the concentration camp was born.

World War One Still the epitome of military futility.

Iran-Iraq An eight-year war over nothing that cost 500,000 lives.

Falklands/Malvinas Collision between Argentine dictatorship and the last writhings of the British Empire.

Football War The 1969 war between Honduras and El Salvador sparked by a World Cup soccer match between the two countries.

5 nominees for the Hitler/Stalin Tyranny Prize

King Leopold II of Belgium No paternalistic nonsense about a 'civilizing mission' here. Until 1908 the Congo was his personal province and playground whose people existed only to produce rubber.

General Augusto Pinochet Chile's dictator wrote the most brutal chapter in Latin America's recent history, breaking new ground in torture and right-wing economics.

Mobutu Sese Seko Unlucky Congo has two of its rulers as nominees. His ruthlessness a byword, Mobutu stole over $4,000 million in his 32 years in power.

Pol Pot (Saloth Sar) Unleashed a holocaust on the Cambodian people; 1.5 million died in his chilling attempt to design a new society without cities or education.

Idi Amin Dada The most notorious of Africa's dictators was no joke to the estimated 250,000 tortured and killed during his nine-year rule of Uganda.

5 classic resistance texts

The Second Sex Simone de Beauvoir
Open Veins of Latin America Eduardo Galeano
Pedagogy of the Oppressed Paulo Freire
The Wretched of the Earth Frantz Fanon
Monopoly Capital Paul Baran and Paul Sweezy

5 revolutions that raised then dashed Left hopes

Mexico 1911 'The Institutional Revolutionary Party' says it all.

Russia 1917 Stalinist Terror and State Arthritis.

China 1949 Mao stood up for equality but killed millions through his social experiments.

Cambodia 1975 It is little remembered now, but the Khmer Rouge was initially received with enthusiasm by the Western Left.

Ghana 1982 Jerry Rawlings claimed his coup was 'a revolution for social justice' but his regime turned into the IMF's pet.

5 environmental disasters

Chernobyl The explosion of the Soviet nuclear reactor in Ukraine in 1986 which made 10,000 square kilometers uninhabitable and gave at least 21,000 Western Europeans fatal cancers.

Bhopal The explosion in an Indian chemical plant of the US-based transnational Union Carbide in 1984; 2,500 died immediately while at least 50,000 suffered long-term damage.

The Aral Sea As much a polluted dustbowl as a sea now, thanks to the irrigation and pesticides of the Soviet cotton industry.

Western transport policy Or lack of one – 'they paved paradise and put up a parking lot'.

The god of economic growth Before which all but the Greenest few still bow down.

The Battle of the Banana

Corporate coups and the rise and fall of political regimes – all par for the course in the ongoing war to control the banana trade.

Business in bunches

In 1870 Captain Lorenzo Dow Baker landed the schooner *Telegraph* in Jamaica and saw that bananas were popular on local markets. He purchased 160 bunches for one shilling per stalk on Port Antonio docks; 11 days later he sold bunches for two dollars each in Jersey City, making a huge profit. The legendary bounty of the banana trade was established. Bananas were shipped to Boston and New Orleans from Cuba and the Dominican Republic as well as Jamaica. By 1898 some 16 million bunches were being imported into the US.

Uncrowned king

In 1899 the United Fruit Company (UFCO) was formed in Boston and began to develop its own plantations in Central America. In Costa Rica, Minor Keith did a deal with the Government to build – with great loss of life – a railway to the Atlantic coast and planted bananas beside the track. He married the daughter of the President and became known as the 'Uncrowned King of Central America'. UFCO's 'Great White Fleet' totaled 95 ships by 1930. Panama disease or wilting first destroyed banana farms in 1900, and continued to create major problems for UFCO's banana plantations thereafter.

Sam the Man

Samuel Zemurray – 'Sam the Banana Man' – went to Honduras in 1905, where he financed a coup that brought very favorable concessions for his developing banana business. He pioneered new plantation techniques, and in 1915 began production from large new landholdings in the Motagua Valley, on the disputed Honduras/Guatemala border. In 1930 United Fruit bought out Zemurray's holdings for $31.5 million; in 1933, as the largest shareholder, he became UFCO's Managing Director. By then the company owned plantations the size of Switzerland in Central America and the Caribbean.

Imperial unease

The British Government became worried about US influence in its Caribbean colonies. In 1901 it provided a large subsidy for the Elder Dempster shipping company to begin a refrigerated service to Jamaica. In 1913 the Fyffes company was created for the banana trade, but it ran into financial difficulties and was taken over – by United Fruit. The Imperial Economic Committee in London reported in 1926 that an 'organization under American control monopolizes the whole supply of bananas from Central America and Jamaica to the United Kingdom'. A strategy of providing financial assistance to associations of banana growers, who would supply the British market independently of UFCO, was implemented. By 1938 Jamaica produced 78 per cent of British imports.

War of the Worlds

The Second World War brought the banana trade to a halt – boats were requisitioned for the war effort and shipping was disrupted, causing great hardship in the region. In 1945 bananas returned again to Britain, shipped from Jamaica under the control of the Ministry of Food. The Moyne Commission published its pre-War findings on the dreadful conditions in Britain's West Indian colonies. It recommended financial support for small-scale banana production, particularly in the Windward Islands. On 6 December 1950 a ship arrived at Liverpool from Sierra Leone with a cargo of bananas of which 78,000 were too ripe; 3,000 dock workers were asked to eat all they could and got through 37,000. The British taste for bananas had survived the war.

Carve-up

In 1952 the British Government 'reprivatized' the banana industry. Imports paid for in US dollars – which, in bankrupt Britain, were extremely scarce – required a licence. In 1954 Geest, a company owned by Dutch brothers based in Britain, signed a 10-year contract with all the growers' associations operating in the Windward Islands. In 1958 the Windward Islands Banana Growers' Association (WINBAN) based in St Lucia was formed. By 1959 banana imports to Britain had for the first time surpassed the pre-War high. Between 1964 and 1966 a mini Banana War broke out between Geest and Fyffes, who eventually agreed to split the British market between them. In 1969 Fyffes unilaterally broke its contract with Jamaica, importing low-cost fruit from Côte d'Ivoire and Surinam instead.

Miss Chiquita

UFCO launched a 'Miss Chiquita' (pictured right) advertising campaign in the US in 1944. Technical changes were also made to the production process. In 1961 bananas were pre-cut and placed in boxes instead of bunches, to protect against bruising. Following a period of unrest on its plantations, in 1954 the company orchestrated a coup against the Government of Guatemala. After an anti-trust suit in 1958, UFCO was slowly broken up into the 'Big Three' banana companies. Between them, they increased their domination of the European market,

by now the world's largest importer. All three were subsequently absorbed into a succession of transnational conglomerates.

Bust and boom

The Windward Islands faced two major setbacks in 1973; the oil crisis which increased the cost of shipping and chemical inputs, and the accession of Britain to the European Economic Community. Here it joined France, whose 'Overseas Departments' in Martinique and Guadeloupe were guaranteed two-thirds of the French banana market. Britain negotiated a 20-per-cent tariff on 'dollar' bananas. Then, in 1975, the first Lomé Convention guaranteed 42 former colonies in Africa, the Caribbean and Pacific ('ACP') trading terms on a par with the best of the preceding years. From the late 1970s to the early 1990s a 'banana boom' swept the Windward Islands.

Rules of engagement

In 1992 the Single European Market and European Union (EU) were designed to remove internal trade barriers. A single new banana 'regime' imposed tariffs and quotas for each exporting country, overall quotas for 'dollar' bananas and 'traditional' or ACP countries, plus additional tradable licences. Chiquita decided to oppose the new EU regime altogether at the World Trade Organization (WTO) after it was established in 1995. On three separate occasions the WTO has found against the EU regime. In early 1999 Chiquita persuaded the US Government to impose punitive import tariffs on EU imports. The latest skirmish in the Banana War continues – but an increasingly effective international network of trade unions, campaigns, organic and fair-trade producers has now joined the fray to change the rules of engagement.

BRIEF HISTORY **2**

The Blue Jeans Story

Or how 'waist overalls' for gold diggers and gunslingers got smart, clothed the American Dream and conquered the world.

Denim
'Denim' is probably a corruption of the French *serge de Nîmes*, a twill-weave fabric made in Nîmes during the 17th century. Another European fabric – a 'fustian' made from a cotton, linen and/or wool blend – was known as 'jean' after the sailors of Genoa, Italy, who wore it. By the 18th century, as slave labor, trade and cotton plantations developed, jean cloth was being made entirely of cotton and was valued for its durability. Indigo blue, extracted from plants in the Americas and India, became a familiar color for workwear.

Settlers
Immigrant weavers from Yorkshire, England, produced heavy cotton fustians – cotton-twill jeans – from a cloth mill in Massachusetts as early as 1638. In 1789 George Washington toured a mill in Massachusetts that was weaving both denim and jean. By 1849 a New York manufacturer was advertising topcoats, vests and short jackets in blue jean. Mechanics and painters were wearing overalls made of blue denim; others wore more tailored trousers made of jean.

Gold
Early in 1848 James Wilson Marshall, a carpenter from New Jersey, picked up nuggets of gold from the site of a sawmill he was building by a

river near Coloma, California. By August the Gold Rush had begun. In 1853 Loeb Strauss (who later changed his name to Levi) arrived in San Francisco from New York and set up a wholesale business. Demand from miners for hard-wearing work clothes was strong. The Pacific Rural Press of 28 June 1873 observed: 'Nothing looks more slouchy in a workman than to see his pockets ripped open and hanging down, and no other part of the clothing is so apt to be torn and ripped as the pockets.'

Rivets

In 1872 Levi Strauss received a letter from Jacob Davis, who had been making riveted clothing for miners in the Reno area. Davis had no money to file for a patent and offered Levi Strauss a deal if he would pay for the patent. Levi Strauss began to make copper-riveted 'waist overalls' (as jeans were then known). In 1886 Levi's 'Two Horse Brand' leather patch,

showing the garment pulled between two horses to prove its strength, was first used. By 1890 lot-numbers were being used for Levi products: 501 was assigned to copper-riveted overalls. In 1902 two back pockets were added.

Movies

During the 1930s, Western movies from Hollywood elevated 'authentic' cowboys, who were often portrayed wearing the garment, to mythic status. Easterners headed west for experience on dude ranches, and brought denim 'waist overalls' back east with them. Customer complaints led to the restitching of the Levi back pockets in 1937 so that the rivets were covered and did not scratch furniture or saddles. Suspender buttons were removed, though all customers were still supplied with a snap-on set.

War

Restrictions on the use of raw materials during World War Two led to a decline in the production of 'waist overalls'. The crotch rivet and back cinch were removed to save fabric and metal. As GIs fanned out around the world the 'waist overalls' they sometimes wore while off duty carried American style and abundance to countries devastated by war.

Denim became less associated with work and more with leisure. In 1947 Wrangler introduced the first 'body fit' jeans. In 1948 an old pair of jeans was found in an abandoned silver mine in the Mojave Desert, California. The woman who found them patched them up and wore them for a while. Then she wrote to Levi Strauss, who bought them for $25 and a few new pairs. Made around 1890, they are said to be the oldest pair of blue jeans in the world.

Rebels

After the War, Levi Strauss began selling its products outside the US West for the first time. New rivals, such as Wrangler and Lee, began to compete for market share. Denim-clad 'juvenile delinquents' and 'motorcycle boys' featured in films and on TV; James Dean wore denim in the film *Rebel Without a Cause*. Some school administrators in the US banned denim altogether. In 1958 a syndicated newspaper report claimed that 'about 90 per cent of American youths wear jeans everywhere except in bed and in church'. Teenagers used the term 'jean pants', and the name stuck. The bad reputation – and the healthy sales – of jeans grew still further when 'college kids' wore them during the protests of the 1960s and at the Woodstock music festival in 1969.

Art

In 1964 a pair of Levi jeans entered the permanent collections of the Smithsonian Institution in Washington DC. In 1969 American Fabrics claimed: 'What has happened to denim in the last decade is really a capsule of what happened to America. It has climbed the ladder of taste'. Embroidered, painted, sequined and 'psychedelic' denim took an outing on city streets. US jean manufacturers claimed that they regularly received begging letters from 'behind the Iron Curtain' and as far afield as Pitcairn Island. Jeans became a symbol of 'Western' culture – or 'decadence' – and a weapon in the Cold War.

Label

With the liberalization of world trade from the late 1970s onwards 'sweatshops' using cheap – usually female – labor in the Global South began to replace factories in the North. Jeans appeared on city streets – even on miners and rural laborers – in the Majority World. In the rich world, the 1980s 'designer jeans' craze took the garment firmly upmarket. Booming sales of branded 'sports shoes', often worn with jeans, reinforced the trend. Chain stores and fashion houses promoted their own lines of jeans. A vast number of new 'labels' appeared. Established brands often missed the latest fad, like baggy jeans, and went for nostalgia instead. Sales rocketed. The global jeans empire shows no sign of losing its sway.

BRIEF HISTORY **3**

Chocolate: from Maya to Market

The history of humanity's growing passion for chocolate – and the shifting source of the magic bean from which it springs.

Oh, divine chocolate!
They grind thee kneeling,
Beat thee with hands praying.
And drink thee with eyes to heaven.
Marco Antonio Orellana

Chocolate follies

Sacred spice

The first known use of the cocoa bean to make a spicy (not sweet) chocolate drink dates back to the Mayan empire of what is today southern Mexico and Guatemala. Here the cocoa bean can still be found growing wild in the bush of coastal Chiapas and neighboring northern Guatemala. For the Maya, cocoa and the thick 'chocolatl' drink that it rendered were a symbol of sanctity, evoking both fertility and prosperity. Mayan priests are the first to have made the drink during the classical Mayan period from about 250 to 900. The bean was so highly valued that it was used as a form of currency at a fixed market rate – you could get a rabbit for 10 beans, a slave cost 100 and a prostitute went from 8 to 10 'according to how they agree.'

Spoils of war

With the inexplicable and much-debated collapse of Mayan civilization the use of chocolate spread north (probably carried by Mayan traders) to the hierarchical Aztec empire of central Mexico. Here the drink was restricted to the élite of warriors, merchants and priests who held sway over

19

Aztec life. It is interesting that Aztec warriors carried light high-energy chocolate on military campaigns and that later chocolate gained its post-World War One popularity after it was used in soldier's ration kits. Cocoa beans continued to be used as a currency (there were even bean counterfeiters!) so those who could actually afford to 'drink money' were privileged indeed. The Aztec emperors stored beans as a way of hoarding wealth and are reported at one point to have had some 960,000,000 beans in the royal coffers. Much of this was undoubtedly tribute from subject peoples invaded by the warlike Aztecs. When chocolate was prepared it was with great ceremony, paying careful attention to the foaming process and adding a delicate mixture of spices, honey and flowers to get the recipe correct.

Spanish prize

Unlike the Aztecs' gold, chocolate was not immediately to the taste of the barbaric Spaniards who slaughtered any Amerindians who would not accept the domination of the Spanish Crown. One commentator at the time shook his head at the bitter-tasting drink, claiming it was more fit for pigs than people. But innovation through the adding of sugar transformed chocolate for the sweet European palate and it grew in popularity, particularly with the ladies of the Spanish court. Other innovations included taking the liquid hot rather than cold and producing it as a tablet that was readily transportable and crumbled into a powder from which the chocolate drink could be concocted. For nearly a century chocolate remained a secret of the Spanish aristocracy virtually unknown in the rest of Europe. Rumor had it that the strong taste of chocolate was useful for covering up poisons. The fanatical Charles the Second of Spain is reported to have sat sipping chocolate while observing victims of the Inquisition being put to death.

Disputed character

When chocolate finally escaped the Iberian peninsula it remained an item of luxury consumption to be consumed only by people of means. Even with the establishment of chocolate houses in London, a tax kept the price out of reach of most ordinary folk. The spread of chocolate led to a debate as to its medical and temperamental value that still rages to this day. Early theories of human metabolism were based on the balance of hot and cold 'humors' and various experts disputed whether chocolate would cool the overheated ardor or heat normally cooler passions. This anticipates later debates as to the aphrodisiac nature of chocolate and its effects as a dangerous stimulant to the emotions or relatively harmless substitute for alcohol and other drugs. The Marquis de Sade's status as one of the earliest-known 'chocoholics' adds a certain spice to such speculations.

Chocolate for the masses
For some 28 centuries chocolate had been a drink of the élite from Aztec emperors to French courtiers and the English bourgeoisie. But the invention of a cocoa press by the Dutch Van Houten in the late 19th century – to extract the cocoa butter out of the beans leaving a powder of cocoa solids – changed all that. Not only was the noble trade of cocoa grinder put into jeopardy (over 150 such grinders plied their trade in Madrid alone, where they formed their own guild) but a vast new confectionery industry came into being. The Cadbury company which brought the press to England was soon churning out both powder and candy bars as fast as the machinery would work. They were quickly joined by Rowntree in Britain and by Milton Hershey and Forest E Mars who set up plants in Pennsylvania and Chicago respectively. To this day these and a few other firms from continental Europe, most prominently the gigantic Nestlé corporation based in Switzerland, dominate the ever-growing global chocolate market.

Source of the bean

If you want to send your children to school, it is cocoa
If you want to build a house, it is cocoa
If you want to marry, it is cocoa
If you want to buy cloth, it is cocoa
If you want to buy a lorry, it is cocoa
Whatever you want to do in this world
It is with cocoa money that you do it.
Ghanaian 1950s high-life tune

Slavish devotion
Despite all the talk of Swiss and Belgian chocolate, the source of cocoa has always been in tropical or semitropical agriculture. The Spanish empire in the Americas initially used Amerindian labor in first Mexico and Guatemala and then Ecuador and Venezuela to provide the raw material for the favored drink of the European aristocrats. But by the end of the 17th century all but 10 per cent of the original native population had

succumbed to a combination of harsh repression, disease and slave labor imposed by their Spanish overlords. The new source of agricultural labor was slaves ripped from their societies in West Africa and transported across the Atlantic in the now infamous 'triangular' trade by which shiploads of cocoa eventually arrived in Spanish ports. Nor were the Spanish alone in this dark enterprise as the French, English, and Portuguese used African slaves to expand cocoa and other agricultural raw-material production in their New World colonies. The Dutch brought as many as 100,000 unfortunate slaves a year through their tiny Caribbean colony in Curaçao.

Shifting production

Today less than two per cent of cocoa comes from Mexico where the Mayans first sipped their sacred but bitter concoctions. In a rich historical irony and a major prefiguring of today's global economy, world cocoa production shifted to West Africa at the end of the 19th century. The region that had once provided the slaves to grow the New World's cocoa now became the major source of global supply. From the island colonies of Portuguese Africa – São Tomé and Fernando Po – cuttings of the cocoa tree were transported first to the Gold Coast and then Nigeria and finally in 1905 to the French colony of Côte d'Ivoire which is today's largest producer. In Ghana it is held that the cocoa seedlings were not an imposition of colonial merchants but were smuggled into the country by a Ghanaian carpenter named Tetteh Quarshie in 1878. Ghana was to be the world's largest supplier of the bean from 1910 to 1979 when poor prices combined with other circumstances to disillusion many of the small farmers who were the backbone of Ghana's cocoa economy.

Price and quality

In colonial times the British-based companies who purchased Gold Coast (the rather wishful British name for their colony in Ghana) cocoa beans such as the United Africa Company also held the monopoly for the sale of industrial goods in the local market. This provided a significant advantage to these firms, who could profit by high charges for what they imported and the lowest possible price to the farmers. The beans were then sold on to the big chocolate manufacturers. Under this system there was naturally increasing resentment amongst farmers who seldom benefited from increases in the international price but were made to pay for any price drops. In an attempt to resist arbitrary price-setting, farmers simply refused to sell their beans to buyers. One such boycott following the 1929 Wall Street Crash led to the formation by Tete-Ansa of the West African Co-operative Producers Association as an alternative marketing channel that would break the expatriate stranglehold. Another boycott in the late

1930s held cocoa beans off the market for many months and led to the establishment of the Nowell Commission to investigate pricing policies. Also at this time there was a struggle between Cadbury and the United Africa Company over the quality of beans. In those days Cadbury wanted high quality for their chocolate while the United Africa Company was primarily interested in quantity and price. To this day Ghanaian beans earn premium price for their high quality.

Nkrumah and cocoa

The late 1950s and early 1960s were exciting days in Ghana as the country became the first independent state in sub-Saharan Africa. The leadership of Kwame Nkrumah with his radical nationalism and Pan-Africanism had an ambitious vision for Ghana's future. Plans for industrialization, electrification, import substitution and a revolution in education had to be underwritten by the foreign exchange earned from minerals, timber and, most importantly, cocoa. Given the boom prices of the 1950s (although most profits never made it back to the Gold Coast) this did not seem unrealistic. But although production increased by a third, the international price fell by more than this. Newly independent Ghana's first seven-year economic plan was based on an international price of £180 sterling a ton but by 1965 the price of cocoa had fallen to £65 a ton. Enemies of Nkrumah's radical model for Africa were quick to bring massive pressure to bear. The Ghanaian Cocobod (the national marketing board) was forced into unpopular cuts in the price paid to farmers. Poor prices not only undermined Nkrumah's ambitious economic program but helped sap his political support, leading to the military coup which eventually was his downfall.

The price rollercoaster

After Nkrumah's fall the revenue earned from cocoa became an ever-more important source of financial support for the Ghanaian state. As a result the percentage of the price paid to farmers went into steady decline until the early 1980s. A low world price in the early 1970s gave way to a boom by the end of the decade with prices peaking at nearly £3,000 a ton in 1977. This was partly due to poor weather conditions affecting supply and partly due to speculation. But with internal purchase and price controlled by the powerful Cocobod, farmers ended up suffering far more from low prices than they ever benefited from the price boom. As a result many Ghanaian farmers voted with their feet, cut down their trees for timber and planted food crops instead. This, combined with very dry weather and a disastrous series of bush fires, resulted in a plunge of Ghanaian cocoa production from about 30 per cent of the world total to less than 12 per cent by the early 1980s.

The era of liberal competition

After a more modest price boom in the mid-1980s the chocolate companies, wholesale buyers and aid agencies encouraged a number of new countries to get into cocoa production as a high-value 'miracle' commodity. As a result a number of Asian countries like Malaysia and Indonesia (and soon Vietnam) set up large cocoa plantations and Brazil and other Latin American countries increased their production. The result was as intended – an increase in supply and a drop in price. In West Africa, particularly Ghana, cocoa remains a smallholder crop and massive agrochemical plantations are rare. A regime of liberal market economics, according to recipes developed in the Washington kitchen of the International Monetary Fund, is now the economic orthodoxy of the region. While this has resulted in a better internal cocoa price for Ghanaian farmers, new health and education charges, skyrocketing prices for agricultural chemicals and a stagnant world price have mostly undermined any improvement.

King Cotton

Cotton: the stuff of Roman robes and royal apparel, of slaves and satanic mills, and of a new empire of capital that still holds sway today. For Gandhi, simple and homespun, the cotton *khadi* shirt was a symbol of a resurgent, democratic India. Today cotton clothes the world, still handing out wealth and misery in equal measure.

Prehistory
Rumors of an odd cross between an animal and a plant helped sell the travel books of the fabulist Sir John Manville and other European travel writers in the Middle Ages. Stories of a marvelous half-lamb, half-plant ignored the fact that the Romans and Greeks knew cotton as a luxury import from India via camel caravans. Cloth discovered in the Indus Valley dates Indian textile manufacture back to at least 2300 BCE. Perhaps even earlier, cotton was being cultivated on the Pacific coast of Chile and Peru. From India it spread west to Egypt and Turkey; from the Pacific north to Central America and the Caribbean. Cotton, coming from at least two different points on the globe, is in a real sense the common property of humankind.

The cotton trade
Cotton cloth gradually became one of the most sought-after goods for the emerging urban markets of Renaissance and Enlightenment Europe. Vasco da Gama opened up the Asian sea trade, replacing the old caravan route and allowing for much heavier loads. A Calico and Chintz craze swept the continent. By 1664 the East India Company was importing a quarter of a million pieces into England alone. Indian craftspeople and dyers had for centuries kept the secret of how to create colorful patterns. But some converted to Christianity and were betrayed by a French Catholic priest, Father Coeurdoux, in an early act of industrial espionage. Although sworn to secrecy, he published a step-by-step guide in France. The European textile industry got a leg up.

Industrial Revolution
The Lancashire textile mills were the engines of the English Industrial Revolution. They were characterized as 'satanic' due to the deplorable working conditions – poverty wages, child labor, an 18-hour working day.

Richard Arkwright created the first factory system, using stolen spinning and weaving technology, powered by water, to create a textile empire under his absolute authority. The new looms were subject to midnight raids by artisan weavers (the Luddites) put out of work by the factory system. By the 1790s James Watt's invention of steam power was being successfully applied to textile production. In 1839 Manchester's cotton mills used nearly 200,000 children. Life expectancy amongst the poor in Manchester was 17, with 57 per cent of live births dead by the age of five. Karl Marx made the trip to Lancashire dozens of times. After all, he was writing *Das Kapital* – and this truly was capitalism 'red in tooth and claw'. And, measured in output and profits, it was incredibly successful. It set the brutal way that cotton is worked 'downstream' that holds to this day, from Dhaka in Bangladesh to the Shenzhen Special Economic Zone.

Mohandas K Gandhi

Empire

The Lancashire textile boom could never have taken hold without the protection of high tariff walls against the world's great textile workshop in India. Indian hand weavers, whose quality was high and wages low, had been the center of world production for centuries. But British protectionism, in combination with the extension of imperial power through the East India Company (an early example of a 'public-private' partnership), changed the rules of the game. British policy transformed India from an exporter of textiles to a supplier of raw cotton for Lancashire factories. The tactics were brutal. They included smashing the hands and cutting off the thumbs of Indian weavers, while implementing a system of usurious taxes favoring cotton production – sometimes provoking famine in the process. When Gandhi led the movement against imported British textiles and in favor of Indian handlooms, Winston Churchill caught the temper of British attitudes, famously denouncing Gandhi as 'half naked... a seditious Middle Temple lawyer'.

Slavery

The histories of cotton and slavery are intimately intertwined. Slaves were brought from the west coast of Africa. While they were used for many purposes, two dominated: working in plantations of sugar and cotton. Millions of souls were ripped from their families and societies to create the wealth of the New World. A 'triangular' trade took slaves west, cotton east and manufactured goods south. From Brazil to Georgia, 'cottonpickin'' became a synonym for human beings used as chattels. The oral history of US slavery is full of the rhythms of the cotton field. By 1860 the US South was providing 80 per cent of Britain's cotton and two-thirds of the world's supply. The Indian farmer could not compete with slave labor. But the Loom Lords who ran the textile industries of Britain, and increasingly the American northeast, began to feel the heat of abolitionist opinion. The days of slavery were numbered. 'Free labor' was the rallying cry, although the distinction between slavery and sweatshops eluded some.

Africa

The cotton culture of the US South and the agricultural economy that spawned it never really recovered its position of dominance. The 'cotton famine' that hit European textile industries during the US Civil War, and increasing global demand for the 'white gold', soon had the European Loom Lords looking elsewhere for raw cotton lint. Diversification was the name of the game. Their own colonies provided coerced labor and cheap product. West Africa (and Mozambique) became a new source of supply. Taxes and other extra-market means once again induced cotton cultivation and discouraged local textile production. The treatment of the producers was particularly brutal in the Belgian Congo and the Portuguese colonies of Angola and Mozambique, where it bordered on outright slavery. Cotton cultivation restructured rural life in Africa. It required between 100 and 185 days of labor per hectare, leading to the neglect of food crops. But Africans were not passive victims. They adopted a number of survival and resistance strategies: overt revolts, particularly in the Portuguese colonies; neglecting their tasks in the cotton cycle (seen as 'laziness' by the authorities); clandestine inter-cropping; a black market in cotton and an indigenous textile industry seen today in the beautiful Kente cloth of Ghana's Ashanti country.

Unequal exchange

After independence, much of West Africa was left with an unhealthy dependence on cotton as a foreign-exchange earner. Low labor costs allowed it to compete with the hi-tech production of the world's biggest producer of cotton lint: the US. But then the US Government started spending billions of dollars on subsidies. This depressed the world price to the point where even African and Indian farmers could not keep body and soul together. An additional burden on small farmers has come with the expensive regime of chemical inputs demanded by industrial agriculture. The effects have been widespread hunger and devastation – and, in India, farmer suicide. Meanwhile, US cotton subsidies provide

Workers in a Lancashire cotton mill in the late 19th century.

a dramatic example of rich world hypocrisy: demanding free trade of everyone else, while practising protectionism at home. But time may be running out for the 'good ole boys' at the National Cotton Council. Brazil launched an action at the World Trade Organization in 2005, accusing the US of unfairly helping its own farmers, distorting the price of cotton and making it harder for developing nations to compete. The complaint was upheld by the WTO in 2007, which expressed its disappointment with meager US efforts to reduce its subsidies.

From Loom Lords to Brand Barons

Power in 'downstream' cotton has shifted from the giant textile mills that used to dominate the industry in Lancashire, the New England states and Western Europe. The labor-intensive textile industry has led the global shift of industrial production to low-wage areas – first the US South and southern Europe and now India, Bangladesh, China and the free-trade zones of Latin America where labor can be bought for a fraction of wages in the industrialized world. But while the industrial production may have shifted, economic clout has remained in the Global North. Big retail chains and brands – Nike, Marks and Spencer, Gap Inc, Wal-Mart, Gildan Activewear and a slew of others – now dictate prices and terms. Today branding is where the money is, with consultants and brand developers known as 'identity consultancies' – such as Futurebrand and the Grey Global Group – doing the 'creative'. There are even 22 Immutable Laws of Branding developed by a guy named Al Reis. These brand names contract textile companies throughout the Global South, demanding textile cotton production of high quality and low cost. While the work is welcome to desperately poor workers, the low wages and often deplorable working conditions are not.

BRIEF HISTORY 5

The Great Tunafish Sandwich Hunt

South Pacific islanders were the first to venture out in search of tuna during the Stone Age. Today, over half the tuna caught in the South Pacific is shipped to the US, mostly to fill sandwiches.

Tuna's Christopher Columbus

The Portuguese showed North Americans how to catch the crafty tuna, teaching Californians to chum (attract and keep the fish near ships by throwing live bait overboard) and string lines from boats. But consumers had not heard of tuna till 1903 when a Californian fish packer was having trouble getting enough sardines and began processing albacore tuna instead. Customers liked the 'white meat' fish and more canneries sought tuna. In 1932 the 'Christopher Columbus of tuna', Joaquin Medina, set out from San Diego in the largest fishing vessel of the time, the Mayflower. He traveled almost 14,400 kilometers and fished for yellowfin tuna around Hawaii. Four years later, in a tuna clipper named Cabrillo, he sailed to the Marquesas and the Galapagos Islands and returned with even greater catches, stimulating more interest in long fishing expeditions.

Enter the big net

US fishers were the first to adopt the purse-seiner – boats with a giant net which sweeps up everything in sight including dolphins, sharks, coral and other fish species. Fisher Lou Brito started the craze in 1958 when his Southern Pacific, the first purse-seiner to operate from San Diego, returned with a large catch. In the next five years, 97 tuna-boats were converted to purse-seiners.

North American fishers also reaped the rewards of a US Government position that claimed tuna were not located within any country's national jurisdictions. Seizure of US boats for illegal fishing did not deter the poaching – the US Government punished countries seizing American ships by reducing its foreign aid. For a period of about 25 years, US purse-seiner fishers were able to fish where they liked and how they liked – without paying a cent in compensation.

Dead dolphins aren't fun

Until the 1980s the US primarily fished in the eastern Pacific, where tuna and dolphins swim together. About 400,000 dolphins were killed each year in nets of the US tuna fleet – then the largest in the world. But Sam La Budde's dramatic footage of dolphins dying in tuna nets, filmed by him while he worked undercover on a Panamanian tuna-boat, sparked popular outrage. In January 1988, environmentalists launched a successful consumer boycott of three major tuna processors in the US – Heinz's Star Kist label, Chicken of the Sea and Bumble Bee – which announced in 1990 they would no longer accept tuna caught in nets that kill dolphins.

'Tuna is fun food,' explained Ted Smyth, Vice-President of Heinz, referring to its common use in kids' sandwiches. 'If it's associated with the harassment and killing of a noble creature like the dolphin, that's not right.'

Tuna Wars: round one

Beginning with scuffles over US illegal fishing in the early 1980s, the US-Mexican 'tuna war' became global in the late 1980s. Under pressure from environmentalists, the US embargoed Mexico for producing tuna that was dolphin-unsafe. Initially, this had little economic effect on the Mexican tuna fleet – now the largest in the world, supplying the big markets of Europe and Japan. But on 20 April 1991, the US extended the ban to all European countries that brought Mexican tuna to can and re-exported it to the US. This affected $4-5 million worth of exports from France, Italy and Britain. The Mexican Government, followed by Europe, took the US to the General Agreement on Tariffs and Trade (GATT) Panel which ruled that 'regulations governing the taking of dolphins incidental to the taking of tuna could not possibly affect tuna as a product' and that countries could not embargo a product for how it is produced. But GATT's ruling was never enforced and the US was let off the hook.

A touch of arrogance

As controversy raged in the eastern Pacific in the 1980s, the US fleet headed west. But South Pacific nations soon became fed up with continued poaching and the US found itself in another tussle over tuna. Despite ship seizures, the US was still aloof to local concerns until Kiribati gave the Soviet Union access to its fishery for a fee of $1.5 million a year. The Pentagon panicked about this Soviet encroachment into 'friendly waters'. According to Island Business: 'It spurred the US to work harder for a multilateral treaty. At previous talks, the Americans had displayed what island delegates initially described as a good deal of ignorance, insensitivity and more than a touch of arrogance'. Signed in early 1987, the subsequent fishing agreement established a program of payments for regional economic development.

Globalization in a can

Today, tuna consumed by US customers may have been harvested in the South Pacific, shipped to Thailand, bought on the spot market, canned in a plant leased to one corporation, then labeled and distributed by another.

Canneries founded in Puerto Rico in the 1970s lost an average of 1,000 jobs per year in the 1980s when tuna processing shifted to American Samoa – popular for its favorable tax rates, easy export to the US and cheaper labor. The Pago Pago canneries consumed around a third of water and electricity supplied by the Government, leaving the country dependent on US aid.

Globalization of the industry became complete in the 1990s as the canners turned to booming Asia. Asian-based firms bought two of the big three canned-tuna companies – Bumble Bee and Chicken of the Sea. Half of the world's canned tuna is caught in the South Pacific, but almost all of the profits from fishing tuna go to the US, Taiwan, Japan and Korea. Just three corporations supply 81 per cent of the fish that makes up an American icon – the tunafish sandwich. They now increasingly offer tuna as fillets and steaks instead of just in cans. They have faced a public image battle recently over the levels of mercury in their product – the US Government recommends that pregnant or breastfeeding women and young children should limit their consumption of tuna.

Sugar and Slaves

Sugar was not the only crop that consumed the lives of slaves – cotton and tobacco took their toll as well – but its production relied entirely on their labor. Most of the 10-12 million who survived the passage to the New World died within a decade, since they were cheaper to replace than to feed.

Origins

Arabs were probably the first to cultivate and refine sugar around the Mediterranean. From the 11th century Europeans developed a taste for it during their Crusades to the 'Holy Land'.

Both Arabs and Europeans overcame strong religious and cultural objections and relied on slaves in the labor-intensive process of sugar cultivation. Sugar cane was first carried to the 'New World' from the Canary Islands by Columbus on his second voyage of 1493. It was cultivated by African slaves in Santo Domingo, from where it was first shipped to Spain in 1516. Sugar and slavery followed the trail of Spanish conquest to Mexico, Paraguay and the Pacific coast of South America.

By 1526 the Portuguese were shipping sugar to Lisbon from northeast Brazil, which rapidly became the center of the trade. Slaves in Bahia originally included indigenous people, but Africans were preferred – and fetched three times the price. Some 50,000 African slaves reached Brazil between 1576 and 1591.

Expansion

In 1619 the British established their first New World colony at Jamestown (Guyana), bringing with them both sugar cane and their first enslaved Africans. In 1654 Dutch soldiers expelled from northeast Brazil arrived in Barbados with their slaves – and their knowledge of sugar. By 1667 there were 745 mostly British owners of sugar plantations in Barbados using over 80,000 slaves. In 1655 the British invaded Jamaica and introduced slave sugar there too. The French were doing likewise in Martinique. The French, Danish and British Governments copied the Dutch West Indian Company, setting up privileged national slaving companies. They established themselves on the west coast of Africa, where they built forts and made deals with local traders, supported by their governments and protected by their national navies. The infamous 'triangular' trade got under way: slaves were taken from Africa to the New World, commodities (of which sugar was the most lucrative) from the New World to Europe, and manufactured goods like cloth and weaponry from Europe back to Africa. Enormous profits were made, primarily in Europe, from each side of the triangle.

El Dorado

Between 1701 and 1810 Barbados – an island of just 430 square kilometers – received 252,000 African slaves; Jamaica 662,400. Annual sugar consumption per person in Britain rose from 5 pounds in 1700 to 18 pounds in 1800. Britain came to dominate both the slave and sugar trades, which financed its imperial expansion.

In 1713 the Treaty of Utrecht (which also ceded Canada to Britain) contained an 'El Dorado of commerce': the contract or *asiento* to import slaves to the Spanish Indies. The British Government sold this privilege for $12 million to the South Sea Company – there were hopes that the entire British national debt could be eliminated by this trade alone. Feverish speculation followed. Shareholders in the South Sea Company included the entire royal family, 462 members of the British House of Commons, the Swiss canton of Berne, King's College, Cambridge, the writers Daniel Defoe and Jonathan Swift as well as the 'father' of modern science, Sir Isaac Newton. The company sold 64,000 slaves before the speculative 'bubble' burst in 1731.

Two-thirds of the slaves shipped to the Americas in the 1770s worked on sugar plantations. In 1771 alone Liverpool sent over 100 ships to Africa to capture more than 28,000 slaves; London 58 ships for 8,000; Bristol 23 ships for 9,000; even the small port of Lancaster sent 4 ships for 950 slaves. In France, Nantes became the pre-eminent slaving port, followed by Bordeaux, Le Havre and La Rochelle.

The inferno

Rebellions on slave ships were frequent – at least one every ten journeys. In 1532 the 109 slaves aboard the Portuguese ship *Misericordia* rose up and killed all the crew except the pilot and two sailors. In 1650 a slave ship sailing from Panama to Lima was wrecked off Ecuador. The captives killed the surviving Spaniards. The rebel leader, Alonso de Illescas, established himself as a lord in Esmeraldas. In 1742 the galley *Mary* was driven ashore by local people on the River Gambia. The slaves on board killed most of the crew and kept the captain and mate prisoner for 27 days.

The utmost brutality was needed to prevent or subdue rebellion. Slaves were habitually shackled. Exemplary torture was commonplace. In 1709 the ringleader of a failed uprising on the Danish vessel *Friedericus Quartus* had one hand cut off and shown to every slave. The next day his other hand was cut off – the day after that, his head. His torso was then hoisted into the ship's rigging. The other mutineers, after torture with thumbscrews, were whipped and had ashes, salt and pepper rubbed into their wounds. In 1717, reporting the loss of all but 98 of the 594 slaves on board the South Sea Company's ship *George*, the captain cited 'the length of the journey' and 'bad weather' as the culprits. Suicides were frequent: in 1767 Ashanti slaves on sale in Elmina (in present-day Ghana) cut their own throats.

Revolt

Initially, few uprisings were recorded in the slave colonies themselves – but they soon began. The most effective was in the French colony of Saint-Domingue (present-day Haiti). Slaves were excluded from the promise of liberty that came with the start of the French Revolution in 1787 – Nantes had its best-ever slaving year in 1790. But on 22 August 1791 rebels led by Toussaint L'Ouverture set fire to the cane fields in Saint-Domingue. They took, and kept, control of the colony – a truly astonishing achievement at the time. From 1807 onwards revolts became almost annual events in Bahia, Brazil. Some were led by educated Muslims. Mullahs accused of teaching friends to read the Qur'an in Arabic received whippings of 500 strokes or more.

In 1843 and 1844 there were repeated revolts in Cuba – by then the largest producer of sugar in the Caribbean. The Escalera Conspiracy was named after suspects who were tied to a staircase and whipped until they confessed. Some 3,000 people were summarily tried, and 80 were shot. Written histories tend to focus on European or American 'abolitionists', before the slave trade was eventually banned in Europe and slavery itself abolished in the US, Brazil and elsewhere. The resistance of the slaves themselves is either downplayed or ignored altogether. The sugar industry adapted with relative ease to a system of contract labor, which included the transport of 'indentured' Indian workers to new areas such as Fiji and Mauritius. Working conditions changed very little.

BRIEF HISTORY **7**

The Secret Life of the Apple

Apples have been with us since the dawn of recorded time, in countless varieties of color, shape and size. But the modern world is in danger of squandering its heritage.

Prehistoric wildings   8,000 BCE
Human beings have been munching apples since prehistoric times. They spat out apple pips in neolithic Britain. And 10,000 years ago they left apple remains to carbonize around their Swiss and Italian lakeside homes. In Switzerland and in the regions adjoining the Caucasus mountains, ancient humans even appear to have dry-stored apple-halves for winter. But these were wild crab apples, tiny wizened fruit which, in Ancient Britain, came to be known as 'wildings'. They had little in common with the apples we know today.

Early ancestors   **2,000 BCE**

The exact origins of what we recognize as apples are rather obscure but they are generally thought to come from the Caucasus Mountains in Asia Minor, near where 17th-century historians located the Garden of Eden. By 2,000 BCE they had reached the eastern Mediterranean, probably carried by merchants and travelers down the prehistoric trade routes which crossed the Middle East. From Palestine apples were taken to Egypt and cultivated in the Nile delta during the 12th and 13th centuries BCE, where they were regarded as a luxury. Apples were also taken west to Greece and Italy, and Homer refers to them in The Odyssey, which was written between 900 and 800 BCE.

Roman roots   **300 BCE**

As apples spread around the world, different varieties emerged to cope with their new environments. And the Romans added to this range by deliberately breeding apples for taste and size. Writers like Virgil, Cato and Pliny were able to list two dozen varieties of apple. And a contemporary of theirs, Columella, describes and recommends distinct kinds like the Armerian, the Cestine and the Syrian, showing that apple-growers used the same system of naming as today – generally naming the variety after the finder, some benefactor or notable person, or the place where the apple originated. Apples became a favorite fruit for the Romans, and they were dried and served as a relish in winter or eaten sour in the summer as refreshment after arduous work. The Roman armies carried apples across Europe, planting pips wherever they settled. And in this way apples marched northwards.

Norman knowledge   **1000 CE**

From the Romans the French learned great fruit–growing skills which were developed in the monasteries. This knowledge – which included expert cider-making – was taken to Britain during the Norman Conquest in 1066, along with new varieties of cider and dessert apples. Several kinds of apples still remained in Britain from Roman times, like the dessert apple Decio – thought to have been introduced by the Roman general, Etio. But most Roman varieties were unsuitable for the British climate and the Norman varieties rapidly took precedence. British monks continued experimenting and developing new apples, and it is from these varieties that Western apples are largely descended.

Medieval favorites   1200

Several kinds of apples became established in Britain during the 13th century. The Old English Pearmain, recorded in 1204 and so named because of its pear-like shape, was the main dessert apple until well into the 18th century. Its cooking partner was the Costard, which was sold in the markets of Oxford from 1296 until the end of the 17th century and bequeathed us the word 'costermonger' – meaning someone who hawks fruit and vegetables in the street. But prosperity declined as the country was hit by successive droughts, the Black Death and the Wars of the Roses. Fewer apples were produced and more were imported. This went on until the 16th century when Henry VIII ordered his chief fruiterer, Richard Harris, to visit France and learn about apple cultivation. Harris returned with 'a great store of grafts' including the famous Pippins, from which he grew the first ever modern-style orchard at Teynham in Kent.

Settler treasure   1700

By the 17th century apples were so popular in Britain that the first settlers who sailed to Canada, Australia, the US, South Africa and New Zealand took apples and apple-pips with them, counting these among their most treasured possessions. Captain Bligh of the *Bounty* took the first apples to Australia; Jan van Riebeeck, the founder of Cape Settlement, took them to South Africa; and the Pilgrim Fathers (and Mothers) who boarded the *Mayflower* carried them to America. In North America the most famous apple-planter was John Chapman or 'Johnny Appleseed'. Born in 1774, he planted seedling nurseries from Pennsylvania in the east through Ohio into Indiana in the west. The Indians regarded him as a medicine man and his apple-tree enthusiasm, odd clothing and religious devotion – he distributed religious tracts torn into parts for widespread circulation – started many folktales. He was said, for example, to be so kind to God's creatures that he even 'slept with bears'.

American apples   1800

Many different varieties of apples emerged in the US and its apple industry was set in motion by Henderson Luelling – a fortune hunter who went west during the gold rush in a covered wagon full of soil and apple trees. He was left behind by the rest of the wagon train because his vehicle was so cumbersome. But he met a William Meek in Washington State and together they started planting orchards. Apples were in great demand from the gold prospectors in the western states. And by the time local demand declined, a railway had been built, enabling apples to be distributed across the entire North American continent.

Modern Delicious   1850

About the same time in Iowa, a Quaker farmer called Jesse Hiatt discovered a sucker sprouting from the roots of a dead tree. The shoot grew into an apple tree bearing a totally new apple which Hiatt named 'Hawkeye'. He sent it to a fruit show and on biting into one the judge exclaimed 'delicious, delicious'. In 1895 the apple was introduced to the trade as a 'Delicious' and became one of the most widely grown apples in the world.

Granny Smith   1850

Another of the most famous modern apples was discovered in Australia by Maria Anne Smith. The daughter of transported convicts, Maria was fiercely independent, rejecting both the criminal life of her parents and the bureaucratic hypocrisy of the colonial administration. She worked as a midwife in the small township of Eastwood in New South Wales where she was known as 'Granny Smith' because she had delivered so many babies. But as her husband's health declined she took on responsibility for maintaining the farm and orchard which was the family's main source of income. One day in 1868 she found a small tree pushing its way through a pile of discarded fruit. She transplanted it and before long was harvesting the world's first major crop of green apples, soon to be famous all over the world. When asked how the tree came about, she said: 'Well, it's just like God to make something useful out of what we think is rubbish' – a comment referring not only to the fruit but also to her own convict origins.

Uniformity rules   1950 onwards

Apples are now grown all over the world from Himachal Pradesh in northern India to small luxury orchards throughout Africa. Most, though, are grown commercially and come from just half a dozen varieties – usually chosen for their red skin or because they travel well rather than because they taste good. A plague of uniformity is sweeping the world, numbing the taste buds and reducing the gene pool. While amateur gardeners in Britain have kept many old apple varieties alive, the US has lost forever most of the apples it had 100 years ago.

But consumers are starting to demand more variety. We can't leave the responsibility of saving diversity in our apples – or any other food – up to the random selections of amateur gardeners. We must insist on a world where natural diversity is valued and protected for the benefit of all.

How History has been Hijacked

From national destiny to the certainty of progress, from 'the good old days' to conspiracy theory, history is often wreathed in myth for political ends.

National destiny

Nationalist chauvinism is perhaps the main distortion of historical understanding all over the world. It's an old story – my country right or wrong. For all too many historians, their own countries have a special destiny and represent superior values to their devious and barbarous neighbors.

Double standards abound. The English attack the excesses of the French Revolution but prefer to forget they also executed a king. The French blame the English for the persecution of Joan of Arc – forgetting the complicity of their own Catholic Church. Jewish history talks of the struggle to be free of the evil Pharaoh but does not deplore the Hebrews' own massacres and conquests. US history, meanwhile, is one of expanding human rights and freedoms – except for natives, blacks, radicals and small countries in Central America.

The good old days

This is a potent myth going back to the story of the Garden of Eden. The idea of a lost 'golden age' is particularly appealing to the old and those displaced from positions of wealth and power. The appeal often lies in the clarity and stability of the former age: when women and servants knew their 'place' and the prerogatives of empire were unchallenged; when there were still 'family values' and respect for authority. But as these examples imply, one person's good old days were another person's nightmare.

This kind of nostalgia fuels a fundamentalist reading of history: an era of true belief (Victorian England, the natural authority of the Tsars, the 'right-thinking' caliphs of early Islam) can be returned to by rooting out the immorality of the decadent present. This can be tricky. Real things are lost in the course of history: the destruction of community and commons by the Industrial Revolution, for example. But appreciation easily gives way to idealization.

Manufactured tradition

Tradition cloaks the powerful and their institutions in the robes of respectability. But these are often skin-deep and of quite recent vintage. A plethora of patriotic symbols created to inspire mass loyalty – flags, national anthems, equestrian statuary – date only from the latter part of the 19th century. Such traditions were even exported to Africa, where elaborate British, Portuguese and German rituals of imperial monarchy were fused with African symbols. Favored ethnic groups were encouraged to create 'tribal traditions' of land tenure, political authority and customary law which did not exist in pre-colonial Africa – and worked to the detriment of women, youth and people from other ethnic groups. A relatively fluid set of pre-colonial identities was frozen by rigid 'traditions' from which Africa still suffers to this day.

Conspiracy theory

A time-honored view of history that ascribes society's misfortunes to the plotting of Catholics, Jews, Communists, Freemasons, Capitalists or what-have-you. This idea is particularly popular with the Right in general and fascists in particular, who see the world as controlled by a vast network of unlikely conspirators. According to works like the fantastical *Protocols of the Elders of Zion*, Jewish bankers and atheist communists made common cause to promote oppression, cultural decadence and race-mixing. Modern fascists like British historian David Irving spill a great deal of ink to convince a skeptical world that the Nazi concentration camps were a public-relations invention of these same Jews and leftists. The Cold War playground of spies and subversives provided excellent raw material for the eager conspiracy historian. Latterly a whole host of conspiracy theorists have got their teeth into 9/11. But this type of history easily gives way to gossip: less dramatic notions such as economic interests and political influences explain superpower behavior better.

Eurocentrism

History is too often seen only through the eyes of Europe – or those European settlers, missionaries and fortune-hunters who ended up colonizing the rest of the world. This form of tunnel vision sees all progress and development as flowing from European innovation and genius. European culture is civilization; the rest of humanity is simply what anthropologist Eric Wolfe calls 'peoples without history'. Africans, Asians and native Americans are reduced to irrational resisters, passive victims or silent witnesses. Their contribution in work and culture – whether African labor or native American agriculture, Islamic mathematics or Chinese science – is trivialized. Their histories begin only when they encounter Europe. Even when the terrible costs of European colonialism are realistically calculated, these peoples are seldom granted their due as historical actors in their own right.

The nobility of the oppressed

Those who resist the forms of history that celebrate the virtues of the winners stand in danger of romanticizing the losers. Cartoon histories of noble workers and fat capitalists give little real sense of the flesh-and-blood struggles against oppression. Such an approach to 'history from below' tends to portray women, black people or the underclass as either passive victims or brave resisters. Their contradictory humanity and how it changes over time is reduced to a flattering but sterile nobility. Their hopes and fears, idiosyncrasies and ambitions, are flattened to a dull sameness.

From the top down

This is history from the perspective of the winners. A series of great men – usually politicians (referred to as 'statesmen'), war heroes, entrepreneurs, monarchs and important thinkers – are responsible for the progressive evolution of society. Its repetitive storyline sees the members of a revolving élite falling in and out of grace. They hand down reforms – the right to vote, the abolition of slavery, the right to form unions, universal education, welfare programs – to a passive and grateful public. This view minimizes the hard struggles of ordinary people to force these concessions out of recalcitrant and reactionary holders of power. The careers of the rich and famous are substituted for the rich diversity of popular culture and its many forms of resistance.

The certainty of progress

The notion that history has a definite goal has often seduced humankind. Old-fashioned versions tended to see history as the enactment of God's will on earth. More modern variants include the Marxist notion of a classless society and the various techno-fantasies of believers in the forward march of progress. Most of this is wishful thinking which ends up cramming people and societies into categories where they simply do not fit. It can make for crude history and pretty ruthless politics. The by-products of 'progress', not least of which is the potential ecological collapse of the planet, should lead to a healthy skepticism about any pre-ordained results for humanity's historical adventure.

BRIEF HISTORY **9**

A Brief History of Ethics

From Socrates to St Paul, Al Ghazali to Marcuse, Mahavira to Derrida, Wollstonecraft to Gandhi, humans have come up with a wide range of philosophies. Here is a basketful – or two – of ethical stances to choose from.

The Greeks

The horny, violent and amoral gods of Greek mythology were hardly role models for humans and certainly didn't offer an ethical system. Maybe as a result, secular philosophy flourished in Classical Greece. For Socrates (c 469-399 BCE) the human capacity to question was all-important: an unexamined life is not worth living. Real knowledge and right behavior exist – but you have to discover them for yourself. Socrates also had a knack for asking questions that revealed how little we really know about anything. Plato (c 428-354 BCE) thought there were two kinds of knowledge: empirical knowledge, which we obtain through the senses, and the 'vastly superior' knowledge we get through using our reason. Only a few experts ever discover the latter and these experts should be put in charge of everyone else. Plato was an élitist and a moral absolutist who believed that morality is a part of the structure of the universe itself. But Aristotle (384-322 BCE) thought ethics should be determined by ordinary practical people, exercising common sense and moderation. He believed that we are programmed with the capacity for justice, fairness and courage, and that we become moral by working at it, much as we learn to play the piano by practising.

Chinese ethics

Chinese ethics is more social and less individualistic than Western philosophy. In classical Chinese philosophy, ethics consists of two parts: *dao* and *de*. A social *dao* or 'The Way' is what guides us and the job of ethical thinkers is to reflect on how to preserve, transmit or change this way. *De* or 'Virtue' consists of the character traits, skills and dispositions induced by exposure to *dao*. Both *dao* and *de* encompass more than morality proper but also apply to fashion, etiquette, economics, prudence and even archery. Kung Fu-tzu or Confucius (551-479 BCE), the most influential of Chinese ethical thinkers, saw himself not as a philosopher but as a historical scholar, transmitting a code of social conduct inherited from ancient sage kings. Utilitarian and pragmatic approaches emerged with the later philosophers, Mozi and Xunzi. Contact with the West brought new influences – socialism and pragmatism being the most attractive to Chinese intellectuals and political leaders.

Hinduism

Hindu ethics tend to be complex and unworldly. The Upanishads (c 900-200 BCE) are the key philosophical texts. In these, metaphysical pursuits are placed above worldly pursuits. The idea of social responsibility is almost dispensed with. But there are other more socially aware Hindu texts, such as Manu's Law Books, which make it mandatory for kings to attend first to the welfare of their citizens and to protect the rights of the individual within a group. The Ramayana and Mahabharata popular epics explore the struggles, paradoxes and difficulties of coming to terms with the evolving idea of *dharma* (moral and social order). The message is: you must do your duty according to your 'nature' and duty is determined by your place or class in society. These epics, however, do manage to resolve the deep conflict between asceticism and duty by synthesizing the two in the concept of *nuishkama karma* or 'disinterested action' – an idea that was to provide part of the foundation for Gandhism.

Buddhism

The Buddha, Prince Siddharta Gautama (born 563 BCE), was born into such luxury that he did not even know suffering and death existed until he glimpsed them one day outside his palace walls. He set off on a spiritual journey. The result was an ethical system characterized by simplicity, frugality and compassion. In Buddhist ethics, motives are what matter most. If an action has its roots in greed, hatred and delusion, then it is unwholesome or bad; if in liberality, compassionate love and wisdom, then it is good. But the consequences of actions also matter, as do working towards the material and spiritual welfare of others. Actions in this life and the accumulation of merit will affect future reincarnations. But sin, guilt and worry about past offenses play no part in the Buddhist conception of wrong-doing. The five core Buddhist values are: abstain from killing and hurting living creatures; from stealing; from wrong indulgence in sensual pleasures; from lying; and from taking intoxicants.

Jainism

Jainism is both a philosophical system and a way of life in its own right. It originated in India and was founded in 500 BCE by Mahavira, an ascetic and unorthodox teacher. Like Buddha, with whom he has been compared, he was non-theistic, rejecting a 'supremely personal God'. Jains believe that every entity in the world has a *jiva* or a sentient principle whose distinguishing features are consciousness, vital energy and a happy disposition. The most fundamental principle is that you should not harm any sentient being, even the tiniest insect. These concerns make Jains the earliest protagonists of 'animal liberation' and vigorous exponents of vegetarianism. Truthfulness and non-possessiveness are also central to the Jain ethical system.

Judeo-Christianity

Practical perfection in this world is the main aim of Jewish ethics. The central doctrine is that human beings are created in the image of God and can reach their most perfect self-realization through worship and imitation of God. One of the best ways to do this is through decent, humane and moral relations with one's fellows. You should love your neighbor as yourself. The best known of the ethical teachings of the Bible are the Ten Commandments. Meanwhile, Jewish mysticism (or the Kabbalah) teaches that the physical and the spiritual are in a constant state of active interpenetration so that the moral actions of humans can have a profound impact on the very structure of the universe. Jesus of Nazareth (died 33 CE) was a Jew who took the Jewish notion of reciprocity one step further. He taught that we should not only love our neighbors as ourselves but also love our enemies, and there should be no limit to our forgiveness for injuries. Jesus did not give any precise moral rulings. He said nothing about war, capital punishment, gambling, equality, sex, slavery or contraception. But he challenged society's standards in his attitudes towards the poor, heretics, prostitutes, adulterers, lepers and women. His followers, especially St Paul, were less restrained in making specific moral pronouncements and condemnations.

Islam

Islam is rooted in the idea of 'divine command', of God's revelations to the Prophet Muhammad (died 632), recorded in the Qur'an. This provides a basis for a moral order and presents humanity with a clear distinction between right and wrong which is not subject to human vicissitude. The Prophet's actions, sayings and norms – known collectively as the Sunnah – provide a human model for how to live; while God's commands and prohibitions are formulated into Shari'a laws. The job of Muslim ethics is to create rational awareness that sustains the validity of the revelation. The Qur'an's ideals and commands are translated at a social level through the Muslim concept of community. The Qur'an also strongly emphasizes the ethics of redressing injustice in economic and social life – including improving the status of women. Several different traditions exist within Islam. In Shi'ism, for example, imams – holy men – are believed to be divinely guided and have the power to act as custodians of the Qur'an and interpreters of its vision for individuals as well as society. Sufism is more mystical and esoteric. For Sufists like Al

Ghazali (died 1111) the important thing is to cultivate an inner personal life in search of divine love and knowledge. True moral action links this inner awareness to outward expression and practice.

Mayan ethics

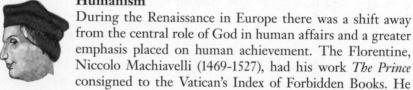

According to the Mayan vision of the cosmos, every form of life emerges from the same origin or seed. Some seeds become trees, others flowers, others water, others human beings. Thus each creature is inextricably linked to all others and what one does to a tree affects not only the tree, but oneself and other creatures. This inter-relatedness calls for profound respect between people and their Creator, between people and nature, and among people themselves. The aim of the Maya is to keep their relationships with the world around them, and also the inner life of each person, in perfect balance according to the rhythms of the cosmos. No being is superior to another being, merely different, and from this springs the basic Mayan concept of unity within diversity. In the community each person must be included, as each has their specific contribution to make. Evil is recognized as part of reality and wrong-doing is punished so as to restore the equilibrium between the offender and the victim. Mayan ideas have much in common with those of other indigenous cultures of the Americas, especially in their holism and respect for the environment.

Humanism

During the Renaissance in Europe there was a shift away from the central role of God in human affairs and a greater emphasis placed on human achievement. The Florentine, Niccolo Machiavelli (1469-1527), had his work *The Prince* consigned to the Vatican's Index of Forbidden Books. He wrote that the successful ruler needs not only to have virtue but also a readiness to lie, steal, cheat and kill, if need be. 'It is necessary for a Prince who wishes to maintain his position to learn how not to be good,' he says. His view of human nature was pretty pessimistic. So was that of English philosopher Thomas Hobbes (1588-1679). He popularized the doctrine that human nature is basically nasty in a theory called Psychological Egoism. His solution was a legalistic form of the reciprocity idea: the 'Social Contract'. To Hobbes, morality was simply a way for wicked but rational human beings to avoid conflict. French philosopher Jean-Jacques Rousseau (1712-78) took the opposite view. He believed we are born as moral beings with a huge potential for goodness, which is why children's education is so important. But civilization corrupts this innate goodness. Rousseau and other Romantics believed it possible to form a society which virtually dispenses with government.

Utilitarianism

Forget about the motives. It's the consequences that count – and those can be measured – was the line taken by two English radicals and freethinkers, Jeremy Bentham (1748-1832) and John Stuart Mill (1806-73). For Bentham, human beings are ruled by 'two masters': pleasure and pain. Laws should be passed only if they maximize pleasure and minimize pain for the majority of people 'for the greatest happiness of the greatest number'. Mill, however, saw the dangers of tyranny by the majority. He was all for pluralism: a healthy society should have room for difference and oddballs. He was also in favor of normally sticking to a set of moral rules rather than calculating every act in terms of pain and pleasure. Mill and Bentham were responsible for introducing the then radical notion that the chief duty of a government is to make the majority of their population happy. In recent years animal liberationists have drawn much from Utilitarian thinking, especially Jeremy Bentham, who kept a pet pig for company and said: 'The question is not "do they think?" but "can they suffer?".'

Deontologism or duty ethics

Immanuel Kant (1724-1804) was so regular in his habits that the people of his home town in Germany would set their clocks by observing his daily walks. He thought that morality rarely has anything to do with happiness and is all to do with duty. Ordinary people are right, thought Kant, to believe that morality is essentially about sticking to a set of compulsory rules. He just wanted to give philosophical justification to this belief. He stressed that to be moral we have to imagine ourselves on the receiving end of other people's decisions and universalize from there. Kant's system has been criticized for not allowing for exceptions or for conflicts between moral rules. A more modern development of duty ethics is the 'Prescriptivism' of Richard M Hare (1919-2002). He also believed that morality is about obeying rules. But he claimed that a moral statement like 'murder is wrong' is more like a recommendation, or an order not to murder, than a statement of fact.

Marxism

Karl Marx (1818-83) thought morality is just ideology in disguise and that it exists to serve the interests of the ruling class. Underlying society's beliefs about everything is one thing: economics. Capitalism has survived so successfully because the dominant class has monopolized education, religion, the law and ideas about morality. Belief in the disinterested nature of bourgeois 'justice' and 'morality' is just 'false consciousness', according to Marx. Only after a revolution when everyone is free of illusions about an objective morality will it be possible to create a society which is free and just. Post-Marxists like Herbert Marcuse (1898-1979), Roland Barthes (1915-80) and Michel Foucault (1926-84) have examined further how the spectacle of consumerism hypnotizes individual citizens into accepting the 'Morality' of Capitalism.

Gandhism

Though not a philosopher or a religious leader, MK Gandhi (1869-1948) and his ideas have had a huge impact around the world. His core principle is that of nonviolent direct action. He toyed first with the idea of non-cooperation, reinforced by his Quaker friends in South Africa. But eventually he came up with a more confrontational but still nonviolent concept – that of *satyagraha* (truth force). In developing this method he combined Hindu, Jain and Buddhist notions. He put it to work in the civil-disobedience movement which eventually led to Indian independence. Since then it has achieved remarkable results in many freedom struggles, including the US Civil Rights movement led by Martin Luther King. Other nonviolent freedom struggles around the world – from Tibet to Greenham Common – have been influenced to some extent by Gandhism.

Existentialism

The Existentialist philosopher Jean-Paul Sartre (1905-80) believed that every individual is unique so no-one can generalize about 'human nature'. He believed that it is we ourselves who are responsible for our essential natures or characters. We are free to 'make' ourselves and if we deny this freedom we are 'inauthentic' cowards, exhibiting 'bad faith'. Morality comes down to the business of making 'fundamental choices'. There are no moral systems or rules or gurus that can help us. You are totally responsible for your final decision and all the anguish that may result from getting it wrong.

Freudianism

Until Sigmund Freud (1856-1939) started delving into the unconscious, most moral philosophers assumed that we are always in control of our thought processes and that the choices we make are ours. According to Freud, human beings are programmed by instinctive psychic structures in layers of the Unconscious, Ego and Super-Ego. The Unconscious exerts powerful pressures upon us to fulfill our instinctual desires which the Super-Ego insists the Ego deny. The Super-Ego is similar to the conscience. It is like a parental voice reminding us of social norms acquired through childhood. Being moral may not accord with our real natures at all and so to base a moral system on what we essentially are is impossible. Jacques Lacan (1901-81), Freud's most radical modern disciple, went further to say that the self itself is a fiction. It is a linguistic construct and since language exists as a structure before the individual enters into it, then the whole notion of human identity is untenable. So self-knowledge or moral choices cannot be 'ours'.

Postmodernism

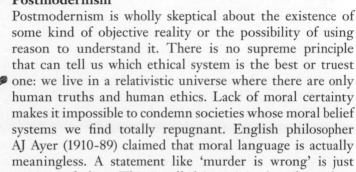

Postmodernism is wholly skeptical about the existence of some kind of objective reality or the possibility of using reason to understand it. There is no supreme principle that can tell us which ethical system is the best or truest one: we live in a relativistic universe where there are only human truths and human ethics. Lack of moral certainty makes it impossible to condemn societies whose moral belief systems we find totally repugnant. English philosopher AJ Ayer (1910-89) claimed that moral language is actually meaningless. A statement like 'murder is wrong' is just someone expressing a feeling. This is called 'emotivism' or 'hurra-boo theory'. More recent postmodernist thinkers like Jean Francois Lyotard (1924-98) and Jacques Derrida (1930-2004) claim that reason is itself a fiction, because it's a human, linguistic construct, not a transcendent entity. Our worship of reason has been the cause of much human suffering and led to dangerous political certainties which insist on the exclusion of 'the other'. The damage done by the 'modernism' of large totalitarian regimes holding on to the objectivity of their utopian visions is stressed by several philosophers. In a postmodern world we are free to shop around for any set of moral values we feel are appropriate. But there are no signposts: we each have to decide for ourselves.

Social ethics

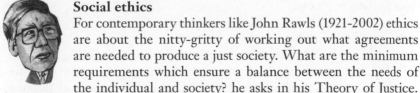

For contemporary thinkers like John Rawls (1921-2002) ethics are about the nitty-gritty of working out what agreements are needed to produce a just society. What are the minimum requirements which ensure a balance between the needs of the individual and society? he asks in his Theory of Justice. Liberty and acceptance of difference are important, he asserts. So is basic protection against poverty. Some people will inevitably do well, others less so, but all should be guaranteed a minimum standard of living, with a minimum wage. Alasdair MacIntyr (born 1929) meanwhile suggests that ethics should concentrate less on individuals and their moral decisions and more on the community and its moral health and welfare. He thinks we should focus on what people should be rather than what they should do. This is known as 'Virtue Theory'. MacIntyr reckons that human beings are unstoppably communitarian and that communal life is held together by those traditions and virtues that groups encourage in individual members.

Environmental ethics

Unlike many indigenous ethical systems of the Majority World, traditional Western approaches to the natural environment have been strictly human-centered. The current plight of the planet as a result of human activity now calls for a more holistic kind of ethic. That may mean accepting that humans do not always have moral precedence over other life-forms. The Gaia Hypothesis of James Lovelock (born 1919) suggests that our host planet is itself a huge, ruthlessly self-regulating biological organism. It is not committed to the preservation of human life at all. So it may be very much in our interest to convince our planetary host that we are worth keeping on as environmentally conscientious house-guests. At present environmental ethics are in the process of evolution with various strands emerging. Some theorists remain human-centered, some animal-centered, others promote a life-centered ecological holism. They range from utilitarian claims that humans need a healthy environment and so should take care of it, to discussions about the rights of rocks.

Female ethics

The idea that virtue is in some way gendered, that the standards and criteria of morality are different for women and men, has existed in Western thinking for a long time. The dominant patriarchal view has maintained that by 'nature' women are more intuitive, irrational, gentle, passive, selfless and sympathetic than men. Early feminist Mary Wollstonecraft (1759-97) attacked this view of female 'nature' as an ideological construct whose primary function was to legitimize male supremacy in public life and to restrict women to the domestic sphere. But more recently, contemporary thinkers like feminist psychologist Carol Gilligan (born 1936) have revived ideas of ethics being gendered. She argues that women's moral responses to problems are 'essentially' different, more co-operative and less aggressive. Such a belief is problematic if one believes, as many feminists do, that the idea of 'female nature' is a social and historical construct. Another modern philosopher Julia Kristeva (born 1941) stresses that there is no such thing as 'essential woman', primarily because of postmodernist doubts about the very notion of identity itself.

BRIEF HISTORY 10

The Politics of Development

From the socialist optimism of the 1960s to the global justice and environmental movements of the 2000s, how ideas about changing the world have continued to shift – and how they have been reflected in the pages of the *New Internationalist*.

The socialist vision

When the *New Internationalist* first appeared in 1973, the poor in what was then routinely called the Third World faced hunger and disease on a massive scale. Only socialism seemed to offer any solution – with land reform and free health services high on the agenda. The poor had been exploited by colonialism and they continued to be exploited by capitalism. Socialism seemed like the way to put an end to all this; only state planning could organize the massive redistribution of wealth required.

The new Third World

Newly independent Third World countries had also taken a broadly socialist line. India, which had achieved independence in 1947, launched its series of Five Year Plans in 1955. The Chinese Revolution of 1949 was communist-led. President Julius Nyerere of Tanzania set out in his 1967 Arusha Declaration a blueprint for African socialism. And those countries still fighting for freedom – like Vietnam, Southern Rhodesia and Portugal's African colonies, Mozambique and Angola – were also Marxist-inspired.

The aid lobby

Sympathizers in the West who wanted to help the Third World – the 'aid lobby' – tended to follow much the same line. They might have called themselves Marxists, socialists, liberals or even conservatives. But they tended to adopt a quasi-Marxist vocabulary to describe the problems, such as 'imperialism' and 'exploitation'. Something had to be done quickly. Almost everyone argued for aid in the form of cash or food. But change of a more permanent kind was also required. Hence the idea, originally raised by US President Harry Truman in his 1949 inaugural address, of 'development' – a vague notion that indicated some kind of positive change or progress that could be made almost regardless of a country's political system.

Trade wars

Third World leaders used the United Nations to argue for development funds and to protest about the injustices of international trade. They were supported by Marxist economists, whose 'dependency' theories argued that Third World economies had been reduced to mere 'peripheries' of Western capitalism. Poor countries were suppliers of raw materials like coffee or cocoa (for which they were badly paid) and had to buy manufactured goods (for which they were charged a lot). This implied two solutions. First, that Third World countries might achieve greater independence by trading amongst themselves and trying to industrialize – one group of South American countries set up the 'Andean Pact'. Second, that as sellers of raw materials to the West they should get together to charge higher prices. OPEC with its oil-price hikes in the 1970s started to show the way. 'Trade not aid' was the new slogan.

From liberation theology to ecology

Most of the inspiring ideas of the 1970s derived from Marxism. It fused with Christianity to form 'liberation theology' as radical priests in the shanty towns of Latin America realized that religion and politics were inextricably linked. Meanwhile Brazilian educator Paulo Freire was showing how the process of learning should be one of political empowerment. But there were other new ideas – on the environment, for example. There was widespread concern about the exhaustion of the earth's resources– the **NI** devoted a theme issue to this in 1976 (*Trash and Grab – the looting of a small planet*). And EF Schumacher's *Small is Beautiful* argued that sophisticated Western equipment was destructive in poor countries. They needed an 'intermediate' technology.

In general, it was easier for people to propose radical solutions in relation to the Third World, where injustice and repression seemed much more clear-cut than in the West. Many of these new ideas were aired at a series of UN conferences throughout the 1970s – on Food, Environment, Population. The boldest result was a call in 1974 for a New International Economic Order that would set the world aright – producing healthy flows of aid and more equitable trade.

Disillusion sets in

But there was to be no completely new order. Many of the ideas (like those on the environment) did become part of conventional development wisdom. But many others, particularly on trade, died. Mutual trade pacts collapsed because the political and economic interests of different countries collided. And élites in the Third World tended to be quite happy for the West to exploit their countries so long as their own wallets expanded. Aid was increasingly discredited. It was either diverted by corruption or financed projects like dam-building which destroyed the livelihoods of the poorest to benefit the rich. Some started to argue that only socialist countries should be aided – since new resources poured into an unjust society will inevitably flow towards the powerful.

Socialism faltering

But socialism too came into question. Eastern Europe had always been an embarrassing precedent. Now socialism had also taken some disturbing twists and turns in the Third World, ranging from authoritarian isolationism in Burma to military dictatorship in Ethiopia. Cuba was still well regarded for its social-welfare programs and China was considered to have had remarkable success in meeting basic needs. But there were increasing doubts about political freedom in both countries. And Tanzania, even under the inspiring leadership of Julius Nyerere, had made little progress towards a truly egalitarian society. Marxists, it seemed, could explain why people were poor. But they were less convincing when it came to solutions. The Nicaraguan revolution of 1979 was a symbolic turning point. It had the moral drive of socialism but accepted the contribution of personal enterprise.

The personal is political

In the West too, new ideas began to cut across a purely class-based socialism. Feminism showed how most political parties had treated women as invisible. Socialism had little to say about human relationships based on gender, race or sexual orientation. And socialist countries had been as exploitative of the earth as capitalists. Feminists now argued that the 'personal is political' – that our lifestyles and our personal attitudes and relationships have ramifications for the whole of society. From the early 1980s the **NI** started to write on themes like 'lifestyles' or 'sex'.

Capitalism in trouble

State socialism had been found wanting. But the capitalist countries of the Third World had done little better. Many were in economic trouble by the early 1980s. Governments kept people under control by repressive methods – often by military dictatorship. This 'stability' attracted Western banks. But a good credit rating proved a mixed blessing. Countries like Brazil and the Philippines which had accepted the largesse of friendly international banks finished up deep in debt. Now they came under the dismal influence of the International Monetary Fund, which insisted they cut down spending on social welfare and adopt monetarist 'adjustment' policies. The debtor nations agreed not because such IMF policies worked (they were uniformly disastrous) but because the IMF, under US influence, held the purse strings.

The Right exultant

The late 1980s and 1990s saw the political tables turned. The once-dogmatic Left was reassessing socialism while the Right stuck more rigidly to its ideology. The rapid collapse of the Soviet Union and its satellite states put the Right in triumphalist mode: this, apparently, was 'the end of history' and all humans had to look forward to was rampant consumerism and the free market. The 'structural adjustment' inflicted on poor countries was in the 1990s applied to the former communist states, which were catapulted to the opposite extreme – wholesale privatization and abandonment to the free market in its rawest (often criminal) form. As the Millennium approached, right-wing observers claimed the 20th century as their own, the century of 'freedom', 'capitalism' and 'America'. According to this narrative, the multifarious struggles of the world's people for greater control over their own lives, for decent standards of health, education, nutrition, for social justice, for peace and civil rights, were reduced to one central story: the ultimate victory of the particular model of democracy and capitalism patented and promoted by the United States of America.

The Left licks its wounds

By the turn of the century the very word 'socialism' had largely passed into disuse, as if considered inappropriate in polite company. Democratic socialist parties in the rich world recast themselves as 'social democrats' or as 'New Labour' and effectively accepted the neoliberal economic orthodoxy, whether they were in government or in opposition. The issues of social class, poverty and exploitation remained but there was no longer an accepted political language in which to talk about them – nor a mainstream political alternative prepared to take issues of social justice seriously.

Development in ruins

The whole idea of 'development' also came into question. The *New Internationalist* in 1992 published a series of essays by the German thinker Wolfgang Sachs called *Development: A Guide to the Ruins*. It argued that development meant nothing more than projecting the American model of society onto the rest of the world. 'This heritage,' said Sachs, 'is like a weight which keeps one treading in the same spot. It prevents people in Michoacan, Gujarat or Zanzibar from recognizing their own right to refuse to classify themselves as "under-developed"; it stops them rejoicing in their own diversity and wit. Development always entails looking at other worlds in terms of what they lack, and obstructs the wealth of indigenous alternatives.'

He went on: 'The idea of development was once a towering monument inspiring international enthusiasm. Today, the structure is falling apart and in danger of total collapse. But its imposing ruins still linger over everything and block the way out. The task, then, is to push the rubble aside to open up new ground.'

Green revolution
In the 1970s and 1980s many on the Left tended to be scornful of environmental activists as 'insufficiently political' – the implication was that concern for nature was a bit like holding a fluffy bunny and not to be compared with the serious business of combating exploitation. The penny dropped as the implications of climate change became evident to all those prepared to notice during the 1990s: environmental politics were actually at the heart of the matter. At first there was talk of a Red-Green alternative emerging – the **NI** came out with an issue in 1998 with the optimistic title *Red and Green: Ecosocialism comes of age.* But most of the creative political energy of the 1990s and 2000s has come from the Green side. The **NI** has been arguing for much of the last two decades that the Emperor of Economic Growth has no clothes – though there is still not a political party close to power anywhere in the world prepared to advance that notion. The implications of a low- or no-carbon lifestyle will be profound; the political challenge will be to make sure that it does not arrive on the basis of 'apartheid', with high-carbon pleasures for the rich and the rest left to grub about in the darkness.

The global justice movement
The environment aside, the other 'new ground' lay in the emergence

of a global justice movement. Globalization was proceeding apace – if 'development' (now thought to require inverted commas) involved projecting the American model of society onto the rest of the world, then globalization was its realization, as Starbucks and McDonald's opened for business in every major city and Nike sought its workers in the 'free economic zones' and sweatshops of Asia. But there was a flipside to this in the globalization of resistance. At the World Trade Organization meeting in 1999, 100,000 demonstrators converged on Seattle to protest against the concerted attempt to open up markets for corporate exploitation in what was now being called the Global South or the Majority World.

A new 'movement' was born, loose in terms of organization, internationalist in scope and practice. Since 2001, the annual gathering of the rich and powerful for a World Economic Forum in the Swiss ski resort of Davos has been mirrored by a World Social Forum at which activists and intellectuals, farmers and alternative economists, map out their myriad alternatives. There is a marked (even determined) absence of specific ideology – all are conscious of the damage done by the Big Ideas of the past. But all are confident that – in the words of another *New Internationalist* magazine title from 2002 – 'Another World Is Possible'.

BRIEF HISTORY **11**

The Rise (and Falling) of the Nation-State

Nationalism is a relatively new idea and its dominance is already on the wane in the face of globalization.

Lords and their lands

The imperial armies of Ancient Rome and China conquered in the name of the emperor not the nation. In Europe in medieval times ordinary people owed their allegiance not to a state but to a feudal lord. Wars were fought between local aristocrats – like the Duke of Bourgogne or the Earl of Warwick – not kings or queens. In other parts of the world, societies were divided along cultural or ethnic lines, but again, borders as such were fluid and ever-changeable.

The nation-state arrives

The business of nation-building has always been a bloody one. Feudal lords were forced to give up their regional autonomy by kings who wanted to rule over larger areas. It took the Hundred Years' War (1337-1453) to disentangle England from France, and the murder of thousands of Albigensians to establish France as a nation. Nation-states finally became a reality in North America and Western Europe in the latter half of the 18th century and in Latin America soon after.

Creating a nation-state was one thing; making the people who lived there believe in it was quite another. As writer and former Prime Minister of Piedmont, Massimo d'Azeglio, pointed out when the nation-state of Italy was created in 1861: 'We have made Italy, now we have to make Italians'.

Motherlands and other lands

'As a woman, I have no country,' wrote Virginia Woolf. In most of the new nation-states women and the working class were not regarded as citizens. Those without property could not vote and they were unable to stand for Parliament. Many nation-states built their identity through displays of military prowess and often by means of military conflict – from which women were also excluded. Leaders spoke of 'the Motherland' but nationalism was essentially a means of co-operation between moneyed

patriarchies. As the vote was extended to women and to the working class, it became necessary for those patriarchies to be able to manipulate national identity in order to maintain loyalty and control.

The nation of the 'people'

'The principle of Sovereignty resides essentially in the Nation: no body of men, no individual, can express authority that does not emanate from it,' asserted the French Declaration of the Rights of Man and the Citizen in 1792.

American Independence and the French Revolution created new national models which relied heavily on written constitutions, national flags and anthems. They also introduced a new concept of democratic citizenship – one which stirred ordinary people to revolt against the monarchy. Popular revolts in Europe were paralleled in the New World – in 1791 Toussaint L'Ouverture led an insurrection of black slaves that produced the independent republic of Haiti in 1804. Patriotism became the ultimate loyalty, supposedly superseding all other ties.

Nationalism exported

As European empires expanded to the Americas, Asia, Africa and the Middle East, the new rulers not only imposed colonial rule but also brought their own model of the nation-state, which was alien to most of the indigenous populations. The colonial powers divided up the world along straight lines which separated village from village and family from family in the name of imperial allegiance. Quite different – and sometimes antagonistic – peoples were enclosed within the same boundaries. Muslims and Hindus in India, Hutus and Tutsis in Rwanda were played off against each other, and the peoples of those nations are still paying a bloody price for imperial nation-building.

As empires shrank and newly independent states declared their nationhood in the 20th century, they did so – regardless of political credo – in the manner of those who had colonized them and in traditional style with guarded borders, flags and national anthems. Inevitably their power was resisted by those with other ethnic, religious or pan-nationalist loyalties.

Fire in the belly

Of all the main political credos, nationalism has been the most successful. The emergence of national economies regulated by the state combined people's sense of economic security with their sense of geographic place. This has proved to be a potent blend to capture hearts and minds. In Russia and China communism not only failed to subvert nationalism but was taken over by it. Nationalism – often ethnic, sometimes religious – provides a convenient and believable credo for people trying to root themselves in the world. It is something to believe in, to belong to. And it suits those in power very well. It is easy to manipulate. It is a convenient tool for rulers to be able to whip up support as Slobodan Milosevic did with Serbian nationalism in the 1990s.

The nation-state dominant

Today the whole world – with the exception of Antarctica – is divided into nation-states and crisscrossed by boundaries. National identity has become as much a part of our psychological make-up as gender, race or class. The major conflicts being fought in the world today are almost all struggles to form new national identities – often based on supposed race or ethnicity.

The irony here is that of the 192 nation-states that make up the United Nations there are perhaps only a handful which do not include as part of their make-up large 'minority' groups. Nation-states today are essentially multicultural, which is why separatist movements are often forced to create identities from the past and resurrect former supposed glories in order to create new 'imagined communities'.

The nation sandwiched

But the story does not end here. Though the number of nation-states is still on the increase – as countries like former Yugoslavia and the USSR have splintered in recent years – their control is being eroded. Many of the original functions of the nation-state – welfare, defense, state ownership of production, railways, and crucially, communications – are either in the hands of the international community or have been privatized. Giant transnational companies and international banks bestride the world stage. To quote the UN's *Human Development Report*: 'The nation-state now is too small for the big things and too big for the small'. At the same time, ordinary people have less faith than before in the trappings and structures of the state – the monarchy or presidency, parliament and politics. Where the state collapses – Somalia, Iraq, Afghanistan – local warlords re-emerge. The wheel has come full circle.

BRIEF HISTORY **12**

The Roots of Feminism

The term 'feminism' may belong to modern times – but the roots of feminism go back much further.

Rebels and thinkers

There have always been independent feminists. In sixth century BCE Greece, Sappho wrote lesbian poetry and ran a girls' school. The 15th-century French writer Christine de Pisan is now regarded as a feminist thinker. In the 17th century English adventurer and political activist Aphra Behn was getting embroiled in the West Indian slave rebellion – and writing 13 novels. The radical way in which some men were thinking during the Age of Reason incidentally changed attitudes towards women. Thinkers like Newton, Locke, Voltaire and Diderot believed that science and reason could explain the world. They began to analyze women in terms of what they deemed 'natural' rather than what was divinely ordained. This was not necessarily better for women.

Mothers of the revolution

Women played a major role in the 1789 French Revolution and the ideal of 'Republican Motherhood' took shape. But, some argued, if women had the task of 'bringing up the new citizens', they should also have status. Feminist pamphlets proliferated. In her *Rights of Woman*, Olympe de Gouges wrote: 'Woman is born free and her rights are the same as those of man... if women have the right to go to the scaffold, they must also have the right to go to Parliament.' Parisian women formed political clubs and associations to campaign on issues affecting them. But the male leaders of the Revolution were basically hostile and in 1793 they outlawed all women's clubs. A woman's place was in the home, they ruled. This hostility persisted through the 19th century. The Napoleonic Code gave all management of family funds to the husband. Not until 1909 did French women have control over their own earnings. Not until 1944 did they get the vote.

Radical sparks

Meanwhile, in North America, women took part in the independence struggle and exercised their power as consumers to boycott British goods. Even in Britain there was a rash of radical – and reactionary – writing about women. Closely watching events in France was British journalist and translator Mary Wollstonecraft. She worked to support her family but in 1787 came to London to live by her writing. She joined a radical circle of intellectuals. A year after Thomas Paine wrote *The Rights of Man* (1791), Mary Wollstonecraft produced her *A Vindication of the Rights of Women*. It  was the first full-scale book favoring women's liberation and was widely read. She was dismissed by the male conservative press as 'a strumpet'.

Missions and manacles

For black women living in slavery in the US, the late 18th century was a turning point, as Protestant evangelism combined with the anti-slavery movement. Women made up a large part of revivalist congregations – both in white and black churches. Women were not supposed to preach but some – like the former slave Jarena Lee – ignored this. Black women realized that freedom from whites was not enough. They had to have freedom from men too.

But uniting white and black women was not easy. When black feminist Sojourner Truth stood before the Second Annual Convention of Women's Rights in Akron, Ohio, in 1852, racist white women tried to stop her speaking. There were many black women activists but Sojourner Truth was the most outspoken, arguing publicly that black women should have the vote.

Industry and protest

During the Industrial Revolution unmarried women left home to work in the cities, often for low wages in appalling factory conditions. Meanwhile the idea of female education became firmly entrenched and middle class women demanded access to a much wider range of occupations. On both sides of the Atlantic women started taking part in industrial action. During the 1808 Weavers Strike in Britain *The Times* singled out striking women weavers as 'more turbulent and insolent' than the men. In the US, the first all-women strike took place in 1828 at Cocheco Mill, New
Hampshire. In Britain, in 1854 Barbara Leigh Smith drew together for the first time a group of women who called themselves feminists and campaigned to change laws. A strike by women in an East London match factory helped create the British trade union movement.

Invasion and rebellion

In Asia and Africa women were resisting both traditional and colonial oppression. Chinese feminists who joined the Taiping Rebellion of 1850-1864 called for an end to foot-binding and demanded communal ownership of property and equal rights for women and men. Colonizing Europeans made alliances with groups that were the most conservative and often most oppressive of women. So the British in India encouraged the dowry system, arranged marriages and education for men only. But by 1905 Indian women were participating in the Swadeshi movement to boycott foreign goods and in 1917 the Women's Indian Association was set up with links to the British movement for women's suffrage. In parts of Africa women were banned from entering the cities and their traditional access to land – as Africa's principal farmers – was also denied. But in 1923 the Egyptian Women's Federation was formed and in 1924 it got the age of marriage for girls raised to 16.

Suffering for suffrage

Women's call for the vote was echoing around the world. It was first answered in New Zealand/Aotearoa in 1893. In Britain mass meetings organized by Emmeline Pankhurst and her two daughters Sylvia and Christabel drew crowds of up to 500,000. Determined  militants chained themselves to railings and caused civil disturbances. In 1908 the Pankhursts were arrested and imprisoned. They went on hunger strike and were force-fed – causing public outcry. But only in 1918 did women (over the age of 30) get the vote in Britain. The US followed in 1920. In India Provincial Assemblies were allowed to enfranchise women in 1919. And in 1931 the Indian National Congress Party pledged itself to sexual as well as caste and religious equality at independence. The first Latin American country to give women the vote was Ecuador in 1929, followed by Brazil, Argentina, Cuba and Chile during the 1930s.

Reds and beds

Karl Marx and Friedrich Engels saw women's liberation as part of the socialist revolution and Rosa Luxemburg, Clara Zetkin and Alexandra Kollontai became respected political leaders. In 1918 the first Women's Conference was held in Moscow and during the 1920s – under Lenin – the Soviet Government promoted equal rights. Marriage, divorce and contraception were made simple. But in the 1930s and 1940s Stalin turned the clock back. Divorce was made difficult, abortion banned, contraception restricted. In China the 1949 Revolution brought formal equality for women and men. But both here and in the USSR women did the housework as well as their jobs. In the West feminism lay dormant. Radicals were preoccupied with fighting unemployment, fascism, then McCarthyism.

The Second Wave

But during the 1960s feminism burst into life again in the US as part of a radical culture that included Civil Rights and sexual liberation. Betty

Friedan's *The Feminine Mystique* was a bestseller in 1963. Feminist groups campaigned on issues such as childcare, health, welfare, education, abortion. Consciousness-raising groups proliferated. In Europe, Canada and Australasia too, new ideas and laws were changing society. Germaine Greer's *The Female Eunuch* was an eye-opener. And in 1975 the United Nations announced an International Decade for Women. Revolutionary movements in Zimbabwe, Angola, Mozambique and Nicaragua included women's liberation in their ideology. In Europe the peace movement became the focus for feminist activism – especially at the US air base at Greenham Common, England. And feminism boomed in Latin America after the restoration of democracy during the 1980s.

Women's rights today

It is as a result of the pressure these feminists exerted that many women's lives have improved. Today, more are working, more girls are being educated, women are living longer and having fewer children, there are more females in business and in politics. The laws on personal relationships have improved too: there is legislation against domestic violence, in some countries there are more liberal marriage laws, and in others, same-sex relationships are now recognized in law. In six African countries female genital cutting has been outlawed. The UN Convention on the Elimination of All Forms of Discrimination Against Women has now been ratified by 185 countries.

Yet the brutal facts remain. The vast majority of the world's women still have very little power, at work, in their relationships at home, or in the wider world. Worldwide, 70 per cent of those living in poverty are women, as are two-thirds of illiterate adults. One in four women is beaten by her husband or partner. Every day, 1,450 still die unnecessarily in childbirth or during pregnancy. It is largely women who are exploited by the multi-billion-dollar pornography industry; women who are trafficked from country to country as commodities in the sex trade; women who do the part-time, low-paid jobs in appalling conditions that have arrived as part of globalization. Meanwhile, the rise of religious extremism has resulted in heightened legal and social restrictions on women.

So while middle-class white women in the West are unlikely to lose the rights they have won, there is a danger that rights elsewhere are being slowly, silently and inexorably clawed back. The feminist battle is only half won.

The Rich History of Pan-Africanism

From Prince Hall to Marcus Garvey, from Kwame Nkrumah to the African Union.

Roots

Pan-Africanism has a rich history which dates back at least to the 18th century. It came originally from the New World rather than from Africa itself. Crushed by the brutality of slavery in the Americas and the Caribbean, people of African origin naturally yearned for their ancestral homeland and the dignity and freedom it represented – even those who had been born in captivity. Prince Hall, a black cleric in Boston, campaigned  unsuccessfully in 1787 for help from the State Assembly in returning poor blacks to Africa. Another black Bostonian, Quaker shipbuilder Paul Cuffe, took matters into his own hands in 1815 by setting sail in one of his ships with 40 other black Americans and founding a settlement in Sierra Leone, which the British had established as a refuge for freed and runaway slaves in 1787.

Past glory

The issue of 'repatriation' was contentious, though, particularly among free black Americans in the northern US of the 19th century: Frederick Douglass, for example, argued that the idea was a conspiracy to avoid giving American black people their rights. Nevertheless, the efforts of the American Colonization Society (largely white liberals) resulted in the establishment of another slave refuge: Liberia. Former slaves also returned to Africa from the Caribbean and Brazil.

Pan-African resistance took other forms, too. The racist idea of white superiority and African backwardness was challenged, for example, by the publication in 1829 of David Walker's Appeal, which drew attention to Africa's glorious history, including that of ancient Egypt. By the mid-19th century these notions were being actively promoted within Africa, too, by James 'Africanus' Beale Horton and James 'Holy' Johnson from Sierra Leone and by the Liberian Edward Blyden, who campaigned tirelessly against racism and British imperialism. Yet all of these early Pan-Africanists were pro-Western: they wanted to create autonomous African nation-states that would develop both economically and educationally along orthodox Western lines.

Carve up & congress
In 1884 the major European powers convened the Congress of Berlin, at which they agreed how Africa would be carved up between them. This naked scramble for Africa gave new urgency to the Pan-African response. In 1886 George Charles, president of the African Emigration Association, declared to the US Congress that his organization planned to establish a United States of Africa. Pan-Africanists convened their own Congress on Africa in Chicago in 1893, at which they denounced the partition of the continent and discussed the French threats to the independence of Liberia and Abyssinia in particular.

This new organized solidarity bore fruit in the launch of the African Association in 1897. Its key figure was Henry Sylvester Williams. Williams might be called the grandfather of Pan-Africanism. Born in Trinidad, he studied law in London and it was there that he convened the first Pan-African Conference in 1900. Like all the early Pan-African meetings, the participants at the first Pan-African Conference were drawn almost entirely from the Caribbean, American or European diaspora rather than from Africa itself. The delegates talked of creating a movement campaigning for African people's rights – and sent a petition to Queen Victoria denouncing Britain's treatment of people in its African colonies.

Garvey & Du Bois
The twin giants of the Pan-African Movement in the first half of the 20th century were both based in the US: Marcus Garvey and WEB Du Bois.

Marcus Garvey lived his early life in Jamaica but his Universal Negro Improvement Association (UNIA) failed to achieve lift-off until he moved to New York in 1916. In Harlem, however, his ideas about black pride struck a chord almost immediately. By 1920 he was being talked of as the 'Black Moses': he held an international convention with delegates from 25 countries and led a 50,000-strong parade through the streets of Harlem. His most popular slogans were 'Back to Africa' and 'Africa for the Africans', sentiments which ironically suited the racist Ku Klux Klan. In 1925 Garvey's dream fell apart when he was imprisoned for mail fraud connected with his Black Star shipping line: after two years in jail he was deported to England and never regained his influence. But Garveyism remained the most popular form of Pan-Africanism in the Caribbean and resurfaced long after his death in the reggae scene of the 1970s.

WEB Du Bois was an altogether different figure from Garvey, rooted in rigorous academic research into the social condition of African-Americans. Co-founder of the National Association for the Advancement of Colored People (NAACP), he edited its newspaper *The Crisis* from 1910 to 1934. Du Bois saw the problems of Black Americans and Africans in an internationalist way, as part of a general struggle for justice. He organized another Pan-African Congress in Paris in 1919 to coincide with the Versailles peace conference at the end of the First World War, hoping in vain to persuade world leaders that US President Wilson's lofty principle of self-determination should be applied to Africans, too.

Harlem renaissance & négritude
Du Bois organized three further Pan-African conferences in the 1920s. But by the 1930s the main impetus of Pan-Africanism in the Americas was cultural, deriving from the Harlem Renaissance in which a generation of black writers and artists looked to Africa for their inspiration and identity, including Zora Neal Hurston, Claude McKay, Langston Hughes and Paul Robeson.

Another important strand of Pan-Africanism was *négritude*. This was a term identified with nationalists and intellectuals from France's Caribbean and African colonies, such as Aimé Césaire and Léopold Senghor, who propounded it in Paris in 1933. The key idea was that all Africans, whether in exile or at home, shared an 'African personality'. In practice the movement became an argument for African nationalism that was peculiar to the French colonial context; when its leaders eventually took power in an independent state, as Senghor did in Senegal in 1960, they held power on behalf of a Westernized, pro-French élite. Most prominent among the critics of négritude was the writer Frantz Fanon, a doctor from Martinique who put his own Pan-Africanism on the line by joining the anti-colonial struggle in Algeria.

Nkrumah takes up the flame
The fifth Pan-African Congress in 1945 had Du Bois, now 73, as its honorary chair and Amy Ashwood, Marcus Garvey's first wife, presiding over its first session, but the torch had in reality passed to a new generation of Pan-Africanists from the continent itself, including Kwame Nkrumah and Jomo Kenyatta.

Nkrumah soon became the voice and organizing force of Pan-Africanism. In the late 1940s and 1950s he promoted the idea of an independent West African Federation, seen as the first step towards a United States of Africa. When, in March 1957, he became leader of the newly independent state of Ghana, one of his first thoughts was to use his new position to help other Africans transcend the old colonial boundaries and work towards uniting the continent. He convened a Conference of Independent States in 1958, though at that stage there were only eight independent countries in Africa. He also went immediately to the aid of independent Guinea when France victimized it for rejecting membership of the post-colonial African franc zone. Nkrumah and the Guinean leader Sekou Touré agreed on a union of their two countries which they hoped would prefigure wider African unity.

Crossroads & Congo

This was the key moment of decision for Africa: should it pursue Nkrumah's goal of Pan-African unity or that of national independence? In general the former French colonies were much less keen on the idea of unity, preferring to retain their ties with Paris; as a result they boycotted the second Conference of Independent States in 1960. The crisis in the former Belgian Congo helped to bring this division to a head. The first prime minister of Congo, Patrice Lumumba, was an enthusiastic supporter of Nkrumah's Pan-African vision. Backed by a mining transnational and by Belgian troops, soldiers from Katanga province took up arms aiming to secede and soon had Lumumba in captivity (eventually murdering him four years later); the United Nations (with the US looming large) sent peacekeepers seen as favoring anti-Lumumba forces. A group of francophone independent states held a conference in Brazzaville which praised the Belgian/UN action in Congo; the other independent states held a separate meeting in Casablanca which denounced it.

The political divide was important. The Brazzaville group believed Pan-African socialism would frighten the West away and rob Africa of the aid and investment it needed for development. The Casablanca group argued that Western economic exploitation meant it was more important to develop an African common market and institutions than to go cap in hand for aid. Another conference in Monrovia in 1961 involving both sides failed to bridge the gap.

Nationalism ascendant

In effect the nationalists won the day. There were still idealistic attempts to move unity along – notably the proposed East African Union in which Julius Nyerere of Tanganyika and Milton Obote of Uganda agreed to merge their countries with Kenya under that country's leader, Jomo Kenyatta. But even this initiative foundered on the rocks. It was too easy to run with the model of the independent nation-state favored by the West, which preferred the stability of handing over power to an indigenous élite within the old colonial boundaries. Besides, it was a time full of optimism that the new nations of the Third World, now finding their voice in the United Nations, would be able to compete on the world stage.

Instead of the United States of Africa dreamed of by Nkrumah, the Organization of African Unity (OAU) came into being in 1963 with a headquarters in the Ethiopian capital, Addis Ababa. The OAU proved to be a fairly ineffective collection of nation-states, much like any other regional grouping. Although it retained in its constitution the ideal of Pan-African union, in practice this remained a moribund, forgotten project for decades. It was only as the end of the 20th century loomed – as the unsustainability of the African status quo and the inexorable progress of globalization became ever more evident – that the Pan-African vision came back into sharp focus.

The African Union

The African Union (AU) was established in Addis Ababa on 9 July 2002, superseding the OAU and the African Economic Community. All the nations of the continent have joined, with the single exception of Morocco, which objects to Western Sahara's membership.

There is already a Pan-African Parliament, based in Midrand, South Africa, as well as numerous other institutions in varying states of creation. The avowed goal is eventually to have a single currency (the Afro) and a single integrated defense force. In reality there are still significant divisions over how far to move towards a United States of Africa with Libya among the keenest to embrace full union while many southern African states are more skeptical. Early attempts to show the AU to be a more powerful and meaningful force for Pan-African peace and co-operation than its predecessor have largely foundered, most notably in the signal failure of the African Union force to end the killing in Darfur.

But Pan-Africanism as an idea is still resurgent – and may yet bring a United States of Africa into being.

BRIEF HISTORY **14**

Highways into History

Historical truth, like beauty, is in the eye of the beholder. But people's understanding of the past has been shaped by certain key philosophies of history – here is a guide to them.

The traditional past

Origins Traditional notions of the past reside in the rhythm of the seasons; they are attempts to understand how humankind should adapt to nature. They usually involve some sort of creation story and thus are mixed with religion.

Philosophy The histories of early hunter-gatherer societies were morality tales about how to interact with nature and each other. Gradually these morality tales came to focus on the behavior of the priest, ruler and warrior class as the political state emerged from ancient Egypt to imperial China. But history remained a series of 'lessons' telling (often in remarkable detail) of the great deeds or shortcomings of past rulers and their consequences: glorious conquest, the collapse of cities or deadly offense given to some moody god. These histories were either static or cyclical with little sense of the evolution and direction of society.

Politics The shift in focus from ancestors to rulers was vital: in the process history fatefully moved from being everybody's story to that of kings and priests. History now glorified ruling families and their deeds but could also contain veiled criticism.

Typical Works Oral historians have worked hard to gather the folk tales of hunter-gatherer societies in Africa and the Americas. A contemporary appreciation of this type of history is Calvin Luther Martin's *In the Spirit of the Earth*. Ancient priest/emperor histories were designed to provide proper conduct guides for contemporary rulers – the Roman Tacitus and the Chinese Ssu-ma Chi'en are just two examples.

God's will

Origins Traditional notions of the past based on many whimsical gods gave way to one that unfolded according to the purpose of the one true God of Judaism, Christianity and Islam. The nature gods of hunter-gatherers yielded to the sky gods of settled agriculture. These new religions grew

69

up in Asia Minor and spread rapidly throughout the world.

Philosophy The eye here was directed to the future as much as to the past with events leading inevitably towards some final day of judgment. In general a 'chosen people' or community of the faithful (either by birth or conviction) have been anointed to carry out God's will on earth. History is a battleground between their purifying religious values and those who stand in their way. Just who was God's true agent and who an imposter became the trickiest of historical questions.

Politics Defending holy scripture as historical truth became the main buttress to the power of religious and secular authorities. Religion was politics. Heretics with a different view of the past were usually not tolerated. Both revolt and repression were carried out as if they were God's will.

Typical Works The Bible and the Qu'ran were among the first history books. The scholars of Islamic universities and the holy orders of Medieval Europe held the keys to human memory. Classic books of the period were those of St Augustine, St Bernard or the 12th-century Islamic scholar Ibn Al-Athir.

The Gospel of progress

Origins This is a major point of departure for 19th-century history. Here the influences of natural science in general and Charles Darwin in particular helped shape a cult of objective historical truth. History could be a value-free science reflecting in its methods the same march of progress that it was chronicling.

Philosophy The notion of progress born in Enlightenment Europe hardened into a sense of the inevitability of human advancement. At its best the new emphasis on historical accuracy gave a more balanced view of the past. At its worst it led to an automatic belief in the goodness of modernity.

Politics The crude use of Darwin's 'survival of the fittest' idea suited industrial society's need to justify the winners without too much thought for the losers. Marxism, another form of the gospel of progress, turned Darwin on his head to provide revolutionaries with a scientific faith in the inevitability of progressive socialism. Today crude certainties about what historical truth is and where it leads us have been shattered.

Typical Works EH Carr's *What is History?* is a classic and intelligent case for the progressive interpretation. The optimism of generations of Marxist historians has stumbled on the realities of 'actually existing socialism'. Ironically the main proponents of progressive optimism today are conservative historians concerned to defend the victories of the modernizing market.

Patriotic history

Origins The growth of the nation-state called for a different kind of past. The first secular theory of history can be traced to the work of 19th-century German historian Leopold von Ranke. It soon spread across Europe, forming the dominant mode of history-writing in the 19th and early 20th centuries. This kind of history is still a staple of school textbooks.

Philosophy The nation and whatever noble predecessors it can claim are the centerpiece of this history – almost always a success story. The sense of a common past is the glue that keeps a country together. The nation's spiritual beginnings are traced back to the kings of ancient Gaul, to powerful African emperors or noble tribes in long-gone Teutonic forests. The nation takes up the mantle of 'the chosen people' from religion, and patriotic history is the unfolding of this people's special destiny.

Politics While the politics of this history varies from radical republicanism to jingoistic conservatism, a sense of special national destiny is always its motor force. It revolves around the deeds and qualities that made the nation great and, in the case of Europe, how this greatness was transported abroad to civilize lesser peoples. Much patriotic history in the Majority World is a reaction to Western paternalism but takes on many of its characteristics, as with the murals in post-independence Ghana which attributed to Ghanaian genius the invention of the alphabet and the steam engine.

Typical Works The French historian François Guizot set the tone in the early 19th century and has been followed by scores of other European historians ranging in approach from the radical Jules Michelet to the High Tory Winston Churchill. At its worst this degenerates into militaristic saber-rattling history, but at least the cruder justifications of the West's 'civilizing role' are now gone.

History from below

Origins This is not properly speaking one of the 'grand governing narratives' that are usually identified as philosophies of history – it makes few claims about the overall meaning of history. But social history is a democratic response that accompanies the growth of political rights, literacy and a taste for their own history by those people left out due to their gender, color, class or beliefs. It started in the late 19th century but only flowered in the 1960s.

Philosophy The social historian tends to look at society from below, concentrating on the issues of everyday life: the organization of work, consumer habits, family patterns and the dynamics of class and gender. Social history often focuses on the part rather than the whole: a local village, a particular industry, the influence of a church, gay or bohemian subcultures. Larger meanings are illuminated by these shafts of light from below.

Politics This kind of focus tends towards a sympathy with people at the bottom of society. This is in sharp contrast to much of national history, which engages us with those in power and their problems in 'managing' society. The conclusions of social historians can be conservative but the overall political tendency of this kind of history is on the Left.

Typical Works There are many fine works of social history but EP Thompson's *The Making of the English Working Class* is as good as any. The French Annales school of the early 20th century, led by historians like Marc Bloch and Fernand Braudel, was a major influence in starting the social-history revolution, using local studies to give a vision of the whole society. Contemporary social history has narrowed its focus. Many feel that this leaves the overall analysis of historical meaning too open to those with less democratic inclinations than the social historian.

BRIEF HISTORY **15**

A Short History of Architecture

From the European Tradition (Chartres Cathedral) to the Vernacular (Machu Picchu), from the International Style (the Seagram Building) to Postmodernism (the Gherkin), the ideas behind the buildings.

THE WESTERN TRADITION – Location: Europe

Form: Europe's rich architectural tradition ranges from the temples of ancient Greece to 19th-century government buildings that evoked the grandeur of the nation state. Its many styles – from the heavy flamboyance of Gothic with its gargoyles and flying buttresses to the ordered formality of the Renaissance – still give us pleasure and a sense of well-being. Construction took a long time: Chartres Cathedral took 25 years to complete and at the time that was considered miraculously quick. Every detail was handcrafted and each major building was seen as inescapably part of a larger vision of the age.

Examples: Any guidebook of Europe is crammed with the architectural treasures of Western civilization. The grandeur of imperial Rome can be experienced through the Colosseum and Pantheon that draw millions of visitors each year. The most outstanding of many beautiful Gothic cathedrals is probably that at Chartres in France. One of the great architects of the classical tradition was the Venetian Andrea Palladio (1508-1580) who started out as a stonemason and became the designer of the *palazzi* and villas of the mercantile aristocracy. Palladio's concern with classical form and proportion had an influence far beyond both his century and his native Italy. Christopher Wren, who rebuilt St Paul's Cathedral after the Great Fire of London, sought to combine both classical and baroque elements in a period rich in design solutions that were hybrids of past styles. By the 19th century the 'gothic revival' movement inspired by John Ruskin was reacting against the discipline of the classical tradition.

Philosophy: Each style within the Western architectural tradition had its own set of ideas to underpin design. The imperial architecture of Versailles or St Petersburg speaks to the expansive self-image of empire. The spires and domes of cathedral architecture suggest the glory of God while intricate detailing lower down addresses the finer points of theology.

Impact: It is on the Western tradition that our mind focuses when we think of architecture. These classical designs and their features – the loggia, the arcade and the well-proportioned facade – have provided pleasure to both user and onlooker for centuries. It is also to this tradition that critics such as Britain's Prince Charles turn when they look beyond modernist sterility. Although it is possible to learn from the classical tradition it is certainly not possible to recreate the bygone eras that gave rise to particular styles and forms of building. Also unlikely is a return to the handcrafting and painstaking attention to detail that characterized the classical era.

REVOLUTIONARY MODERNISM – Location: Germany/Russia/France/Holland

Form: This movement in architecture bloomed in Europe after the First World War. The inclination was to use the sharp clean lines of the machine as a model for building. The expressive features of this new architecture were the ramps, stairways, lifts, heating ducts, chimneys, escalators and structural supports which were suddenly made visible after centuries of being hidden behind thick walls of masonry. Technology was not something to be hidden away but something to be glorified. The use of reinforced concrete allowed for much more flexibility in design. As Le Corbusier, one of the pioneers of modern architecture, put it: 'the house is a machine for living in and the chair a machine for sitting in'.

Examples: A central goal of the pioneers of modernism such as the German Bauhaus school was to create healthy housing projects for the workers as an alternative to the dark TB-ridden slums of European cities. These often combined living spaces with recreational and educational facilities – or with workplaces, as in the case of Walter Gropius' design of the Bauhaus school itself.

Philosophy: These modernists were inspired by the Russian Revolution, and the Soviet constructivist school was an attempt to put technology at the service of the Revolution. The inspiration was radical and idealistic: to sweep away the corrupt old world of buildings that were simply dishonest monuments to the powerful and embrace a technology that could liberate all humanity from want.

Impact: The early modernists had trouble getting commissions. But the buildings they did get a chance to erect stood out like a sore thumb from their more traditional surroundings. Their desire to 'start over' set the stage for the later wholesale destruction of neighborhoods for commercial development or urban renewal. What was old was bad and what was new by definition better. The constant rectangles, machine-like shapes, and lack of decoration made the new buildings difficult for even the workers to accept. While modernism was inspired by socialism it was very much the product of 'grand designers and planners' and there was little attempt to involve the user in the design process.

THE INTERNATIONAL STYLE – Location: United States

Form: The revolutionary innovations of the early modernists quickly gave way to the international style. But here a social vision was reduced to a mere architectural style. The clean lines and mechanical forms remained but utopian experiments in worker housing disappeared. Many of the corporate skyscrapers and high-rise apartment blocks that we are familiar with today are variations of the international style. Glass curtain walls shroud these often hermetically sealed megaliths that tower over their surroundings. One of the founders of the international style was the prolific Mies Van der Rohe (an ex-Bauhaus architect), who sought pure Platonic forms for his soaring buildings. The international style fitted the needs of developers for cheap and fast construction in the US economic boom and the rebuilding of Europe after World War Two.

Examples: German architects like Van Der Rohe and Gropius fled to the US to escape Hitler's crusade against such non-Aryan tendencies in design as flat roofs. They quickly began to have a profound influence on US-style high-rise development. Van Der Rohe's 1950s Manhattan headquarters for the Seagram liquor company is a key example. The US skyscraper certainly predated the international style, going back to architects like Louis Sullivan (the Guaranty Building in Buffalo) and later Frank Lloyd Wright's buildings in the US midwest. Even in the early days Sullivan saw the high-rise as not simply a work of art but 'the joint product of the speculator, the engineer, the builder'.

Philosophy: The international style tended to maintain those modernist prejudices that were most acceptable to the real-estate developer – those that reduced costs and increased usable space. Purity of form meant cheaper prefabricated material and no time and money wasted on hand-crafted ornamentation. The office high-rise began to be seen as a 'package'. In residential development the tower block was a 'quick fix' to the housing crisis - particularly in parts of the Third World and the Soviet bloc. Le Corbusier had argued for urban density that allowed for 'sun, space and greenery' in a *ville radieuse*. But open and green spaces dwarfed by high rises quickly fell into disuse.

Impact: The international style has become the main vehicle for modern commercial and residential towers. The cell-like living associated with high-rise dwellings has led to a destruction of public community and increased isolation of the individual. Cheap pre-fab public housing is prone to physical deterioration and vandalism. Two prime examples are the once highly regarded Pruitt-Igoe flats in St Louis and the Quarry Hills flats in Leeds. The curtain walls typical of the international style are highly energy efficient - taking on heat in the summer and losing it in the winter. For most of us these towers are an inevitable part of modern life – 'like traffic jams or plastic forks'.

POSTMODERNISM – Location: North America/Europe
Form: In the 1970s and 1980s the international style began to fall out of favor with both architects and building users. The sterility and uniform repetitiveness of this type of architecture was wearing thin. Some postmodernists, like the Luxembourg architects Robert and Leon Krier, started radically rethinking modernist assumptions about style, scale, building materials and even the purpose of design. But the dominant postmodernist tendency – as seen in the work of US corporate architect Philip Johnson – is merely to tinker with the 'engineering aesthetic' of the modernists. This is often done by stylizing otherwise modernist designs with the addition of an elaborate roof or the odd column on otherwise conventional high-rises.

Examples: The term postmodernism covers a wide range of differing architectural practices. It attempts to counter the alienation of stark modernism by the use of curved shapes, pitched roofs, different building materials and more ornamentation. It  speaks to the need of the captains of finance and industry for a more flamboyant celebration of their power (Johnson's AT&T building in New York for example) than modernist austerity allowed. Like many other art forms, postmodernism has fallen prey to a preoccupation with producing buildings as mediagenic events and elevating the architect in question into a cultural superstar.

Philosophy: There is little that unites postmodernism but the rejection of strict modernism – the most recent manifestations of which are the 'high-tech' work of the British architects Richard Rogers and Norman Foster such the City of London's Gherkin. Postmodernism represents a breakdown in the modernist consensus and an opening of the door to different approaches to design. At best it tries to recover a sense of 'place' denied by a modernism that looks the same whether it is in Tokyo or Nairobi. At worst it is mere decoration devoid of any social vision or sense of public responsibility. As one cartoon of an old couple has it: 'We used to be old-fashioned but now we are postmodern'.

Impact: The hope for postmodernism lies in the sense of new possibilities combined with a willingness to learn from (rather than deny) past architectural achievements. The danger is that it will degenerate into a self-enclosed culture of competing in-groups debating the use of clever historical references that no-one else can understand or even see. What on the surface seems a rich variety of views tends in practice to a drab uniformity of buildings: differences are only in detail with essentials shaped by the commercial interests of the client. An eye to publicity and self-promotion is no replacement for a more fundamental rethinking of the relations between architecture and society that includes the community and the users of buildings as a vital part of the process of design.

THE VERNACULAR – Location: Almost anywhere
Form: By most estimates between 90 and 95 per cent of buildings are designed without the help of professional designers. Local designs evolved in accordance with the demands of economy, climate and

topography. Unlike industrialized architecture such buildings have a much closer connection to local materials and must fit into the social and natural environment. The vernacular is the source of many interesting innovations in building. The arcade, the porch and the gable all predate the arrival of the professional designer. There are vernacular versions of floor-heating, air conditioning, light control – and even elevators. There is also a widespread use of natural features: hillsides, caves and trees have been integrated with living and public spaces.

Examples: Vernacular architecture varies from spectacular temples such as the Incas' Machu Picchu or the Mayan Tikal to more humble dwellings such as the Asian sampan or houseboat. Dwellings, granaries, religious institutions and fortifications are the most frequent vernacular structures. They often include ingenious adaptation to local conditions such as the scoops on top of houses in the Sind district of Pakistan that channel wind from the roof into each building. Summer temperatures of 120 degrees Fahrenheit are by this means cooled to a 'pleasant' 95 degrees by these breezes.

Philosophy: If there is a belief system behind vernacular architecture it is a combination of divine inspiration and common sense. The evolution and adaptation of these forms over centuries involves drawing from experience and consultation within the community as to what works best. While temples and ceremonial buildings were designed primarily by priests, they tended to reflect a consensus of communal belief that does not often exist in the modern world.

Impact: Many movements in architecture have sought inspiration in the vernacular. It is of course possible to romanticize vernacular architecture – to ignore the multiple discomforts and inconveniences. But its fit with nature and community stands in sharp contrast to design formulas where the developer and architect, in their search for the profitable masterpiece, pay scant attention to such details. Vernacular architecture also shows that ordinary people have a design capacity that, if tapped, might reduce not only costs but also their own alienation from the urban environment. This is particularly true in the Majority World, where there is simply not the capital available to solve the housing crisis without the active participation of the homeless in designing and building their own communities.

BRIEF HISTORY **16**

Key Moments of Islamic Civilization

From the invention of algebra through the foundation of physics and medical treatment to the first statement of animal rights.

570 Prophet Muhammad is born in Mecca. At the age of six he becomes an orphan and is taken into the care of his grandfather. When the latter dies, the young Muhammad is entrusted to his uncle.

610 Muhammad receives the first revelation while meditating in the cave of Hira near Mecca. He hears a commanding voice addressing him and becomes the Messenger of God.

622 After persecution in Mecca, Muhammad migrates to Medina. The migration – hijra – marks the beginning of the Islamic era.

623-631 After three battles, Muhammad conquers Mecca and forgives all his enemies. A written constitution is established as the basis of governance. The foundations of the Muslim civilization are laid in the city-state of Medina.

632 Prophet Muhammad dies after giving his 'farewell sermon'. Abu Bakr, a close companion of Muhammad, is unanimously selected as the first caliph of Islam.

633-643 After Abu Bakr's death, the Prophet's companion Umar al-Khattab is elected as the second caliph. Syria, Iraq, Egypt and Palestine come under Muslim rule. Jerusalem is captured, but Caliph Umar declares that Christians will be honored and protected. He introduces the Islamic calendar consisting of 12 lunar months.

644 Caliph Umar is murdered. An 'Electoral Council' elects Uthman ibn Affan, the Prophet's son-in-law and close companion, as the third caliph.

650-652 Caliph Uthman compiles the Qur'an as it exists today. Islam expands into the Maghreb or northwest Africa.

653-656 Islam spreads to Persia and Byzantium. Unrest spreads in Muslim lands. Caliph Uthman dies in a revolt. Ali Abi Talib, the Prophet's

cousin and son-in-law, becomes fourth caliph, but his selection is disputed. Muawiya, Governor of Syria, declares himself the 'first king in Islam' in defiance of Caliph Ali.

661-680 The Muslim world begins to fragment. Caliph Ali is murdered. Disputes arise between those who want political leadership to be elected and those who want political and religious authority to reside within the family of the Prophet. Hussain, the Prophet's grandson and son of Caliph Ali, is killed at the Battle of Karbala, which becomes the formative event in the emergence of the Shi'a tradition, splitting the Muslim community into two groups – the Sunnis and the Shi'as. The Umayyad dynasty is established in Syria.

700-750 Islam extends into India. Muslims enter Spain and reach the borders of France. The advance of Muslims is halted at the Battle of Tours on the Loire river in France in 732. The battle becomes a seminal event in shaping European stereotypes of Muslims. In Baghdad the Abbasid dynasty is established. The paper industry emerges and Iraqi jurist Al-Shaybani publishes his famous work, *The Concise Book of International Law*.

751-800 A sophisticated book trade evolves, backed by a thriving publications industry. The great compilers of hadith – al-Bukhari, Abu Dawood, al-Tirmidhi, ibn Maja and al-Nasai – publish their works and 'authenticate' the sayings of the Prophet. Ibn Ishaq publishes the first biography of the Prophet Muhammad. Islamic Jurisprudence (*fiqh*) is codified and six 'Schools of Thought' emerge as the orthodoxy. A massive project to translate works of Greek thought and learning into Arabic begins. The Rationalist school of philosophy (the Mutazila) emerges. The Spanish Umayyad dynasty is established in Cordoba and the Arabian Nights stories make a first appearance. Abu Hanifa al-Dinawari publishes *The Book of Plants*.

800-850 Al-Kindi becomes the first Muslim philosopher, Jabir ibn Hayan establishes chemistry as an experimental science. Al-Khwarizmi invents algebra. Ibn Qutayba, an 'Inspector of injustices' in Basra, publishes his seminal *The Book of Etiquette*. Translation of the works of Greece, Babylonia, Syria, Persia, India and Egypt reaches its peak. Muslims conquer Sicily.

851-900 Muslim astronomers measure the circumference of the earth and Iraqi scientist Ibn Hawkal publishes *The Book of the Shape of the Earth*. Al-Farghani publishes his *Elements of Astronomy* and al-Battani publishes *On the Science of Stars*. The Musa Brothers, who are engineers, publish the *Book of Ingenious Mechanical Devices*. Philosopher al-Farabi publishes his celebrated commentary on Plato, *The Perfect State*.

Afghan scholar and advisor to administrators, Al-Harawi, publishes his pioneering work, *The Book of Public Finance*.

901-950 Philosopher and physician al-Razi publishes his observations on smallpox and measles and Al-Tabari publishes his history of the world, *Annals of Apostles and Kings*. The Postmaster General of Baghdad, Ibn Khurdadhbih, publishes *The Book of Routes and Kingdoms*, a comprehensive work on the distribution of post throughout the Muslim world. Mystic Al-Hallaj causes controversy by declaring, in a state of ecstasy, 'I am the Truth'. And theologian Al-Ashari establishes the anti-philosophical Asharite movement.

951-1000 Physicist Al-Haytham publishes his monumental study *Optics*, containing the basic formulae of reflection and refraction, and announces that experiment and empirical investigation is the foundation of all scientific work. Al-Baruni publishes his *Determination of the Co-ordinates of the Cities* and travels to South Asia to study Hinduism and yoga. Philosopher and physician Ibn Sina publishes *Canons of Medicine*, the standard text for the next 800 years. Al-Azhar University, the first in the world, is established in Cairo. Humanist Al-Masudi lays the foundation of human geography and philologist Ibn Faris publishes his linguistic masterpiece, *The Law of the Language*.

1050-1100 Intellectual war breaks out between theologians, philosophers and Muslim mystics or Sufis. Thinker and theologian Al-Ghazali laments the decline of Muslim civilization, publishes *The Revival of Religious Sciences in Islam* and launches a monumental attack on Greek philosophy, *The Incoherence of the Philosophers*. Iraqi political scientist, Al-Mawardi, publishes his *Rules of Sovereignty in the Governance of an Islamic Community* and Libyan scientist Al-Ajdabi publishes his great work on meteorology, *Seasonal Periods and Atmospherics*.

The Crusades, a series of Christian wars against the Muslims, begin with the first crusade in 1095.

1100-1150 Sicilian geographer Al-Idrisi produces his map of the world and Sufi psychologist Ibn Bajja publishes his psychological masterpiece, *The Knowledge of the Self*. Spanish philosopher Ibn Tufail publishes *The Life of Hayy*, a philosophical novel and prototype of Robinson Crusoe; and Moorish physician Ibn Zuhr brings out *The Book of Practical Treatments and Precautionary Measures*. Mutazalite philosopher Ibn Rushd answers Al-Ghazali with an equally monumental defense of philosophy, *The Incoherence of the Incoherence*.

1150-1200 Timbuktu is established as a great center of learning and book production. It is the furthest point of the Muslim Empire and home of Sankore University. Geographer Yaqut al-Hamawi publishes his great Geographical Dictionary and Spanish horticulturist Ibn Al-Awwam brings out

The Book of Agriculture. Iraqi engineer Al-Jazari publishes his great illustrated work on mechanics, *Integration Between Theory and Practice in the Application of Mechanics*.

The Kurdish Salahuddin Ayyubi ('Saladin') takes on the Crusaders.

1150-1200 Al-Hariri publishes his linguistic masterpiece, *The Assemblies*, and Fakh al-Din al-Razi tries to reconcile philosophy and religious thought in his book *The Substance of the Ideas of Classical and Later Philosophers and Theologians*. Persian philosopher and mystic Al Suhrawardi tries to establish an Islamic basis for philosophy in his work *Philosophy of Illumination*.

1200-1250 Al-Zarnuji publishes his celebrated pedagogical work, *The Method of Learning* and Spanish physician Ibn al-Baytor publishes *The Comprehensive Books of Drugs and Diets*. Fakhr al-Din Razi publishes his great *Encyclopaedia of Science* and biographer Abu Khallikan establishes philosophy of history as a distinct discipline. Mystic Jalal-al-Din Rumi publishes *Masnavi*, his influential anthology of mystical poetry and anecdotes. Spanish thinker Ibn Saad publishes his ideas on multiculturalism in the *Introduction to the Classes of Nations* and Moorish Spain is fully established as a multicultural society. Ibn abd as-Salam formulates the first statement of animal rights.

1250-1300 Mongols sack Baghdad and burn down the great House of Wisdom and the city's other 36 public libraries with their vast store of manuscripts. The Abbasid Caliphate ends but the Ottoman Empire is established.

Biologist Ibn Nafis accurately describes the circulation of blood and Iraqi musician Al-Urmawi publishes his great *Book of Musical Modes*. Astronomer Nasir al-Din Tusi completes his major work *Memoirs of the Science of Astronomy* at the Maragha Observatory, Persia, setting forward a comprehensive structure of the universe; and develops the 'Tusi couple' enabling mathematical calculations to establish a heliocentric worldview.

After the eighth crusade, when the last Christian city, Acre, falls to the Muslims, the Crusades come to an end.

1300-1400 Ibn Khaldun establishes sociology as a distinct discipline and publishes his celebrated *Introduction to History*. Ibn Battuta travels the globe and describes his adventures in *Travels of Ibn Battuta*. Al-Damiri develops the idea of zoological taxonomy in *The Comprehensive Book of Animal Life* and Egyptian vet Al-Baytar brings out *The Complete Compendium on the Two Arts of Veterinary Practice and Horse Training*. Syrian jurist Al-Jawziyyah publishes his great work on jurisprudence, *Methods of Judgment in the Administration of Islamic Law* and Ibn al-Ukhuwwah brings out his book, *The Clear Exposition of the Principles of (Public) Accountability*.

The religious scholars close the 'gates of *ijtihad*' ('reasoned struggle'); and establish *taqlid* (blind imitation) as the dominant mode of thought, leading to ossification in science, learning and innovation.

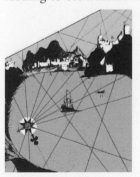

1400-1500 The Ottoman Empire expands after the fall of Constantinople. Muslims are expelled from Spain after the fall of Granada. Jewish refugees from Spain take refuge in the Ottoman Empire. Persian mathematician Al-Kashi publishes his theory of numbers in *The Key to Arithmetic*; and Cheng Ho, Muslim admiral of Ming China, leads voyages of discovery to Africa. Arabian navigator Ibn Majid publishes *The Book of Instructions in Principles of Navigation and Regulations* and pilots Vasco da Gama from Africa to the Indian coast.

1500-1600 The Mughal dynasty is established in India. Ottoman architect Sinan builds the Blue Mosque complex in Istanbul. Turkish jurist Tashkopruzade publishes his elaborate classification of knowledge, *The Key to Highest Attainment and Light of Leadership* and Egyptian jurist Ibn Nujaym brings out his celebrated work of legal logic and reasoning, *Similars and Parallels: Analogues and Precedents*.

1600-1700 The Taj Mahal is completed in Agra, while the Ottomans lay siege to Vienna. Persian mystical thinker Mulla Sadra publishes his work on mystical philosophy, *The Signs of Divine Grace*. Europe embraces Islamic humanism wholeheartedly.

1700-1800 European imperial powers begin to colonize the Muslim world. Universities and institutions of higher learning are closed; Islamic medicine is banned; and Muslims are barred from pursuing higher education.

Muhammad ibn Abdul Wahhab establishes the Wahhaby movement in Arabia, Syria and Iraq, insisting on a literalist interpretation of the Qur'an.

1800-1900 The 'Mutiny' in India is crushed. Indian educationalist Sir Syed Ahmad Khan establishes the Aligarh University to 're-educate' the Muslims.

1900-1950 Reformer Jamal al-Din Al-Afghani, together with the Mufti of Egypt, Muhammad Abduh, establish the pan-Islamic movement for reform and *ijtihad* ('reasoned struggle'). After eight centuries, the Ottoman Empire collapses. In the Arabian peninsula, Ibn Saud brings warring tribes together to establish Saudi Arabia.

Philosopher and 'Poet of the East', Muhammad Iqbal, publishes his epic poem *Complaint and Answer*, asking God to explain the reasons behind the lamentable state of Muslim people.

Pakistan is established as the first 'Islamic state'.

1950-2000 Muslim states in Asia and Africa obtain their independence. The Muslim Brotherhood in Egypt and Jamaat-e-Islami in Pakistan become the main components of a global Islamic movement. The Organization of Islamic Conference (OIC) is established as a 'Muslim United Nations' and great hope is pinned on the emergence of OPEC as a global player.

'East Pakistan' breaks from 'West Pakistan' and becomes Bangladesh. After the collapse of the Soviet Union, six new Muslim countries emerge in central Asia. The revolution in Iran is hailed as the first 'Islamic revolution' but soon leads to despair and pessimism. The 'Taliban', a group of semi-literate students, take over Afghanistan.

2001-2050 Two possible futures. Crisis after crisis leads Muslim cultures to the edge of chaos – and over. Alternatively, Islam is reformulated, Muslims redefine modernity in terms of their own categories and concepts, and Islam re-emerges as a dynamic, thriving civilization.

BRIEF HISTORY **17**

River Water and Human History

From the Yangtze to the Nile, civilizations have depended on rivers, while modern development has often relied, for better or worse, on big dams. A guide to the promise and the pitfalls of harnessing water.

Subsistence agriculture

Irrigation is almost as old as agriculture itself. It was practised on a small scale to grow food for local consumption (and even surplus). Elaborate canal systems to water the crops of the Papago or 'bean people' allowed these native Americans to survive some of the harshest conditions of the Sonoran desert. Intricate systems of small reservoirs or *qanats* and spring tunnels were used to capture precious  run-off in a belt stretching from Palestine to Iran. The lighter the touch in dealing with delicate dryland eco-systems, the better the chance of avoiding waterlogging or salt-poisoning of fertile topsoils. Today such locally controlled irrigation is still in operation from the ricefields of Bali to the 100,000-odd irrigation co-operatives that dot the Japanese countryside.

Oriental despotism

Larger-scale irrigation systems are integrally tied to the development of the absolutist state that came to dominate small villages in the valleys of major rivers from the Tigris-Euphrates to the Yangtze and Yellow rivers of China. The city-state itself arose in the drylands of the Middle East where it co-ordinated the  major works of irrigation and water control. The trade-off was simple: dependable water supply and relative safety from floods for tribute, labor and obedience. Huge armies of laborers had to be mobilized first to build and then to maintain elaborate systems of dikes and irrigation canals. The Nilometer measured the Nile's crucial flood – 16 cubits was ideal. Religions of sacrifice and the worship of river gods – Isis and Hapi on the Nile, Ninurta in Mesopotamia and Ganga in ancient India

– were part of the cosmology of a ruling priesthood. The bending of rivers to human will occurred at the same time as bending the will of the many to the dictates of the few. Today most of their great waterworks lie in ruins.

The mystical source

For the European culture of the Renaissance and the Enlightenment the sources of the world's great rivers took on a symbolic and metaphoric importance. The source of the Nile in particular became associated with everything from the Garden of Eden and the Horn of Plenty to the nourishment of political liberty. The fountains of Bernini made use of ornamental water hydraulics that were later to shape modern engineering and featured classical figures of crouched or reclining (but always well-muscled) river gods of four continents. Early European explorers such as Sir Walter Raleigh were obsessed by the idea that rivers of the New World (such as the Orinoco) would lead them to the gold of an elusive El Dorado. In later literature, writers like Joseph Conrad used the river as inspiration to explore the journey into the human psyche.

Cadillac desert

The Western notion of the river mirrored first in the great Roman aqueducts was a linear highway to be shaped by destination and purpose. European rivers such as the Rhine have been heavily engineered mostly to accommodate shipping. But modern hydraulic society reached its highest expression in the American West. Here a vast wilderness was flooded with settlers looking for the promised land and finding mostly arid and semi-arid desert. Many went to the wall before billion-dollar investments in water infrastructure made the desert bloom. The Mormons led the way with a rigid theocracy directing the irrigation of Utah. By the 1930s the construction of the Hoover Dam on the wayward Colorado River had initiated the era of the mega-dam. Today California's Imperial Valley, one of the world's great food-producing regions, and thirsty and energy-hungry desert metropolises such as Los Angeles, Phoenix and Las Vegas are lavish testimony to the taming of the Colorado, Columbia and myriad other Western rivers.

Dams for development

This model of a prosperous US West bewitched modernizers around the world and led to an era of large dam construction starting in the

early 1960s. Generally dam-building and large irrigation projects came to be seen as progressive steps in the march to independence. The High Aswan Dam across the Nile – completed in 1964 with Soviet help – was a symbol of Third World independence from neocolonial control. Since then the Volta, the Zambesi, the Ganges, the Indus and the Paranai are just a few of the great rivers of the Third World breached to supply dependable water for irrigation and the voltage necessary to jolt an industrial take-off.

A powerful consortium of nationalist politicians, multilateral lenders and transnational engineering and construction firms have reshaped river eco-systems as a vital part of industrial infrastructure. Advantages and wealth for some came right away, except for those uprooted from their homes (four million at the last count); the costs have been slower to accumulate. The curse of salted and waterlogged fields, coastal erosion, ruined fisheries, staggering debt, and escalating repair bills are just now beginning to hit home.

Respecting the river

Dam sites these days are usually surrounded by barbed wire and armed guards. With good reason. The movement to resist river engineering has gained real momentum in the last two decades. In the industrialized North, dams are becoming almost as controversial as nuclear power plants. Costs and environmental impacts undergo minute scrutiny. The number of new dams has fallen dramatically.

In the Global South, resistance has proved more difficult with 'resettled' farmers and green activists getting blows from police truncheons rather than seats at assessment hearings. Still, some notable victories have been achieved – a number of dams have been stopped in Thailand, the corruption-ridden Bangladesh Flood Action Plan has been scaled back dramatically and the World Bank has been forced to withdraw from several mega-dam projects on the Indian subcontinent.

The movement is, moreover, putting alternatives on the agenda – energy development that works with a river rather than trying to reshape and conquer it. Traditional small-scale methods of irrigation are also being revived, from Karez in western China (small-scale water catchment) through the stone lines used in arid Sahelian Africa to the rebuilding of age-old raised fields to aid drainage by Quechua Indian farmers near Lake Titicaca in Peru.

The Changing Face of Work

Work has not always been what it is today – a measure of our personal worth and a goad to our guilt if we don't do it. In a world in which formal employment is becoming more scarce, we need to understand that every age has had a different idea about work.

The barest minimum

In early hunter-gatherer societies work was something people only indulged in when they had to – when food was running low or shelter needed repair. They had no desire to work more than was necessary to survive. There are still a few tribal societies which live in this way – deep in the Amazon rainforest, for instance, where food is available in plenty. The fact that they still live as they did thousands of years ago indicates that the desire to work hard to create surpluses and 'progress' is not innate to all humankind, which might have been quite happy to remain as it was had environments more hostile than the Amazon not made better technology a necessity.

The province of slaves

Most ancient 'civilizations' regarded work as something lowly to be treated with disdain. The classical Greek 'civilization' that produced Artistotle and Plato, Sophocles and Homer, had two basic ideas about work: that it was mere physical effort aimed at survival; and that work had no value in itself and should be done by one class of people so as to leave others free to pursue higher goals. Aristotle said that just as the ultimate goal of war is peace, the object of work is leisure. In practice this meant all the work was done by slaves and women so as to leave a male élite free to dream up its lofty ideals and organize wars.

Feeding the lord

Feudal societies were a variation on this Greek theme – the mass of people worked harder on the land than would have been necessary just to feed and clothe themselves. This was because they had to produce a surplus that would keep the lord of the manor in the style to which he was accustomed. And the Greek notions persisted into 20th-century Britain in the shape of an aristocracy convinced of its right to do nothing while being provided for by other people's work.

In subsistence farming, which occupies most people in the Majority World today, work is often very hard but is at least done in your own time and according to the rhythm of the seasons. There is a direct link between how hard you work and how much you produce – even if in so many other ways you are prey to forces beyond your control, from market prices to locusts, IMF policies to corrupt officials. Work has its own meaning and can be bent to the needs of the local culture – it does not need to be defined and organized by the outside world.

Dark satanic mills

The Industrial Revolution which began in the Britain of the early 19th century transformed the whole experience of work. Work now came to mean being employed to produce goods in factories or mines, most often by manual labor. People now lost their
knowledge of how things were produced – the old pride and confidence of the craftsperson disappeared, and work became less creative and less enjoyable. Work became something grim which people would never have chosen to do for its own sake. So a system of rigid work discipline and the threat of poverty and hunger were needed to keep workers at their tasks. This modern idea of work as something for which we are paid and which falls within a fixed number of hours is thus a very recent one – little more than 150 years old.

Between Eden and heaven

Early Christian attitudes to work were very different from the present day. There was no work in the Garden of Eden – instead work was part of Adam and Eve's punishment when they were banished. Until the Middle Ages work was not as important as 'preparing for heaven'. It was associated with physical labor and seen as rather lowly – the Hebrew word for work, *avodah*, is derived from the same root as *eyed*, meaning 'slave'. During the Renaissance the religious view changed: work became good, the will of God, and leisure became idleness. Rising production meant there was new need for reliable labor, and thus the idea that idle hands were the devil's playground became very useful and took deep hold.

Choosing our future

Our view of work now is inherited from the time of the Industrial Revolution – we think of a job as an essential part of life. The jobs we do from 9 to 5 give us our status in the world. But there are fewer and fewer full-time jobs to go around.

Two possible futures lie in front of us. Either we carry on down the same road and wind up in a world where only an élite can work while the mass of people scrabble around trying to survive. Or we can transform our attitude to work – divide what jobs there are properly and fairly, and aim to create a new society built on the constructive use of leisure rather than the worship of work.

BRIEF HISTORY **19**

Cities: a History of Ideas

To the Greeks, the city was simply 'built politics'; to Babylonians and Aztecs, buildings reached towards the gods. Skyscraper architects worshipped 'pure geometry'; development experts have seen the order in slums.

Symbols of order

From around 10,000 BCE nomadic hunter gatherers began to create permanent settlements, whose shape tended to reflect ideas about the cosmic order. Circular designs predominated in societies living close to nature – in the traditional villages of African pastoralists, for example. Others favored the stark artifice of the grid. The Chinese of the 1800-1200 BCE Shang Dynasty, for example, had a perfect square as the ideal layout for their cities.

Cities from heaven

By 3,500 BCE there were many prosperous walled city-states, with up to 30,000 people, in the fertile river delta of Mesopotamia (present-day Iraq). With their temples, ziggurats and towers these cities indicated the desire for a permanence transcending human mortality. Founding cities was part of the role of priest-kings, seen as mediators between heaven and earth. An Ancient Sumerian document records how five god-appointed kings were given five cities in 'pure places'.

Built politics

Ideas of citizenship and democracy mattered most to fifth-century BCE Athenians. For them the city was 'built politics' – the word 'politics' actually derives from the Greek for city. Living quarters in Athens were modest, with little distinction between rich and poor. Essential civic amenities – theater and gymnasium, for  example – were grander. Socrates saw the city as a place of ideas and he criticized those who had 'filled [it] full of harbors and docks and walls and revenues... and left no room for justice and temperance'. Plato and Aristotle thought the city should be more socially segregated and exclusive. But many were already debarred from democracy and citizenship – women and slaves for a start.

Parasitic city

With a population of a million, by the year 100 Rome was the world's largest city. Unlike Athens, it did not sustain itself by cultivating surrounding areas but relied upon its colossal empire to provide it with food, raw materials and slaves. The culture of exploitation was mirrored within the city itself, the ruling class living in opulence while others dwelt in overcrowded, unsanitary tenements for which they paid inflated rents.

Public hygiene was abysmal – refuse, including human corpses, was dumped in vast piles. 'Pathological' and 'parasitical' is how one commentator described imperial Rome. But the Roman Empire also left towns and cities all over Europe, North Africa and Asia Minor.

Walls of freedom

In the early Middle Ages many flocked from the land to the new 'free cities' of Europe, controlled not by feudal lords but by citizens. By 1200 urbanization was taking hold across the continent. Although citizens gained freedom from taxes imposed by local lords, every able-bodied person was obliged to contribute to maintaining the city walls. These had defensive functions, but they also guaranteed self-determination. The medieval city walls symbolized the 'free' collaboration of merchants, priests, scholars, craftspeople and warriors.

Order and sacrifice

The Aztec city of Tenochtitlan, on which modern Mexico City now stands, was an explicit expression of the intertwining of state and religion. The city, of up to 200,000 people, consisted of a highly symmetrical arrangement of temples, administrative centers, plazas and military schools. Towering above were pyramids where humans were sacrificed to gods. But poet and engineer King Nezahualcoyotl, crowned in 1431, discouraged such cruelty and promoted instead the idea of the city as a cultural and intellectual center.

Embodied humanism
In the 1450s Italian Renaissance architect Leone Battista Alberti initiated the classical city revival, restoring Rome's aqueducts and rebuilding ruined ancient monuments. His vision was to give cities a magnificence that would instill pride. Renaissance cities became the embodiments of a humanistic world view in which people, rather than God or nature, took center stage. Indeed, architect Francesco di Giorgio Martini saw the relation of the city to its parts as 'similar to that of the human body... the streets are the veins'.

Labyrinths of privacy
Traditional Islamic cities, from the 9th to the 19th century, reflected a concern for visual privacy. This determined the placing of doors and windows and the height of buildings. Houses were 'introverted', the appearance toward the street being unimportant.

Religious law prescribed that streets should be wide enough to allow two fully laden camels to pass freely. Organic, labyrinthine medinas (old quarters) were the main characteristics of Islamic cities, to be found in Moorish Spain and Islamic India, as well as the Middle East.

Splendor and oppression
French Emperor Napoleon III wanted a capital worthy of a great imperial power and free from hiding places for anarchists and other 'trouble-makers'. In the mid-1800s city prefect Baron Haussmann was charged with rebuilding Paris, which he did by cutting through the maze of medieval streets and constructing magnificent straight boulevards. This model of social control was copied around the world. It was also imposed in Algeria and other French colonies, where medinas were ruthlessly 'modernized' by military engineers. The British Empire, for its part, created 60 cities around the world as a means of securing trade routes and exercising colonial control.

Territories of poverty
During the industrial revolutions of Europe and the US in the 18th and 19th centuries, cities mushroomed. Factories sprang up, providing jobs for the new urban working classes. Friedrich Engels noted that as

factories grew, so did 'those separate territories assigned to poverty'. In Liverpool population densities reached 3,000 people per hectare. People lived anywhere they could and even cellars were packed full. The new cities became blanketed with acrid smoke and were breeding grounds for bronchitis and tuberculosis.

A city in the garden

In 1898 English architect Ebenezer Howard suggested a solution to pollution and overcrowding: create new 'garden cities' in the country. These moderately sized, self-contained, urban communities would also be socially, economically and ecologically sustainable. Howard also proposed shared ownership of land. But the few garden cities built in Britain (Welwyn and Letchworth) and the US (Sunnyside Gardens, Chatham Village and Radburn) turned out to be leafy commuter-belt travesties, devoid of Howards' social idealism.

King of the sprawl

US architect Frank Lloyd Wright proposed that cities would 'disappear': each family's own home would function as a city center. Cars would shrink distance, giant freeways forming an intrinsic part of the urban 'architecture'. There was also a strong element of traditional American 'homesteading' in his 1930s vision, with each house set in an acre of land for growing food. Trimmed lawns materialized, food-growing did not. Nor did cities 'disappear' as he had predicted. But car-dependent suburban sprawl became the norm – minus the communal social benefits, such as garden schools and farm units, that Lloyd Wright had also proposed.

Geometric assault

Le Corbusier was the guru of the modernism that came to dominate 20th-century cities. 'Houses', said the Swiss watchmaker's son, 'are machines for living in'. 'Pure geometry' was the ideal and he praised the fact that cities were an 'assault on nature'. His designs involved large apartment blocks towering over open, tree-dotted spaces, linked by highways. Le Corbusier planned only one real city, Chandigarh in newly independent India.  But he was the inspiration for Brasilia and other post-1945 cities in capitalist and communist countries alike.

'The design of cities is too important to be left to citizens,' he famously said. Such arrogance enraged critics who labeled Corbusian design as 'ego-tripping' for architects, who were sufficiently privileged not to have to live in the tower blocks or concrete-and-steel wastelands of their creation.

Do-it-yourself city

During the 1950s and 1960s there was a wave of reaction against the 'totalitarian' approach epitomized by Le Corbusier. British architect John Turner was profoundly influenced by his work in the self-built *barriadas* of Lima, Peru. He expected slums. Instead he found orderly, well-functioning, self-managing settlements. As 'the expert' Turner had little to teach the *barriada* dwellers: 'they knew perfectly well not only what to build but how to build it'. He concluded that when people had control over the key decisions concerning their housing and their environments this produced social well-being. When they didn't, their environments became 'a barrier to personal fulfillment and a burden on the economy'.

Non-planning

Similar ideas were taking hold in the industrialized world. In Britain a highly iconoclastic 1969 manifesto – written by Reyner Banham, Paul Barker, Peter Hall and Cedric Price – proposed 'non-planning'. In the US Jane Jacobs campaigned for a return to the density and variety of the traditional unplanned city, while Richard Sennett argued for the democratic benefits 'in extricating the city from preplanned control'. Anarchists in Copenhagen put their politics into practice in 1971 by creating an autonomous free town, Christiania, which still exists today. In the decade that followed several small-scale 'community architecture' projects took off in other parts of the world.

Money, money, money

Marxist studies which explained urban growth in terms of circulation of capital were current in the 1970s. But as those theories became increasingly abstract, the practice of city development became more crude and pragmatic. The 1980s saw economic recession, industrial job losses and the rise of the radical Right; city authorities were under pressure to open doors to business, whatever the social cost. Planning again came under attack – this time from free-marketeers who felt it interfered with enterprise.

Info-city

Information technologies, especially the internet, have taken the world by storm. The fashionable view is that they will do away with the need for cities: anyone can perform any activity anywhere. But Spanish philosopher Manuel Castells detects  an opposite trend: the new technologies have concentrated power in the most dominant metropoli – Los Angeles, New York, London – and boosted the capitalist system. The result, he says, is deepening social inequality and escalating urban violence.

BRIEF HISTORY **20**

The Irresistible Rise of Public Debt

Without borrowing money, Northern governments would not have been able to fight wars – let alone win them, fiddle the balance sheet of history and impose a crippling form of debt slavery on the South. Here we chart the irresistible rise of 'public' debt in capitalist societies – and the repudiations, defaults and write-offs that regularly came with it.

Conquest

Merchants in European city-states like Venice, Genoa and Florence helped fund the Crusades, which aimed to take Jerusalem and the Holy Land from Islamic rule in the name of Christianity. Made rich by regional trade, these merchants eventually wielded enormous political power over governments – including the Papacy. Longer European voyages of discovery and conquest relied on support from monarchs and merchants, both of whom expected a good return on their investment. So colonial expansion was driven by adventurers who were daring and curious about the world but also owed a lot of money.

The theft of gold and silver from the indigenous cultures of Latin America confirmed how profitable such expeditions might be, and enthusiasm for them redoubled. Colonial administrations were set up in the new lands to transfer wealth back to Europe. But there was a troubling problem, particularly in the Americas. Native peoples were decimated by

European diseases and often refused to work for the colonizers – thus threatening the whole enterprise. Eventually, the shipping of enslaved Africans to new sugar plantations in Brazil and the Caribbean and to cotton plantations in the southern US became the most profitable trade of all – and thus the main source of capital for future borrowing.

Revolution

Lending to nation-states in Europe was good business. Governments could ensure repayment by taxing their citizens and they could not legally go bankrupt. So states borrowed heavily – most often to fight wars among themselves.

In 1692 legislation in England pledged the receipts from beer and liquor taxes as security for a loan to the Government of £1 million. 'Public' debt increased steadily and by 1840 had reached £827 million, almost all of it used to fight wars.

Government debt and burdensome taxes were a major source of discontent in France. The revolution of 1789 repudiated two-thirds of the debts then owed by the French Crown. Napoleon financed his military exploits largely from foreign levies, but public debt rose again thereafter. By 1870 it had reached 12 billion francs as a consequence of the Franco-Prussian war – the victorious Prussians demanded 5 billion francs in reparations from France. The Japanese Government borrowed 250 million yen for war with China in 1894 and 1.5 billion yen in foreign bonds for war with Russia in 1905.

Independence

Meanwhile, newly independent governments in the Americas began to borrow too. In 1790 the US Federal Government assumed $75 million of debts incurred by states during the War of Independence. But their prior debts to British banks remained unpaid – in 1842 11 US states eventually defaulted on them. In 1861, when Mexico defaulted on its debts, Britain, France and Spain promptly invaded.

Federal debts incurred during the US Civil War rose to $2.6 billion by 1865. The Canadian Government started off with a debt of 75 million Canadian dollars passed on from the provinces at the time of Confederation in 1867. The Government continued to borrow – but largely to finance railroads.

Hot

The two 'world' European wars (1914-18 and 1939-45) sharply increased public debt. The French Government owed 34.2 billion francs in 1914 and the total rose steadily when war began. British national debt increased from £610 million in 1900 to £7,800 million in 1920 and £21,300 million in 1945 – making Britain one of the world's largest debtors.

Germany's defeat in 1918 led to financial chaos. Excessive war reparations were considered partially responsible for the rise of Nazism. In 1934 Hitler repudiated war debt, then built the Nazi war machine with loans that reached 300 billion marks by 1945. Japan's public debt stood at 151 billion yen at the end of the war.

During the 1930s Britain and other European countries defaulted on their war loans from the US, valued at around $30 billion. In the US, borrowing for the 'New Deal' to mitigate the effects of the Great Depression increased Federal debts to nearly $43 billion by 1940. But the cost of the Second World War was far greater, so that Washington's debt jumped to $269 billion by 1945.

Cold

After the defeat of Germany in 1945, 'hot' war was replaced by 'cold' war against the Soviet Union. In 1951 West Germany was told to use 10 per cent of its exports to repay its debts, but as the Cold War hotted up the ratio was reduced to 3.5 per cent. Eventually the 'London Agreement' of 1953 wrote off two-thirds of what Germany owed. British repayments to the US were capped at four per cent of exports. In 1960, France adopted a 'new' franc that was valued at 100 'old' francs, which meant that the nominal value of its public debt was immediately reduced to one per cent of its previous level.

The US financed the Marshall Plan to promote post-war European reconstruction, while the Bretton Woods institutions (the World Bank, the International Monetary Fund [IMF] and the General Agreement on Tariffs and Trade) were established to promote Western-style

'development'. In 1950 the World Bank made its first African loan to Ethiopia. In 1956 the Paris Club of creditor governments entered its first debt renegotiation – with Argentina. In 1965 President Sukarno, unhappy with loan conditions imposed on Indonesia, withdrew from the World Bank and the IMF. A bloody military coup followed and the new regime of General Suharto, more sympathetic to the West, received massive debt relief and much easier terms from the Paris Club.

Proxy

Lavish spending by the United States on the Vietnam War, combined with an oil-price hike by Arab producers in 1973, massively increased the worldwide circulation of US dollars. Private banks began to lend these 'petrodollars' to governments in the South. At least 20 per cent of the new loans were spent on arms, often to fight 'proxy' wars between the Cold War superpowers.

In 1982, when Mexico told its creditors it could no longer pay, the Third World debt crisis began. Governments stepped in to bail out private banks. Between 1985 and 1988, under the US 'Baker' and then 'Brady' plans, 'private' debt was transformed into 'public' debt. Between 1982 and 1990 developing countries' debt service alone totaled $1,345 billion – the equivalent of six Marshall Plans. 'Structural adjustment' programs were imposed by the IMF and World Bank as a condition of new lending.

Civil

The Cold War ended in 1989 after a decade of US Government borrowing for military projects like 'Star Wars'. The Gulf War against Iraq followed in 1991 – debt relief was offered to Arab countries, and Egypt in particular, in exchange for their support against Iraq. Elsewhere, loans to countries of the former Soviet empire began. In nations as far apart as Yugoslavia, Rwanda and Peru, debt slavery lay concealed behind outbreaks of violent civil unrest. All attempts to organize relief for the South were rebuffed on principle until 1996, when the 'Heavily Indebted Poor Countries Initiative' was launched to make debt repayments 'sustainable'. Meanwhile, private lending resumed to a small number of 'boom' economies in Asia – and ended in a dramatic crisis that began in Japan and brought civil unrest to South Korea and the downfall of Suharto in Indonesia. Speculative debt-driven 'contagion' spread to Russia, then Brazil – within a decade, the 'cold' war was replaced by a 'financial' war .

Jubilee

The worldwide Jubilee 2000 campaign to get the principle of debt relief for the Majority World accepted was remarkably successful, even if the practice left much of the problem unresolved. In particular, the prospect of financing the Millennium Development Goals, agreed unanimously by the UN, got no closer while poor countries still had to devote far larger sums to servicing their debts. Meanwhile, in the US, the budget surpluses of the Clinton years were replaced by the huge deficits of the Bush regime, principally after 9/11 for the War on Terror and the war in Iraq, but also to finance tax cuts for the rich. Then, after the worldwide 'credit crunch' that began in August 2007, public funds were used once again to relieve private debts, this time by bailing out banks in the rich world which only the year before had been pocketing record profits. Governments proved willing to accept bad debts from private banks 'in the public interest', even as the banks refused to accept bad debts from 'sub-prime' mortgage borrowers in the US, whose homes were promptly repossessed.

A History of Reproduction, Contraception and Control

Snake skins and crocodile dung, feminists and fascists, population panic and the Pill: the war over women's bodies has been fierce.

Snake skins and crocodile dung

Women have always found ways of preventing unwanted babies. The 4,000-year-old Kahun Papyrus, the oldest written document on birth control, refers to vaginal pessaries made of crocodile dung and fermented dough. Arab traders were the first to use intra-uterine devices. When taking camels to market they placed small stones in the uterus of female animals to avoid them becoming pregnant on the way. Condoms made of linen and from the skin of sheep, goats and even snakes were used in many societies. In the ruins of Pompeii, the Italian city engulfed and preserved by volcanic lava 2,000 years ago, dilators and curettes were found similar to those used for modern abortions. Other early forms of birth control included bloodletting, glass or metal diaphragms, cotton soaked in lemon, dried fish, mercury and a variety of other herbs and chemicals.

Malthusian misery

In 1789 the British economist and clergyman Thomas Malthus published figures that were to become the cornerstone of the population-control movement. Malthus maintained that world population would rapidly outpace the earth's capacity for food production unless 'preventive checks' were put in place. Otherwise, he claimed, overpopulation would bring untold 'misery' in its wake – poverty, famine, pestilence and war.

Feminists and fascists

At the beginning of the 20th century Margaret Sanger, a socialist and feminist from New York City, coined the term 'birth control'. Sanger and her colleagues saw birth control as a way of freeing women from the yearly tyranny of pregnancy and birth. But there was a fine line between this and dictating who should be allowed to have babies. The famous anarchist Emma Goldman was arrested for distributing a pamphlet entitled *Why and How the Poor Should Not Have Many Children*. And Sanger too moved in that direction.

From there it was a small step to 'eugenics' – the belief that society can be improved by selective breeding. Eugenicists felt that poverty was a sign of genetic inferiority. They maintained that rich people were superior to poor, whites superior to blacks and the able-bodied superior to the disabled. The eugenicists were to become a powerful force in the politics of population control. By 1932 compulsory sterilization laws for the 'feeble-minded' and 'physically defective' had been passed in 27 states in the US.

But it was German fascist leader Adolf Hitler who pushed eugenics to its extreme. In 1933 Germany passed sterilization laws (modeled on those developed by the US Eugenics Record Office) which led to 200,000 sterilizations of 'genetic inferiors' and the murder of millions of Jews, Gypsies and homosexuals in Nazi gas chambers.

Mass sterilization

After World War Two the focus of population control moved to the Majority World, where populations were burgeoning while those in Europe and North America were slowing down. India became a keen advocate of birth control, a policy which eventually culminated in the mass sterilization of 6.5 million people in 1976 during the 'Emergency' of Indira Gandhi. Hundreds died from infections due to botched operations and the program sparked riots and demonstrations in many cities, leading to the Government's fall in 1977.

In the same year Dr Reimert Ravenholt, the head of USAID's population office, publicly hinted that the Agency intended to sterilize a quarter of all women in the developing world. Today 90 per cent of the women who have undergone surgical sterilizations are in the Majority World – 32.5 million as a result of mass campaigns in China in

1983 and 1991. In several Asian nations, substantial rewards, including cash hand-outs, have been offered to people who undergo permanent sterilizations. These financial incentives are difficult to resist when people are poor and hungry. Or indeed, if they are offered no other options for birth control.

Pro-natalism

While mass sterilizations and campaigns to reduce births were going on in some places, elsewhere women were encouraged, even coerced, to have more children. In Britain in 1944 a panel of 'experts' convinced itself that the decline in the birth rate was due to birth control and that it heralded the 'moral decline of the nation'.

Racial supremacy was also the issue in Europe and in the US. In 1905 Theodore Roosevelt warned of the 'race suicide' of America's Anglo-Saxon Protestants if they did not increase their birth rate relative to Asian, Italian and Jewish immigrants.

Where governments feel under threat – from immigration or conflict – they often advocate an increase in population, encouraging women to have large families (especially sons) and to stay at home and look after them. In fact, this rarely occasions real demographic change.

Several European countries have adopted incentives to encourage births; giving government subsidies to those with larger families. Pro-natalist thinking is also returning to the national agenda in the US, where it is linked with the anti-immigration movement.

The Pill

In 1950 the American biologist Gregory Pincus was invited by the Planned Parenthood Federation in the US to develop an ideal contraceptive. Within a few years an oral birth control pill was being tested on 6,000 women – not Americans, but women from Puerto Rico and Haiti. In 1960, the first oral contraceptive (Enovid-10) was launched in the US market. The 'Pill' as it became known, heralded a revolution in birth control. Here at last, women were told, was a method that was both effective and safe. Women the world over embraced this new drug with enthusiasm. Within two years the Pill was being used by 1.2 million women and a decade later the numbers had risen to ten million.

Despite its popularity there were nagging worries about health risks. As early as 1961 studies showed that the Pill carried the risk of blood clots, heart attacks and strokes due to high levels of the hormone estrogen. In 1962 there was evidence of at least 11 Pill-related deaths. Women activists in the US brought these dangers to public attention.

In the early 1970s a 'mini-Pill' with reduced estrogen was finally introduced. But at least three manufacturing companies continued to produce high-dose Pills until 1988. Scientific debate about the health risks of oral contraceptives continues, although it is now accepted that the Pill is unsuitable for certain groups of women.

The business of birth control
The dictates of the market play a major part in family planning and population control. About $5 billion is spent each year on family planning in the Majority World; $1 billion of this is donated by Northern governments, multilateral agencies and private organizations.

Pharmaceutical companies have global contraceptive sales of around three billion dollars per year. This huge economic power enables them to influence the policies of Southern governments and the priorities of the medical establishment. International aid donors, national governments and businesses collude in dictating who shall have children.

In Asia, for example, it is common for employers to offer incentives for using birth control and disincentives for having large families. In South Korea, one company provided housing and loans for employees using birth control. Maternity care was withheld after the birth of a third child and workers having large families were not promoted. Those with more than four children had to leave the firm. In the Philippines, workers were obliged to attend lectures on the 'need' for birth control.

Many private-sector population projects are funded by government aid dollars from the West. According to the UN, contraceptive use in the Southern Hemisphere increased fivefold in the last quarter of the 20th century because of the intervention of foreign-aid donors and international institutions.

The future
The history of women's reproductive health has been riddled with fear and force, ignorance and prejudice, and male control over women. It is easy to forget that women's bodies and lives are at the heart of the debate. And that Malthusian statistics represent the births and deaths of real flesh-and-blood people.

Reproductive issues cannot be addressed in isolation from the wider context of gender and social equality, and of equal access to healthcare, education and economic opportunity. A worldwide women's health movement now lobbies for what is best for women rather than what will best limit world population. Recent UN conferences have adopted some of the language and theories of this movement. In the meantime, women still have to negotiate their way through the debates with information which is always complex and often unclear.

BRIEF HISTORY 22

Migration: a Journey through Time

Homo Erectus was the first migrant, out of Africa, and ever since people have been on the move in search of a better life. Whole new worlds have been both ravaged and regenerated by migrants. But now the rich world is slamming shut the doors.

First steps

Homo Erectus was the first human to set foot outside Africa, about one-and-a-half million years ago. Because they discovered how to use fire, these people could move north and live in Europe's colder climate. But it was Homo Sapiens, the first fully modern human, who really kicked off global migration around 50,000 years ago.

These people's lives were dictated by the movement of ice sheets. In periods of intense cold, water would freeze at the poles and sea levels would lower to reveal land between the continents. Australia and Papua New Guinea formed one territory, for example, which was linked with the Philippines and Indonesia. There was no land bridge to mainland Southeast Asia but around 40,000 years ago people crossed the sea in boats to become the first inhabitants of Australia. Another land-bridge from Korea allowed the colonization of Japan. Further north, East Asia was joined to Alaska. Hot on the heels of animal herds such as giant bison, horses, sloths, moose, large cats and mammoths, humans crossed over from Eurasia to America. Within a few thousand years, they had traveled from the top of North America to the southern tip of what is now Chile. By the end of the Ice Age, 12,000 years ago, humans had migrated further than any other animal ever known.

Itchy feet

Greed and desire spurred leaders and merchants to travel far from their homelands. The Greeks, Romans and Indians were among the first to create vast empires, stretching over sea and land. Merchants used the power of the empire to take from, or trade with, all parts of the world, spreading Christianity and Islam along the way. Traders from the Bismarck Archipelago, New Guinea, started sailing around the Pacific in 1700 BCE in search of untapped resources. Polynesians arrived in small sea-craft in New Zealand/Aotearoa, 700 years later, in the last stage of long and dangerous Pacific Ocean voyages.

Once the Portuguese arrived in the Indian Ocean in 1498, they dominated trade and migration. In 1500 they demanded that the ruler of Calicut, the main spice market, expel all Muslims and allow the Portuguese to seize ships and goods found at sea. They then captured Mozambique, Goa, Malacca and Hormuz. They took Brazil and had a base in China. The Spanish also pursued their aspirations through the conquest of the Philippines. By the 1560s Spain had established itself in Mexico, Peru and Chile.

Shuffling soles

The international trade in slaves began from the shores of the Black Sea. Men were sent to serve in the armies of Egyptian sultans, and women, especially blonde Circassians, were dispatched into domestic service or prostitution in Muslim and Christian areas of the West. In the 1440s Portuguese sailors began to bring African slaves back to Europe.

Around 15 million people were taken from Africa as slaves and shipped to Europe, Brazil, the Caribbean and North America, though at least two million did not survive the passage. Most were gathered from the 20 principal slave markets dotted along the western coastline from Senegal in the north to Angola in the south. Today an estimated 40 million people in North and South America and the Caribbean are descended from those slaves.

Down at heel

Industrialization and competition from the colonies reduced jobs available while Europe's population continued to grow. From 1846 to 1939 around 59 million people left Europe, 38 million of them to the US and almost all the rest to European colonies or former colonies such as Australia, Argentina, Canada and Brazil.

In addition, many people from colonies in the Global South became indentured workers in other colonies – a system that the British Empire pioneered in Mauritius as a way of replacing slave labor involving fixed contracts and conditions that actually were little better than slavery. From 1830 onwards at least 12 million and possibly as many as 37 million people were dispatched to various British, French, Dutch and German colonies. India and China were the largest source of these workers: in 1900 around 30,000 Chinese 'coolies', as they were known, were found in mines in one district of Borneo alone.

In the South Pacific, agents known as 'blackbirders' used deceit and violence to recruit men for work. Around 280,000 Melanesians and Micronesians became *kanakas*, workers exported to other countries in the region. Conditions for indentured workers were harsh: 8.5 per cent of all Indian workers who arrived in Jamaica in 1869 died within a year.

Goose-stepping
Before the First World War, people were generally free to travel through Europe and sometimes overseas without a passport. But as xenophobia grew and then war broke out, control of migration was seen as essential to preserve the 'character' of Western nations. Many countries became opposed to an increase in the number or diversity of immigrants – some on openly racist grounds, such as Hitler's Germany. In Britain, where 120,000 Jews settled between 1875 and 1914, Jewish migrants became the focus of racist marches which led to the restrictive Aliens Act of 1914. Countries considered immigrant-friendly also succumbed to this pressure: the United States banned Chinese and Japanese workers and the Ku Klux Klan became popular by targeting Catholics, Jews and immigrants. Migration slowed substantially in both North America and Australasia between the World Wars.

Treading gently
After the horrors of war, human rights (including the rights of refugees and migrants) became a potent international issue. But the principle of national control and manipulation of immigration had gained ground. Rich countries feared a stampede and remained closed to migrants.

The formation of new countries after the Second World War shifted people as well as borderlines: the partition of India and Pakistan in 1947 involved the movement of 14 million people; and the establishment of a Jewish homeland in 1948 displaced 780,000 Palestinians.

After the mid-1950s governments realized that to spur economic growth they would need cheap workers. South Africa recruited many temporary laborers from countries in the region. The oil-producing states of Saudi Arabia, Oman, Kuwait, Bahrain, the United Arab Emirates, Qatar and Libya were destinations for many contract workers from nearby Asian and Arab countries. Germany was one of the European states which used a guestworker program – special migrant-labor agreements which allowed in workers on a temporary basis.

Other countries sought permanent immigrants to kick-start their economy. Australia actively recruited European settlers and received over two million immigrants between 1945 and 1964.

Shutting the gates
As governments became obsessed with economics, migrants became increasingly valued in terms of their monetary worth. Competition for jobs in the most-developed countries increased after the 1970s and

immigration declined. The tables were turned when countries which had been traditional sources of emigrants such as Italy, Greece, Spain and Portugal became the destinations for immigrant workers from other European and North African states from the 1980s onwards.

In the 1990s, Europe tightened its borders. Ethnocentric and racist right-wing politics reared their head once again. Ethnic minorities became scapegoats for national social and economic problems and potential migrants were stopped in their tracks. Ironically, however, the expansion of the European Union in 2004 led to a significant wave of migration from the east to the wealthier west of the continent.

In general, though, while money and goods flow freely under globalization, people cannot. But humans have moved in search of a better life since the beginning of time. And the pressures to escape from poverty and inequality are not becoming any less intense.

BRIEF HISTORY **23**

A Short History of Food

How people started to take control of their food – and how the international trade in foodstuffs upset the fragile balance of cultivation, land and life.

Managing the magic

About 12,000 years ago there was a revolution in the way people obtained their food. Instead of foraging and hunting, groups began to settle in one place, secure in the knowledge that they would have enough to eat. It was almost certainly women, the gatherers of berries and seeds while men hunted, who realized that plant growing was not completely haphazard, that there was a connection between putting seeds into the ground and harvesting the grains. This made it worthwhile to stay in one place and tend the young plants.

Ancestors of our food

In the Middle East the hairy precursors of modern wheat and barley were grown; in what is now Mexico around 7,000 years ago people had begun to cultivate the corn, beans and squash that still sustain them. Further south, in the Andes, potatoes were the staple fare. In China millet was cultivated in the north and rice in the south; while in Africa millet grew in the Sahara, then lightly wooded, and indigenous 'red' rice in the great bend of the Niger River in what is now Mali.

The domestication of animals such as dogs, sheep and goats began at about the same time as settled agriculture. Techniques for farming improvements abounded. One of the first was irrigation, which in turn led to the growth of larger settlements of people. Another was the selective breeding of plants and animals.

Traditional nutrition

In almost all traditional cultures people ate foods that blended together in a wholesome way. The rice and pulses of Asia; the corn and beans of the Americas and later of Africa; the wheat and dairy products of the Middle East – all complement and enhance each other's protein to produce a nutritional balance that is hard to beat. And these 'twinned' foods tend to be healthy for the environment: beans planted among the rows of corn fix nitrogen back into the soil, replenishing its vitality. Most people gained their protein from pulses and grains – meat was for rich people or for high-days and holidays.

The spice of new horizons

From the beginnings of settled agriculture there was trade in food – at first in spices such as pepper, which enhanced the taste of food, rather than in the foodstuffs themselves. But in the 15th century Europeans started to explore and settle to the west, south and east – and this led to major changes in the patterns of world agriculture. Around 60 per cent of all crops around the world were first cultivated and eaten by Native Americans but spread to the rest of the world following the conquest of the New World.

Local food crops were displaced by crops that suited European needs and palates. To control production, European countries took over tropical regions as colonies, and the wealth from agriculture was transferred back to the colonial power to fuel their own economic development.

Sugar and slaves

Sugar was the first major 'cash' or export crop grown on a wide scale, requiring a huge labor force. From the 16th century through the next 300 years, the Portuguese, Dutch, British and French between them transported 10-12 million Africans to South America and the Caribbean as slaves.

The 'triangular trade' of slaves to the Americas, sugar to Europe and manufactured goods to Africa was lucrative. Sugar became increasingly important in Europe, especially for use in tea and coffee, the new beverages. By the 1670s sugar was so vital for trade that the Dutch were prepared to give up New York to the British in exchange for the sugar lands of Surinam in South America.

Africa's fragile balance

Unlike Asia and South America, Africa was not endowed with rich and fertile earth. Knowing the limitations of their soil, people hunted and gathered, or herded animals for their livelihood. Where there was cultivation, African population rarely outgrew the soil's ability to support it. Sorghum, bulrush millet and finger millet were grown, plants which can tolerate dry soils and light rainfall. The commerce in slaves upset the balance. Apart from robbing the continent of its strongest young people, the trade put the emphasis on fighting rather than on agriculture. Instead of farming, people found themselves led to war by kings and chiefs eager to exchange captives for European guns and blankets.

When the Europeans divided Africa between them, in the 19th century, the old balance was utterly lost. Land which had grown food was now turned over to crops that would satisfy the industrializing nations of Europe: cotton, coffee, cocoa, peanuts, palm oil, bananas, rubber, tea and sisal. Trade restrictions and low prices for these 'commodities' and other raw materials drove African (and most other developing) countries into debt.

Industrialized cheap food

The colonial model continues to shape world agriculture, even in an era when the countries of Africa, Asia and Latin America are politically independent. The global food system is now largely based on providing cheap food in abundance for the markets of the rich world – including the provision by air and sea of fresh produce that used to be seasonal but is now available to consumers all year round – while in the poorest countries hundreds of millions of people continue to suffer routine undernourishment. For a while, the mass production of cheap food seemed to work: world population doubled to six billion between 1970 and 2000, yet the cost of food declined in real dollars. In affluent countries, food took up about 10 per cent of a family's income, a third of what families spent before World War Two.

The 21st-century food crisis

The cheap food era was unsustainable, however. It had enormous hidden costs – in terms of fossil fuels, irrigation, fertilizers, pesticides, waste, transportation, packaging, pollution and poor health – and from 2007 the chickens came home to roost. Shortages of food pushed prices ever higher and by the end of the year the food price index kept by *The Economist* was at its highest since the magazine's founding in 1843. Food riots broke out Mexico, India, Indonesia, Morocco, Yemen, Uzbekistan, Mauritania, Senegal, and Burkina Faso as the shortages bit deep. Many other governments subsidized food costs for the poor to avoid such riots. The soaring prices have, moreover, threatened the capacity of the UN World Food Programme to buy the food it needs to sustain at least 78 million desperately hungry people. Yet the huge food corporations such as Cargill and Bunge, as well as food-retail giants such as Britain's Tesco, France's Carrefour and the US's Wal-Mart, continued to rake in huge profits.

The world still has plenty of capacity to deliver the food that people need. But in the future it will have to be produced in different ways, based on real local needs and not on an industrialized system that feeds vast amounts of grain to animals (about half the US corn crop is fed to livestock because it fattens the animals more quickly than if they ate their natural food, grass – and it takes well over eight kilos of grain to produce one kilo of beef).

The environmental issues, meanwhile, go much deeper than the conversion of food into biofuel for cars. The challenge for the 21st century will be to wean agriculture off two fast-declining resources – fossil fuels and water – and restore it to the 'solar power' that sustained it for millennia.

The Changing Shape of Overseas Aid

New world orders and theories of aid have come and gone – but old world problems have persisted all the while.

Aftermath

The two wars that began in Europe in the first half of the 20th century were 'total': waged by industrial means on civilians as well as between armies, and with devastating results. In the interval between them came the Great Depression – the worst financial collapse in the history of capitalism – and revolutionary upheaval in Russia. The legacy of this chaotic experience pushed Northern governments into more active economic and social intervention. This shift was reflected internationally.

A conference at Bretton Woods in 1944 agreed heavily modified versions of economic ideas for a 'new world order' proposed by John Maynard Keynes. The International Bank for Reconstruction and Development (IBRD – now known as the World Bank) was established to help the post-War reconstruction of Europe. Together with the foundation of the United Nations, Bretton Woods laid down the basic structure of the 'multilateral' financial agencies that has remained in place to this day.

Reconstruction
In 1948 the US Congress authorized the use of two to three per cent of US Gross National Product (GNP) until 1953 to finance grants for the reconstruction of Europe – what became known as the Marshall Plan. With this the present concept of aid was born. Three-quarters of the goods financed under this plan came from the US, mostly in the form of food aid. The recipients agreed to co-operate and make joint requests to the US through what eventually became the Organization for Economic Co-operation and Development (OECD) – today's rich-country 'club' whose Development Assistance Committee (DAC) includes all the major official-aid donor countries. All the new institutions were designed for, and controlled by, the North. Repeated attempts to establish alternatives based on the UN, in which the interests of the South were better represented, were thwarted.

Cold War
The end of the Second World War also ushered in a 'cold' war with the Soviet Union in which aid became a pawn. Massive US aid was sent to the island of Taiwan, to which the opponents of the Chinese revolutionary regime had retreated. Following the Korean War – which began in 1950 – Western aid financed more than 68 per cent of total imports and 60 per cent of investment in South Korea, while aid from the 'Communist Bloc' financed a third of national revenues in North Korea. Former European colonies were becoming independent. A meeting of Southern heads of government in Bandung, Indonesia, in 1955 gave rise to the Non-Aligned Movement. The idea of a 'Marshall Plan for the South' was taken up by Bruno Kreisky, Austria's Federal Chancellor, in 1958. In the same year, the World Council of Churches called for one per cent of the GNP of rich countries to be devoted to aid in the South: an idea adopted by the General Assembly of the UN in 1960.

Development
In response to the glaring post-colonial poverty of the South, the UN declared the 1960s to be a 'Decade of Development'. Most 'bilateral' aid between individual countries was 'tied' to narrow commercial or political

self-interest in the donor country. West Germany would not give aid to any government that recognized East Germany, while the US strategic and domestic agenda prompted aid to Israel. Great reliance was placed on promoting the 'Green Revolution' to meet the food needs of a world population that was expanding rapidly, especially in the South. But the one-per-cent aid target was never reached. In 1969 a Commission led by Lester Pearson, the Canadian Prime Minister, called for 0.7 per cent of rich countries' GNP to be given in aid, excluding commercial loans and military expenditure – the average was about 0.5 per cent at the time. This was accepted unanimously by members of the OECD.

Redevelopment
The Pearson Commission recommended a 'Second Decade of Development' for the 1970s. It got off to a bad start: by 1973 aid levels had fallen to 0.29 per cent of GNP. In 1972 Robert McNamara, head of the World Bank, called for a reorientation of aid towards the poorest 40 per cent of the world's population. 'Targeting the poor' became the new orthodoxy. A series of UN conferences (on the environment in 1972, population and food in 1974, women in 1975, human settlements in 1977) underlined the failures and challenges of 'development' – particularly for women. The oil crisis in 1973 hit the South hard – and the process of recycling the oil-producers' huge cash surpluses through Northern private banks into 'Third World' loans began. In 1974 the UN endorsed the 'New International Economic Order' called for by the Group of 77 developing countries, who argued that aid was no substitute for a fair deal on basic economic issues like trade.

Lost decade
In 1982 a major financial crisis hit Mexico, which threatened to default on its foreign debts. The Brady Plan – the first major 'structural adjustment' program – was negotiated between the US and Mexican Governments to protect Northern banks and prevent a global financial collapse. A crisis of debt began to overwhelm the South as interest rates rose and commodity prices fell. Structural adjustment, requiring cuts in public expenditure, privatization and strict anti-inflation measures, was the formula imposed to deal with it. Aid levels stagnated well below the 0.7-per-cent target. Large-scale projects like dams came under increasing criticism, particularly on environmental grounds. The 1980s became known as the 'lost decade'. The search for 'environmentally sustainable development' began. The economic success of the 'Little Tigers' (South Korea, Taiwan, Hong Kong and Singapore – all of which had at one time been recipients of substantial aid) seemed to offer a new model of 'export-led' economic growth in developing countries.

111

Washington Consensus

In the latest 'new world order' after the collapse of communism, the acceptance of 'adjustment' by recipient countries became a uniform condition of almost all official aid. A 'Washington Consensus' emerged in 1990 as the World Bank declared that, though poverty persisted, only free markets could reduce it. However, growing anxieties about the threat of social unrest resulted in a New Policy Agenda. This demanded 'good governance' and 'ownership' of adjustment policies from Southern governments. An increasingly long list of conditions became attached to aid. Civil conflict replaced the national contests of the Cold War and became the focus of humanitarian crises in Somalia, Bosnia, Rwanda and elsewhere. The proportion of aid budgets devoted to peacekeeping and emergencies has increased markedly; so too has the amount channeled through non-governmental organizations, seen as lighter on their feet and less liable to corruption than governments.

Promises promises

Enhanced concern about achieving the UN Millennium Development Goals led to renewed commitments by rich countries to reach the age-old target of 0.7 per cent of what was by now called gross national income (GNI), notably at the International Conference on Financing Development held in Monterrey, Mexico, in 2002. Some countries have taken these commitments much more seriously than others – there have been notable increases in aid by Austria, Belgium, Britain, Ireland, Luxembourg and Switzerland. Yet over the period from 1990 to 2005, aid as a percentage of GNI fell in as many donor countries as it increased (see table).

Official development assistance, net disbursed (% of GNI)

	1990	2005
Norway	1.17	0.94
Sweden	0.91	0.94
Luxembourg	0.21	0.82
Netherlands	0.92	0.82
Denmark	0.94	0.81
Belgium	0.46	0.53
Austria	0.11	0.52
France	0.60	0.47
UK	0.27	0.47
Finland	0.65	0.46
Switzerland	0.32	0.44
Ireland	0.16	0.42
Germany	0.42	0.36
Canada	0.44	0.34
Italy	0.31	0.29
Japan	0.31	0.28
New Zealand	0.23	0.27
Spain	0.20	0.27
Australia	0.34	0.25
US	0.21	0.22
Portugal	0.24	0.21

Source :
Human Development Report, UNDP 2007/2008

BRIEF HISTORY **25**

The Story of Money

From feathers, teeth and cocoa beans through the Chinese invention of paper money to the inflation and currency speculation of today.

A cunning invention

Money is ingenious. Less cumbersome than barter, basically it is any medium of exchange a group of people agree to call money. The earliest known record of its use is around 2400 BCE in Mesopotamia and Egypt. There are records of money in China and in the Aegean in the 7th century BCE, and in India three centuries later. It has usually emerged when a community has wanted to expand trade with others. But it has also proved useful for paying fines, taxes and levies – and, of course, rewarding labor.

A head for money

All sorts of things are used as money. Perhaps the most varied repertoire has been found in Micronesia and Melanesia, where feathers, cloth, teeth and stone, as well as the common cowry shell, feature. Sumatrans of the 15th century used human skulls, while Mexicans of that period favored cocoa beans. Shells were widely used in India, North America and Africa, while up until the 19th century the Lele people of central Africa preferred cloth. The first people to start making coins from precious metals appear to have been the 7th-century BCE Lydians, who lived on the Asian coast of the Aegean. Gold, silver, copper and brass became the commonest currency, used by the Chinese, Greeks, Romans, Arabs and Indians. But paper money was already being used in China as early as the Song Dynasty of 960-1279.

Immoral income

Ethical qualms have probably always surrounded money. Aristotle despised and distrusted it. Both Jesus of Nazareth and the Prophet Muhammad were acutely aware of the social and moral damage that love of money and the hunger for accumulating it could do. Earning interest by lending money was prohibited in both religions, with some effect until the late Middle Ages. But such qualms ultimately gave way to pecuniary interest and international trade and banking flourished.

Spawning capitalism

The Spanish conquistadors could hardly believe the abundance of gold and silver they saw when they first arrived in the Americas in the late

15th century. First they got their hands on it by looting and kidnapping: King Atahualpa of the Incas was held to ransom by Francisco Pizarro in exchange for a room full of gold. Then they moved on to exploiting the continent's gold and silver deposits, mined by mainly indigenous slave labor under appalling conditions. The massive inflow of precious metals sent Europe into an inflationary spiral, with wages lagging behind prices. Entrepreneurs could make easy money, the poor became poorer, and capitalism was born.

John Law: banker, gambler, murderer
Banking flourished during the European Renaissance in port cities such as Antwerp, Amsterdam, Venice and Genoa. Modern banking, however, began with a Scots gambler named John Law, fleeing a murder charge in England to try his luck in France. He got the go-ahead from the French Regent, Philip Duc d'Orléans, to issue banknotes in the form of loans against the security of the land of the country. The notes soon gained more credibility than hard coin, fortunes were made overnight and the word 'millionaire' entered the vocabulary. But too many were issued and Law fled France in 1720 leaving broken fortunes, falling prices, depressed business and an enduring suspicion of banking.

Making a mint in the colonies
Trade and colonialism had a profound effect on indigenous money systems in Africa, Asia and the Americas. With Portuguese, Dutch, French and British traders and settlers came Western-style money. Local precious metals were exploited and mints established. Sometimes indigenous currencies were manipulated too, as when European traders imported

vast quantities of cowrie shells into West Africa from the Indian Ocean to trade for slaves. In 1835 the East India Company started minting the existing silver rupee and turned it into the standard coinage of India, while in China the First Opium War (1840-42) opened the way for foreign commercial banks issuing their own notes.

Revolutionary excesses
Revolutionaries are always short of funds and have often resorted to printing their own money. The

American Revolution against British rule was financed by vast issues of 'continental' bills – to the tune of $240 million between 1775 and 1779. The Revolutionary Government in France did the same thing in 1789, and went on to finance the Revolutionary Wars with paper money. But lack of financial control led to overproduction and the notes plummeted to about 0.3 per cent of their face value.

Smith, Marx and 'callous' cash
New ideas about money, society and the relationship between them, were sparked off by the Industrial Revolution. The two most important thinkers were Adam Smith (1723-90) and Karl Marx (1818-1883). Smith proposed that the wealth of a nation ought not to be measured in terms of money but in terms of its useful labor force. Marx also argued that 'value' resided in labor, but cash often triumphed. He and Engels wrote in the *Communist Manifesto* of 1848: 'The bourgeoisie... has mercilessly torn apart the motley feudal bonds... and has left no other nexus between man and man than callous cash payment.' Marx went further to attack the unequal distribution of wealth between worker, capitalist and landlord, arguing that it arose out of the capitalist system of production itself.

Inflating fascism
A big problem with money is the temptation to issue too much of it. The adoption of the Gold Standard by Western nations in 1876, however, linked money to gold reserves and provided a relatively fixed exchange-rate system. This collapsed with the outbreak of the First World War. After the War the victors imposed massive reparations on Germany, which responded by over-issuing money. The results were catastrophic. Goods worth 100 marks in 1913 cost 147,479 marks in 1922 and a staggering 75,570,000,000,000 marks in 1923. The conditions were ripe for the rise of fascism and were not helped by the 1929 Wall Street Crash in the US which caused economic depression, poverty and unemployment on an international scale.

Fragile world
The high costs of failing to develop rules for economic co-ordination were clear to all by 1944 when delegates from 44 countries met at Bretton Woods. They agreed to a new international money system of fixed, but adjustable, exchange rates. After a period of relative success, the Bretton Woods system came to an end in 1971 when US President Nixon terminated the guarantee to exchange one ounce of gold at $35. Many countries pegged their currencies to the US dollar or to other 'strong' currencies, while others floated their exchange rates independently. The result was international monetary instability.

As the world's economy has become globalized, its international monetary system has become increasingly fragile and unsustainable. Money flashes across the world at the press of a button and currency speculators hunt in packs when they sense that a country's money is 'wounded'. The global currency market saw an average of $3,200 billion changing hands every day in 2007. A tax on foreign-exchange transactions (often known as the Tobin Tax after the originator of the idea) has been proposed by campaigners – and adopted in principle by the Belgian and Canadian parliaments – not just because of the amount of money it would raise for human development in the Majority World but also because it might dissuade some speculators and thus serve as a stabilizing force.

BRIEF HISTORY **26**

A History of Public Health

Plagues and disease have always been with us but they were largely rolled back in the rich world by the 19th-century pioneers of public health. In the Majority World they never really went away. And now even the defeated diseases are starting to bite back.

Plague days

Plague first appeared in Roman Europe in the sixth century under the Emperor Justinian as the sanitation systems of the ancient world decayed. Later, as the caravans made their way along the Silk Routes of Asia in the 14th century, they took with them yersinia pestis, a plague-causing bacterium carried by fleas and the rats on which they lived. An alternative theory puts the fleas on ships and sailors entering Black Sea ports from the east. In either case these first tentacles of globalization were the source of the 'Black Death' that swept the then-known world from Indochina to northern Europe. Millions died, particularly in the crowded, unsanitary conditions of the newly chartered towns. In response, the first rudimentary measures of public health were adopted: ship inspections, quarantine, leprosariums, mass burials. In the following centuries, as global commerce and conquest spread, infectious diseases hitchhiked along, with devastating consequences for the indigenous populations of the Americas and the South Pacific. A radical change in people's circumstances – contact with outsiders, changing climate, expulsion from land, altered diet, hard wage labor or urbanization – added stress factors and increased vulnerability to disease.

Pioneers of public health

The first significant wave of public-health advocates emerged in response to the slums and desperate working conditions of 19th-century Europe and North America. In centers like New York, London and Berlin, the struggle for proper sewerage, decent housing, clean water, factory inspectors, district health officers and a regime of food inspections was born. Such figures as Herman Biggs in New York and Edwin Chadwick (who introduced the small bore sewer pipe) and John Simon in Britain led the way. The movement was quite diverse, ranging from birth control and family-planning advocates like Margaret Sanger to scientists such as the Frenchman Louis Pasteur, who was concerned with food safety. Other voices included sanitarians, germ-theory zealots, prohibitionists, anti-child-labor activists and a plethora of other campaigners.

The movement was divided. One wing, under the influence of Social Darwinism, blamed ignorant individuals for their own poor health – such as the paternalistic middle-class campaigns to overcome 'maternal inefficiency' (thought to be a major cause of infant mortality) or to teach the poor how to budget properly and stop drinking. Other liberal and radical campaigners concentrated on poverty and strove to improve living and working conditions, bringing them into immediate conflict with the conservative owner class. This same question divides

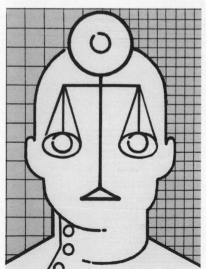

public-health advocates to this day: is health basically an individual responsibility or part of a broader fight for social justice?

The medical model

For all its diversity, the first wave of public-health advocates was remarkably successful. Some 86 per cent of the gains in life expectancy in the industrial world have been due to decreases in infectious diseases, most of which occurred before the discovery of antibiotics and the present development of modern medical techniques and technologies. In the US, less

117

than four per cent of the total improvement in life expectancy can be credited to today's sophisticated medicine. Clean water, decent housing, vaccination programs for children, proper waste disposal, knowledge of personal health needs and practices, plentiful and uncontaminated food and breathable air were the keys. Gradually the slums of early industrialization gave way to more liveable communities and a public-health infrastructure was established. While the medical system should be judged on the basis of its record for cures and care and the equality of access, the fundamental health of a population lies outside its scope. Public health must deal more broadly with the quality of a society – its physical and social environment and the opportunities for a decent life it provides to all citizens.

The Global South

Back in the mid-19th century, public-health pioneer Edward Chadwick compared the situation of a Latin American populace 'sunk into the lowest vice and misery amidst the means of the highest abundance' with 'the wretched population in the vast parts of Glasgow, Edinburgh, London and Bath'. While the situation in the slums of the industrial world has improved dramatically, some five billion of the world's six-and-a-half billion people still live in the global equivalent of New York City's 1890s tenements. While mass vaccination has largely freed the peoples of the South from some diseases (polio, leprosy, smallpox) the basic public-health infrastructure that would provide clean water, ample food and healthy living conditions is not in place for most of the world's peoples. Commitments to primary healthcare have been undermined by debt, exploitation, war and economic stagnation. Even the vaccinations to prevent diseases like malaria and others are proving ineffective as microbial resistance to a number of vaccines is on the rise. Major pharmaceutical companies have simply given up researching drugs for diseases like malaria and tuberculosis – drugs to cure these diseases of the poor are simply not profitable enough. Anyway, as the Swiss medical thinker Henry Sigerist pointed out: 'It is a grim joke to immunize people against disease with one hand and to exploit them into starvation with the other.'

Rats and sucking insects

The science on which public health was traditionally based is running into trouble. Diseases once thought defeated or least controlled, like tuberculosis and malaria, are back with a vengeance and have developed resistance to the drugs once thought to have vanquished them. Hospitals are today besieged by new forms of infection, such as the Staph bacteria, that are resistant to most known antibiotics. In the 1990s, between

100,000 and 150,000 patients died from the infections they contracted inside US hospitals.

A more holistic science is evolving that looks at how humankind alters environments and ecologies, favoring some viruses, bacteria and their hosts. Sometimes it's as simple as overuse of antibiotics or doctors who don't wash their hands. Others are more complex. For example the hemorrhagic fevers appearing today in tropical Africa and South America (ebola, lassa, yellow fever, Marburg disease) are connected to the clearing of land, the elimination of snakes, owls and jaguars who normally eat rodents and the development of grain economies on which rodents thrive. Similarly the development of large Southern cities provide the perfect breeding grounds for Aedes aegypti, the mosquito which carries dengue and yellow fever but is normally a poor competitor in tropical rainforest conditions where more hardy breeds dominate. In the abandoned lots, puddles, water barrels and old tires of tropical slums, Aedes can thrive. Even in the air-conditioned comfort of the modern hotel and office block we have created the rare conditions (chlorinated high temperature) in which the legionnaire's disease bacterium does well. Public-health science needs to pay more attention to the vectors – such as the mosquito, the rodent – of particular diseases and the 'spaces' in our development models and medical practices in which they may find a niche.

A new agenda

Today's public-health movement varies dramatically from the wave of activism in the 19th and early 20th centuries. Then, the main emphasis was on stopping contagion by altering the conditions under which infectious disease spread. This is still a crucial issue in the Global South where the basic necessities of clean water and adequate food top the agenda. In the industrial world, however, the main focus is dealing with chronic diseases (cancer, heart ailments) and their causes. The modern environmental movement, born in the crucible of 1960s discontent, is an important actor in the field of public health. All of its main touchstones – opposition to nuclear power, resistance to chemical pollution in general and agro-chemicals in particular, advocacy for habitable cities, concern over a deteriorating climate and getting the balance right between humans and nature – are also key public-health issues. These are emerging as crucial issues in the South too, where environmentalism links solidly to issues of social justice.

In the early 21st century there is an important coming together of movements around a new public-health agenda based on the environment and social justice. Its scope is as broad as the diversity of issues it must tackle. Public health is no longer the exclusive concern of a few beleaguered government professionals but involves energy and analysis

119

coming from many quarters. There are workers concerned with health and safety; NGOs committed to global equity; medical practitioners who realize the limits of sophisticated medicine; and advocates of alternative medicines and therapies. A common thread of understanding is starting to bind such groupings together: you cannot expect to be healthy if you live in an unhealthy society.

Nonviolence: the Power of the People

Some defining strategies in the rich history of nonviolent action – and the people behind them.

Rise like lions after slumber
In unvanquishable number –
Shake your chains to earth like dew
Which in sleep had fallen on you –
You are many – they are few.
(*Percy Bysshe Shelley*, from **The Mask of Anarchy**, written after the massacre carried out by the British Government on a peaceful rally at Peterloo, Manchester in 1819).

WITHDRAW YOUR CONSENT
Mohandas Karamchand (Mahatma) Gandhi and the people of India.
India – 1930. Fewer than 100,000 British troops control 350 million Indians. Mohandas Gandhi identifies that the British 'have not taken India from us – we have given it to them'. At the beginning of what would be a 17-year campaign of non-cooperation to oust British colonial rule from India, the 60-year-old undertakes a 384-kilometer walk to the beach to gather salt – illegal under British law. After 24 days' walking, on the eve of the law-breaking, he meets with 12,000 supporters on the beach and tells them: 'Hold the salt in your fist and think it is worth 60 million rupees. That is how much the [British] Government have been taking from us

through their monopoly on salt.' At dawn on 6 April 1930, Gandhi picks up a fist of mud and salt. Later, he declares: 'We will practise such non-cooperation that finally it will not be possible for the Administration to carry on.' By midsummer, even with Gandhi and most of India's leaders in jail, the Government has lost control of most major cities. In the years that follow, Gandhi proves a master strategist, advertiser and motivator. His strategies form the foundation upon which many of today's nonviolent actions are built.

STRATEGIZE
James Lawson and the students of Fisk University, Nashville, US.
When the well-dressed black students of Fisk University first sit at lunch-counters reserved for white Americans one Saturday afternoon, they are regarded as a curiosity. This is Nashville in 1960, where white and black Americans are totally segregated so, of course, they are refused service. But by the third Saturday of their sit-in, white tolerance has faded. Police – out in force – beat and arrest the Afro-Americans who are at the lunch counters... only to find a second, then a third wave take their place. Trained for months beforehand to withstand white taunts and physical violence, the students – who have broken no law other than convention – refuse bail. Their imprisonment provokes national sympathy, draws a deluge of recruits – white and black – from throughout the country and leads to a crippling boycott of white stores in downtown Nashville. Their actions start the process of desegregation of all city services that occurs over the following four years. This is an outstanding example of what people-power can achieve through disciplined training based on a carefully planned strategy that anticipates, then neutralizes, the response of the oppressors. Unlike the Indians who responded to Gandhi, these Afro-Americans are a minority who take on a majority – and win.

USE WHAT YOU'VE GOT
Lysistrata and the women of Athens.
It is 411 BCE. The Peloponnesian war between Sparta and Athens is in its 21st year. The Greek women from opposing sides meet and decide that the war must stop. 'We must refrain from the male altogether,' says their chief strategist, Lysistrata. And, if forced into intercourse, Lysistrata advises them to 'yield to their [men's] wishes, but with a bad grace; there is no pleasure in it for them when they do it by force.' And so the sex strike is born, the men's resolve crumples and a treaty of peace is signed.

That, of course, was fiction – a political satire by Greek dramatist Aristophanes (447-385 BCE). Had Lysistrata's grand plan materialized, Athens might not have needed to surrender the war to Sparta in 404 BCE. But the idea is still active – employed by women in a Turkish village in

2001 to get a decent water supply; by Icelandic women in 1979 to help the passage of equal opportunity laws; and in Colombia at a violent moment in the country's drug wars to achieve a brief ceasefire in 1997. The play *Lysistrata* was itself used as a worldwide act of dissent against the war on Iraq with 1,029 productions staged in 59 countries – all on 3 March 2003.

IDENTIFY OPPORTUNITIES
Mkhuseli Jack and the Port Elizabeth resistance against apartheid.
By 1985, violent resistance is failing black South Africans. Even though millions of South Africans are demanding an end to apartheid, the white Government's security forces are widespread, well armed and dealing out death on a daily basis. 'Let us expose this violence and bring it right to the doorsteps of the whites,' Mkhuseli Jack tells the black townspeople living around Port Elizabeth in the Eastern Cape Province. After two months' preparation, Jack urges a huge crowd on 13 July 1985 at a funeral to boycott the white-owned businesses in Port Elizabeth where nearly half a million blacks normally shop. And on Monday, the streets are empty. There is nearly 100 per cent compliance with the boycott in the weeks that follow. When a state of emergency is imposed and the black leaders are arrested, the desperate white store owners pressure the Government to have them released. Another boycott, another state of emergency and another spate of arrests follow over the next 12 months. And although the boycotters' demands – which include withdrawing Government troops and opening public amenities to the black population – are not met immediately, the boycotts shift power to the black communities and help undermine the white regime and its system of apartheid that will collapse eight years later.

PUBLICIZE THE TRUTH
The Mothers and Grandmothers of Plaza de Mayo.
'In order to guarantee the security of the State,' the commander-in-chief of Argentina's military forces tells journalists in October 1975, 'all the necessary people will die.' Five months later, the military seizes power in Argentina and holds it vice-like until 1983. Public executions would make martyrs of its targets, so instead people are 'disappeared': kidnapped, then tortured and murdered away from public view. No-one is immune. As many as 80,000 writs of habeas corpus – applications seeking release from arbitrary detention – are sought from the courts and refused. The resulting terror created amongst the population initially makes it impossible to organize resistance against the regime.

On 30 April 1977, 14 mothers meet in Buenos Aires' Plaza de Mayo wanting, simply, to know what has happened to their children. Despite beatings, threats, arrests and disappearances, their marches become a weekly event and their ranks eventually swell to 2,000 mothers and grandmothers, many carrying pictures of those who have disappeared. Referring to the military as 'assassins' and 'torturers' – and using slogans like 'You took them alive, we want them returned alive' – their example encourages other citizens, then international organizations, to speak out too, exerting pressure on the regime that contributes to its collapse.

Their tool – speaking the truth – puts nonviolent action within everyone's grasp.

NONVIOLENCE HALL OF FAME

THE THINKERS include:

1552-53: French scholar Étienne de La Boétie argues that tyranny can be overthrown peaceably if the majority withdraws its consent: 'It is therefore the inhabitants themselves who permit... their own subjection, since by ceasing to submit they would put an end to their servitude.'

1849: Henry David Thoreau is jailed – for one night – after refusing to pay the Massachusetts poll tax levied for what he believes is an unjust war on Mexico. Urging others to follow his example, he writes *On the Duty of Civil Disobedience*, which argues: 'Under a government which imprisons any unjustly, the true place for a just man is... a prison.'

1955-68: Dr Martin Luther King Jr agitates and organizes for equal opportunity for African-Americans in the US with his rousing public speeches before he is assassinated at just 39 years of age.

1973: Gene Sharp popularizes 'the consent theory of power' (first articulated by La Boétie) in *The Politics of Nonviolent Action*, which includes 198 methods of protest, persuasion, non-cooperation and nonviolent intervention, and is immediately hailed as a definitive study.

1996: Robert Burrowes identifies situations where a ruler's power is not dependent on the consent and co-operation of the people they oppress – for instance, in the Israeli occupation of Palestine – but on the sustained support of élite allies whose consent must be withdrawn for nonviolent action to succeed.

NONVIOLENT MILESTONES include:

1350 BCE: Jewish midwives Shiprah and Puah commit the first recorded act of civil disobedience by refusing to carry out Pharaoh's order to kill Jewish babies.

258 BCE: The world's first successful strike. When the Plebeians – the main constituents in the Roman army – withdraw to the mountains because the Senate prevaricates on granting them certain civil rights, the Senate takes immediate action.

1870s: Kusunose Kita refuses to pay taxes while being denied the vote as a woman, beginning the women's rights movement in Japan.

1930: As Gandhi is defying the British salt laws, trained and uniformed Pashtun recruits form the world's first professional nonviolent army, the Khudai Khidmatgars. 100,000-strong at their peak, they lead civil disobedience strikes and protests that sweep across the Northwest Frontier of India.

1940s: The plans of Minister-President of Norway, Vidkun Quisling, to introduce Nazi indoctrination into schools are scuttled when between 8,000 and 10,000 Norwegian teachers sign a statement of refusal, and 1,000 – removed to freezing conditions and hunger in the North – will not retract.

1943: Gentile women gather at Rosenstrasse, Berlin, to protest the arrest of their Jewish husbands – detained there before transfer to Auschwitz. The crowd grows from 24 to 1,000. After six days' protest, the 1,500 men are released.

1955: Rosa Parks – a black seamstress in Montgomery, US – refuses to surrender her seat in a city bus to a white rider as she's supposed to do under a City ordinance. Following a boycott of the bus company lasting 381 days, a Supreme Court Decision outlaws racial segregation on public transport.

1972: After a series of demonstrations of up to 120,000 people and after many draft resisters are imprisoned, Australia pulls out of the Vietnam War.

1986: When word gets out that Philippines President Ferdinand Marcos has rigged the voting count in the 1986 elections, Cardinal Sin – head of the Catholic Church – calls on Filipinos to place their unarmed bodies between Government troops and 300 army defectors. Hundreds of thousands of people make a human wall around the defectors, offering the soldiers small gifts and putting flowers down their guns. When Marcos orders the troops to attack, they refuse. Marcos flees.

OTHER OPPRESSORS and REGIMES REMOVED FROM POWER when the force of tens, sometimes hundreds, of thousands of people take to the streets to demand that they go include:

1944 – Hernandez Martinez (El Salvador)
1944 – General Jorge Ubico (Guatemala)
1957 – British colonial rule (Ghana)
1982 – Luis García Meza and the Generals who succeeded him (Bolivia)
1985 – Jaafar Nimeiry (Sudan)
1988 – Augusto Pinochet (Chile)
1989 – Egon Krenz, Erich Honecker and the Soviet Union (East Germany)
1989 – Gustav Husak and the Soviet Union (Czechoslovakia)
1989 – The Soviet-controlled Polish United Workers' Party Government

(Poland)
1990 – The Soviet Union (Lithuania, Estonia and Latvia)
1992 – Amadou Toumani Toure (Mali)
1993 – Didier Ratsiraka (Madagascar)
2000 – Slobodan Milosevic (Serbia/ former Yugoslavia)
2001 – Joseph Estrada (The Philippines)
2003 – Eduard Shevardnadze (Georgia)
2004 – Viktor Yanukovych and Leonid Kuchma (Ukraine)
2005 – 14,000 Syrian troops (Lebanon)
2005 – Askar Akayev (Kyrgyzstan)

BRIEF HISTORY **28**

The Growth of Green Ideas

The environmental movement barely existed before the 1960s, yet it forms the single greatest challenge to the status quo in the 21st century, and the future of humanity certainly depends upon its success.

The pioneers

While environmentalism is definitely a child of the 20th century, its philosophical roots hark back to earlier times and it is perhaps the first genuinely internationalist movement in the variety of its origins. It has drawn on everything from traditional native beliefs about the sanctity of nature to the scientific ecology of the German biologist Haechal; from Eastern religions like Taoism and Buddhism to the social analysis of anarchism and Marx; from Charles Darwin to Walt Whitman. The nonviolent civil disobedience of Gandhi has also been a major influence.

The early environmentalists found their homes in wilderness and wildlife protection associations, animal-welfare efforts and the public-health movement. They quickly found themselves in opposition to market liberalism and to the conquest-of-nature mentality of colonialists and of settlers in North America, Australasia and South Africa. Among the first environmentalists were the Americans Aldo Leopold, whose *Sand County Almanac* is an ecological classic, and John Muir, who founded the Sierra Club. The tension within environmental politics was between those who wanted to 'manage' nature in a more rational fashion and those who demanded a whole new paradigm for the relationship between nature and the economy. The tension continues to this day.

Silent Spring

No single ecological work has had as much influence as Rachel Carson's *Silent Spring*, published in 1962. For Carson, a biologist, the lack of birdsong was emblematic of a world poisoned by the first generation of agrochemicals. She traced the impact of chemicals up and down the food chain and in the general environment. *Silent Spring* had a dramatic influence both on public consciousness and eventually on regulatory policy. Despite criticism of her science by the chemical industry and others, 12 of the pesticides and herbicides Carson identified as the most dangerous have since been either severely restricted or banned outright. This of course includes the infamous DDT, now banned in most countries. In Carson's wake, a profound unease about technological progress was loose upon the land and the environmental impact of economic decisions and technological choices was always on the agenda. The main focus of environmental protest in the 1960s was not, however, agrochemicals but the effects of nuclear fallout from weapons-testing and the movement for a comprehensive international test-ban treaty.

Prophets of doom

The early 1970s saw a series of studies published that predicted a dire future for humanity if we did not change our ways. A furious debate broke out between Paul Ehrlich (*The Population Bomb*) and Barry Commoner (*The Closing Circle*) over whether the problem was too many people or too many machines. A group of scientists and business leaders came together to form the Club of Rome and launched an extensive computer-based study extrapolating present patterns of population growth, resource use and other environmental trends. Their alarming results were published as *Limits to Growth* in 1972. The same year another study entitled *Blueprint for Survival* was published in Britain. Their critics accused them (with some justification) of exaggeration and at least some of the doomsday theorists had alarming biases against poor countries, blaming them for population growth and ignoring the vastly disproportionate share of the world's wealth gobbled up by industrial corporations and consumers. But the studies set the alarm bells ringing and made people think about the kind of world we want to live in.

The new environmentalism
Under the impact of a series of major oil spills, nuclear and chemical accidents, species extinctions and mounting evidence of global eco-destruction, in the late 1960s and early 1970s a new generation of more militant environmental organizations started to emerge. Among these were Greenpeace, with its uncanny ability to capture media attention, and Friends of the Earth (FoE), originally an activist splinter group from the more conservative Sierra Club. Both quickly became international in scope and membership, and took a leadership role in exposing and opposing crimes against the environment. Public concern for the environment fluctuated with the business cycle of the economy – waxing in times of prosperity and waning in recession. As organizations like FoE and Greenpeace became established, a new wave of direct-action groups emerged to take up an even more militant position of environmental defense. The anti-nuclear movement in Europe launched massive demonstrations against the secretive nuclear establishment and their power plants, while in the US a loose-knit coalition called Earth First used civil disobedience and sometimes sabotage (which they called 'monkey-wrenching') to defend endangered species and wilderness areas. In Britain direct-action protesters against new motorways are very much in this tradition.

Green politics
The West German Greens were not the first Green political party but they were certainly the first to achieve prominence – and their success helped spawn other such parties, especially in Europe, in the 1980s. The key to whether Greens could organize into effective parties was the political space available to them. Dictatorships or even the 'guided democracies' of the South provided an inhospitable climate. Also the 'first-past-the-post' electoral systems of countries like the US, Britain and Canada made it very difficult for Green parties to break through.

It was under the proportional-representation systems of countries like Germany, France, Scandinavia and Holland that they really gained a political toehold. While their share of the vote has fluctuated between five and ten per cent, their support has been consistent and their influence as part of local, state and now national governments has outweighed their numbers. On such issues as soft energy, pollution controls, planning and human rights they have helped shape policy. But to gain this influence they have often had to compromise on their ideals, leading to a tension inside most Green parties. This was most dramatically seen in the split between the 'realos' (realists) and the 'fundis' (fundamentalists) in the German Green Party but is present throughout the entire Green movement.

The Earth Summit

In 1992 the United Nations convened its second international conference on the global environment, in Rio de Janeiro. The first had been held in Stockholm two decades earlier and saw conflict between industrial countries and the Third World: Southern governments felt they were being expected to bear the brunt of ecological controls which would deny them an industrial future. By 1992 the situation had altered: a grassroots environmental movement had over the two decades gained increasing influence in the South. This stretched from anti-dam protesters in Thailand through the Chipko tree-conservation movement of northern India to Amazonian rubber-tappers' struggle to save the rainforest. Rio's Earth Summit gave voice and weight to such movements, bringing development and environment together. No longer could Southern politicians maintain that the environment was solely a concern of the Northern middle class. But demands for justice as well as sustainability rendered the movement a lot less palatable in Washington and the other industrial capitals, and urgent action on the key problems – from the ravaged global fishery to chemical poisoning, global warming to rampant deforestation – was still manifestly lacking.

It's now or never...

The early years of the 21st century saw environmental ideas take center stage, as the world woke up to the urgent reality of climate change. Global warming – previously treated as the fringe concern of radicals, either dismissed outright or pushed to the margins by politicians and industrialists – became accepted virtually across the board as a threat to the future of humankind as alarming as nuclear war. Apocalyptic pronouncements about the global future in a warmer world became almost everyday events; limiting carbon emissions became a mainstream concern. Yet the politics of climate change remain firmly in the balance. The ideas of Green political parties have been largely vindicated and are taken more seriously but this has not yet translated into votes and influence. Governments seek market-friendly ways of dealing with 'the carbon problem' – trading emissions, offsetting journeys – and balk at setting international targets (via the Kyoto Protocol of 1997 and its successor process, started in Bali in 2007) that fall far short of the measures so urgently needed.

In this political vacuum, the Green movement has never been so important as it is now. Left to their own devices, there is little evidence that rich-world politicians will do anything decisive, addicted as they are to economic growth and rampant consumerism. It will need a groundswell of opposition to 'business as usual' if the emerging climate justice movement is to 'wrestle the earth from fools'.

BRIEF HISTORY **29**

Confronting Child Labor, Then and Now

The Victorian chimney sweep in Britain, the first industrial nation, was once an even bigger symbol of inhumanity than the bonded child laborer of Pakistan and India today. There are lessons we can learn from the past about how to combat child labor – but there are also myths to discard.

Peasant children

Children have always worked. But the nature of their work has changed according to the social conditions of the time – and so has our notion of 'childhood'. In peasant societies children have always participated in the working life of the family – on a seasonal basis in agriculture and more constantly in domestic tasks. The tasks recorded as having been given to children in 16th-century Spain – collecting firewood, herding livestock, helping with plowing, collecting pests from crops – are not dissimilar from those still allocated to children in rural areas of the developing world today.

Factories for four-year-olds

Children have also always participated in light industry – and as industrial activity increased in 18th-century Europe, so the economic opportunities increased too. People in general were rarely troubled by the sight of children working – rather the contrary. When the author Daniel Defoe toured England and reported on what he had seen, far from being concerned at the sight of four-year-olds at work in Lancashire's cotton industry he was delighted that they were finding useful employment.

The philosopher John Locke also wrote reports on how to deal with the children of the poor: 'The children of the laboring people are an ordinary burthen to the parish and are usually maintained in idleness, so that their labor also is lost to the public till they are 12 or 14 years old.' The conclusion drawn by Locke was that poor children should be put to work at three years old with a bellyful of bread daily, supplemented in cold weather by 'a little warm water-gruel'.

The creation of childhood

Locke's views were not extraordinary at the time: childhood had never up to this point been seen as a cordoned-off area of innocence but rather as a period in which children learned skills that made them employable – which is exactly the same view held in many developing countries today. The modern Western idea of childhood is a relatively recent creation which emerged from the Romantic movement of the late 18th and early 19th centuries. The conception of childhood by the poets Blake and Wordsworth as a period of innocence and visionary imagination was nothing short of revolutionary – and Blake directly counterposed to this the bitter experience of child laborers in an increasingly industrial England.

Poor little white slaves

It was another Romantic poet, Coleridge, who coined the term 'white slaves' when he referred in 1819 to 'our poor little white slaves, the children in our cotton factories'. By the 1830s the phrase was in common usage and people routinely contrasted the humanitarian concern for the children of slaves abroad with the apparent indifference to the suffering of child laborers at home. The Factory Commission of 1833 revealed that children were often employed from the age of six and made to work 14-to-16-hour days during which they were kept awake by beating.

Down the mines

The conditions in mines were even worse, and the inclusion of line drawings in the 1842 report on mines profoundly shocked the Victorian public. These helped produce the world's first serious legislation against child labor – but even this only banned children under nine from working in factories and those under ten from the mines. The idea that child labor in Britain was abolished almost single-handedly by the sterling efforts of Conservative politician Lord Shaftesbury has crystallized into a national myth which still affects attitudes to child labor all over the world.

Education, education, education

It was not legislation and inspection that ended widespread child labor in industrial countries such as the US – the first truly effective federal law against child labor did not come until 1938 – so much as economics and education. First, as industry became increasingly mechanized there was less demand for child labor anyway. But just as important in eradicating mass child labor was the provision of universal education, which in Britain was made compulsory for children under 10 in 1880 and free of school fees in 1892 – and the school-leaving age rose steadily throughout the industrialized world in the 20th century. Making school compulsory did not automatically mean children turned up – the process took decades. But if history teaches us that there is a single mechanism most likely to reduce hazardous child labor then compulsory primary education would be it.

Child rights
All but two governments in the world (the US and Somalia) have now ratified the 1989 UN Convention on the Rights of the Child – the fullest embodiment of the modern view of childhood. Article 28 requires governments which have ratified to 'make primary education compulsory and available free to all'. It only remains for them to put their money where their mouths are – and to strike a significant blow against hazardous child labor in the process.

BRIEF HISTORY **30**
Great American Rebels
True originals abound in a country that has much to thank them for – here is just a sample of them.

Daniel Shays (1747-1825)
A veteran of the Revolution who fought at Lexington, Bunker Hill and Saratoga, Shays resigned from the Continental Army in 1780 after not being paid. He returned to his small farm in western Massachusetts. Here, like many others, he quickly fell into debt. Farmers had begun to resist the use of the courts to enforce repayment. When the Supreme Court of Massachusetts indicted 11 rebel farmers as 'disorderly, riotous and seditious persons', Shays organized 700 armed farmers and went to Springfield, where hundreds more joined him. The judges adjourned the court. Confrontations between farmers and militia multiplied in what

became known as Shays' Rebellion. Wealthy Boston merchants raised an army against the rebels. Arrested, condemned to death and pardoned in 1788, Shays eventually died in poverty.

Geronimo (1829-1909)

'I was born on the prairies where the wind blew free and there was nothing to break the light of the sun. I was born where there were no enclosures,' said Geronimo, the last great leader of Native American resistance. His Indian name was Goyathlay ('one who yawns'); he was born to the Bedonkohe Apache group in what is now New Mexico, but was Mexican territory until 1846. He was reputedly given the name Geronimo ('Jerome' in Spanish) by Mexican soldiers. Geronimo was not a chief but a shaman or 'medicine man'. He believed that the spirits had conferred on him an invulnerability to bullets. In 1858 the murder of Geronimo's wife, mother and three children by Spanish soldiers from Mexico increased the level of Apache resistance to a new wave of American settlers. In 1876 the Chiricahua were removed by the US Army to an arid 'reservation' at San Carlos, eastern Arizona. Geronimo escaped three times. The US Army sent 5,000 troops to hunt him down. In 1882 he agreed to return to the reservation, but escaped again in 1885 until the last of all the Native Americans surrendered in 1886. In breach of the surrender agreement, Geronimo and some 400 Apache men, women and children were transported to Florida and then, in 1894, to Oklahoma, where he died.

'I want freedom,' he said, 'the right to self-expression, everybody's right to beautiful and radiant things.'

Emma Goldman (1869-1940)

An influential and celebrated anarchist, Goldman was an early advocate of free speech, birth control, women's equality, labor unions and the eight-hour working day. She was frequently harassed or arrested; her talks were often banned outright. In 1893, amidst mass unemployment in New York, she urged hungry children to go into stores and take the food they needed. She was arrested for 'inciting a riot' and sentenced to two years in prison. Of the rising price of food after the Spanish-American War of 1898 – which centered on American 'interests' in Cuba – she said: 'When we sobered up from our patriotic spree, it suddenly dawned on us that the cause of the war was the price of sugar... That the lives, blood and money of the American people were used to protect the interests of American capitalists.' She worked with the first Free Speech League, a direct progenitor of the American Civil Liberties Union. Her opposition to conscription during the First World War led to a two-year imprisonment, followed by deportation in 1919. Thereafter she was forced to live a peripatetic life, eventually dying in Canada.

Mae West (1893-1980)

'I believe in censorship. After all, I made a fortune out of it.' Mae West grew up as 'The Baby Vamp' on stage in Vaudeville. In 1926 she wrote, produced and directed the Broadway show *Sex*, which led to her arrest for obscenity. In the following year her next play, *Drag*, was banned because it dealt openly with homosexuality. As a result, she made innuendo and self-parody into a fine art, writing the scripts of five out of her nine Hollywood movies. George Raft, whom she was hired to 'support' in the 1932 film *Night After Night*, complained: 'She stole everything but the cameras.' Her 1933 film *She Done Him Wrong* was credited with saving Paramount from bankruptcy. Her popularity reached such heights that sailors named their inflatable life jackets after her: she remains the only actress whose name features in English dictionaries. She was offered the part of Norma Desmond in *Sunset Boulevard* but turned it down.

'When I'm good, I'm very good,' she said, 'but when I'm bad I'm better.' And she coined the immortal: 'Is that a gun in your pocket or are you just glad to see me?'

Paul Robeson (1898-1976)

When asked by the infamous McCarthy 'un-American activities' hearings why he didn't leave the country, Paul Robeson replied: 'Because my father was a slave and my people died to build this country.' Robeson was a brilliant athlete and scholar who quit his New York law firm when a stenographer told him: 'I never take dictation from a nigger.' After working on the stage with playwright Eugene O'Neill, he discovered his singing voice and in the musical *Showboat* began to receive popular acclaim. Traveling the world giving concerts to popular audiences in the 1930s, he thought of himself and his art as 'serving the struggle for racial justice for non-whites and economic justice for workers of the world'. In the Soviet Union he felt 'here, for the first time in my life... I walk in full human dignity'. He developed a commitment to Soviet communism which he never relinquished. He urged black youths not to fight if the US ever went to war with the Soviet Union. In 1950 his passport was revoked and he was 'blacklisted' by concert managers. Unable to earn a living but refusing to compromise his political loyalties, he became depressed by the loss of contact with audiences and friends, tried twice to commit suicide, and eventually died from a stroke.

Rachel Carson (1907-64)

Trained as a marine biologist and zoologist, Rachel Carson spent her early working life in public service, eventually becoming Editor-in-Chief of the publications of the US Fish and Wildlife Service. During the 1930s Depression she supplemented her income by writing lyrical features for the *Atlantic Monthly*. After the publication of *The Sea Around Us* in 1952 she left government service to devote herself full-time to writing. Carson's writing challenged prevailing orthodoxy and was seminal to the growth of the environmental movement, most notably *Silent Spring*, published in 1962, which drew attention to the impact of synthetic chemical pesticides. Vilified as 'alarmist' by the chemical industry and government officials, her testimony before Congress in 1963 (a year before she died from breast cancer) helped to initiate legislation protecting the environment and human health.

Cesar Chavez (1927-93)

Born near Yuma, Arizona, Chavez became a migrant farm worker when his father lost his homestead during the Great Depression of the 1930s. He fought in the Pacific with the US Navy during World War Two; on his return he became an organizer among the huge Hispanic migrant labor force in California. 'You can't change anything if you want to hold on to a good job, a good way of life and avoid sacrifice,' he said after founding the National Farm Workers' Association (NFWA) in the early 1960s. Membership came largely from the vineyard workers. In 1966 the NFWA merged with the United Farm Workers. In 1968 Chavez conducted a 25-day fast to reaffirm the union's commitment to nonviolence. By 1975, 17 million Americans were supporting a boycott of Californian wines. Jerry Brown, the Governor of California, passed a collective-bargaining law which grape growers were forced to support. In 1988 Chavez conducted a 36-day 'Fast for Life' to protest the poisoning of grape workers and their children by pesticides. Like other officials, he received subsistence pay of less than $5,000 a year. Some 40,000 people attended his funeral.

Noam Chomsky (1928-)

A unique combination of eminent academic, political radical and grassroots activist, Noam Chomsky remains the most inspirational radical thinker in America today. Challenging corporate power with forensic skill and seemingly encyclopedic knowledge, his most obvious distaste is for American self-deception and hubris. A self-effacing Professor at the Massachusetts Institute of Technology, his academic reputation rests on a theoretical revolution he created in the impenetrable discipline of linguistics. He says that it was the politics of socialism and anarchism learned from 'the radical Jewish community in New York' that drew him to linguistics. He first came to political prominence as an opponent of the war in Vietnam. Since then he has documented the progress of American interventions around the world and is outspokenly critical of US policy in Israel. A complex network of activists inspired by his work has grown up around him.

The Simpsons (1987-)

America's most famous TV family, the Simpsons, are everybody's subversive anti-heroes. The show champions the struggles of ordinary human beings to get by, pitted against the powerful – whether it's evil Mr Burns the nuclear power-plant owner (allegedly modeled on Fox TV owner Rupert Murdoch), assorted local bullies, crooks, shyster TV presenters, small-town hypocrites, corrupt state politicians or the makers of tasteless Duff beer. Homer naps and eats donuts, his laziness shining through despite his oppressive boss and mechanized, production-line-style workplace. Bart is a one-kid revolution against the stupidity and conformity of high school. Lisa always stands up for what she believes in, whether it's feminist dolls, saving trees, or world peace – but what she wants most is a pony. And Marge will do anything to protect her kids, including taking on Itchy and Scratchy, the violent TV cartoon. Genuine, dysfunctional, contradictory, selfish, altruistic – all of us trying to walk upright in this world have some kind of kinship with the Simpsons. George Bush Senior hated it, saying Americans should be 'more like the Waltons, and less like the Simpsons'. What higher recommendation could one ask for?

BRIEF HISTORY **31**

Landmines: Defusing the Demon

How landmines became such a hit in wars around the world – and how a gathering storm of protest brought about a ban.

Birth of a killer

The first landmines were designed to stop the battle tank, that scourge of trench warfare, during World War One – they were effectively just buried artillery shells with exposed fuses. The development of lightweight explosive TNT in the 1920s made the first reliable anti-tank mines possible. During World War Two, 300 million of these were used, more than two-thirds of them by the Soviet Union. Designed to explode under the weight of a vehicle, these mines were often removed by enemy troops on foot. As a result armies began protecting their anti-tank minefields by using small metallic or glass containers with about half a kilo of explosive, which could be activated by the pressure of a footstep. From improvised hand grenades to the German 'Bouncing Betty', a mine that sprang to the height of two meters before spraying its victims with hundreds of steel balls, the antipersonnel mine had come into its own.

Garbage and butterflies

After the Second World War mine technology advanced rapidly and in the early 1960s the US unleashed its sophisticated 'remotely delivered' mines or 'scatterables' on Laos and then Cambodia, in a vain attempt to stop the movement of soldiers and provisions from North to South Vietnam. Scattered from the air, these mines (nicknamed 'garbage' by the crews carrying them) landed on the ground without detonating. Weighing a puny 20 grams, they were capable of taking off the foot that stepped on them. The randomly scattered mines could not be mapped and US Forces often suffered heavy casualties when retreating through areas previously mined by their own pilots. A decade later the Soviet Union also used random targeting during its invasion of Afghanistan and millions of PFM-1 'butterfly' mines settled gracefully to the ground awaiting victims.

Eternal sentinels

If warfare were conducted according to agreed principles, then landmines would always have been illegal. The Geneva Convention and its two Protocols outlaw the use of weapons that do not distinguish between combatants and civilians and which cause needless injury.

Yet by the end of the 20th century, a plague of landmines had enveloped the world's conflict zones, with an estimated 110 million antipersonnel mines in the ground and an equal number in military stockpiles. Most were supplied by Northern producers to countries thousands of kilometers away, where political and economic instability are common. Cheap and easy to use, they were the favorite weapons in civil wars and wars of insurgency, used by governments and guerrillas alike. These 'eternal sentinels' stand guard long after the conflicts have ended and kill and maim without mercy or discrimination.

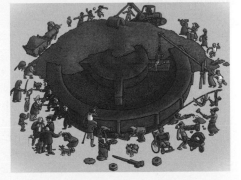

Coward's war

After the Vietnam War, senior US military officials attested to the inability of landmines to stave off an attack, while stressing the horrific injuries they had caused their own troops. In fact between a fifth and a third of all US deaths during the War were caused by these weapons. The earliest calls for a ban, however, grew out of the experience of non-governmental organizations (NGOs) in Afghanistan and Cambodia, where the high rates of injury and death amongst returning refugees presented a crisis of unprecedented proportions. In 1991 Human Rights Watch and Physicians for Human Rights published the first detailed study of how landmines were actually being used in *The Coward's War: Landmines in Cambodia*. The book made a strong case for humanitarian demining, which aims to make the land completely safe for human use – a far cry from stock military mine-clearing techniques.

The ball starts to roll

October 1992 marked the real beginning of the International Campaign to Ban Landmines when six NGOs combined their separate initiatives: Handicap International, Human Rights Watch, Medico International, Mines Advisory Group, Physicians for Human Rights and Vietnam Veterans of America Foundation. None of the six groups on the steering committee of the International Campaign came from the disarmament community. There was also at first a notable lack of indigenous organizations from mine-affected countries, who were hard-pressed enough to deal with the everyday realities confronting them. But by 1995 the Campaign had embraced a multitude of groups from all corners of the world and had been given a huge boost when the International Committee of the Red Cross overcame its usual reluctance to deal with 'political' issues and launched its parallel, well-documented campaign. Attention focused on the political initiatives and conferences but it was the tireless efforts of people on the ground – starting humanitarian mine-clearance, organizing support for those injured by mines, exposing the horrors of mine warfare – which brought a ban closer.

Laws and intentions

In March 1995, Belgium became the first country to legislate a domestic ban on the production, procurement, sale and transfer of landmines and their components and technology, despite opposition from its armed forces. Previously it had been a leading mine exporter, and while a declining market and the receding threat from Eastern Europe were probably factors in the decision, there is no denying the value of Belgium's example. Austria and Ireland followed suit. At the regional level, governments from Central America and the Caribbean announced their intention to create mine-free zones.

The Ottawa process

Bypassing the failure of consensus politics, a Canadian initiative in October 1996 convened an historic conference in Ottawa. The 50 governments who fully participated signed a declaration recognizing the urgent need to ban antipersonnel landmines. At the end Canadian Foreign Minister Lloyd Axworthy boldly announced his country's willingness to hold a treaty-signing conference in December 1997, thus imposing a definite time-scale.

The resultant Ottawa Treaty, which came into force in 1999, was a magnificent achievement for a protest movement – and an inspiring example of how civil society resistance and international co-operation can prompt governments into action. Formally known as the Convention on the Prohibition of the Use, Stockpiling, Production and Transfer of Anti-Personnel Mines and on their Destruction, it has been signed by 158 countries. The International Campaign has become a network of over 1,400 groups in more than 90 countries and received the 1997 Nobel Peace Prize for its efforts.

The battle is far from over: among the 37 countries not party to the Convention are some of the world's biggest countries and mine-producers, including China, India, Russia and the US. Landmines continue to kill and maim people the world over. But the moral argument is certainly won – and the world is closer now to being free from antipersonnel landmines than would have seemed possible a generation ago.

People versus Corporations

For almost as long as corporations have existed, people have lobbied, agitated and legislated to constrain their power and prevent the social and environmental harm caused by the single-minded quest for profit-maximization.

The first corporations

The first corporations emerged in the late 16th century with the aim of encouraging investment in projects of public interest such as roads and hospitals. European states issued 'charters' setting out the tasks each corporation would undertake, and limiting the liability of investors for the company's losses to the amount they had originally invested.

The world's first major corporate scandal took place in 1721 when the London-based South Sea Company, which had falsely promised shareholders fabulous profits from trade with the South American colonies, collapsed. Mobs besieged Westminster and one of the directors was shot by an angry shareholder. Parliament passed the 'Bubble Act' making it illegal to set up new corporations, with very few exceptions, until 1825.

The business of empire

One of these exceptions was the British East India Company. Established in 1600, it monopolized all trade between Britain and Asia and became an instrument of colonial control, given the right to raise armies and rule vast territories on behalf of the Crown. The company attracted public criticism for its unprecedented power and unscrupulous behavior: for violently taking control of Bengal in 1757, exacerbating a famine in which 10 million died of starvation; for the lack of accountability of its managers and investors who engaged in bribery, insider trading and reckless financial speculation; and for its central role in the opium trade with China. It was dissolved in 1858 to give way to direct British rule in India.

Revolt against corporate rule

In 1776 the United States of America declared its independence, kicked off by protests against a British-imposed tax on tea imports, and against the British corporations who ran the American colonies. The new US republic introduced legal measures to limit the ability of corporations to amass wealth and power, including: limits on ownership of land; personal liability of shareholders for the corporation's debts; and the right to withdraw a charter if the corporation failed to serve the public interest.

Megacorporations emerge

The Industrial Revolution, and railways in particular, fueled large-scale enterprise and corporations began to proliferate in Europe and the US from the 1850s onwards. Megacorporations emerged in the 1870s as free trade and unfettered capitalism sparked a period of economic globalization comparable to what we are experiencing today.

Corporations gained enough influence over legislators to rewrite the rules governing their existence, undoing many of the checks and balances placed upon them. Managers were no longer liable for damage a company caused to its workers' health, charters could be granted for an unlimited time, and in 1886 the US Supreme Court ruled that a corporation was a 'natural person' and therefore protected by the Bill of Rights.

'Corporate citizenship'

By the end of the 19th century public concern about corporate exploitation, factory conditions and child labor had hit new heights. Labor movements grew in strength around the world, challenging capitalism and demanding radical social transformation.

Industrialists retaliated against the appeal of socialism with PR campaigns demonstrating that they were good corporate citizens, indispensable to society. They launched welfare programs for workers and a range of philanthropic activities. The language of 'corporate responsibility' began to emerge between the wars, intensified by the Wall Street Crash of 1929 and the Great Depression. It endorsed capitalism and free enterprise, but attempted to humanize it by arguing that well-governed corporations helped society.

Nevertheless, in 1933 Roosevelt's New Deal introduced sweeping reforms to keep corporations in check, including regulation, workers' rights, a social safety net and progressive taxation. Similar legislation was passed in many European countries. Over the next few decades corporations continued to dominate economies, but their rights were relatively evenly balanced with the rights of citizens, through the influence of labor unions and consumer and environmental movements that emerged in the 1960s and 1970s. Newly independent economies began to develop in former colonies, often heavily protecting their own industries from foreign competition.

The neoliberal era

In 1970, free trade guru Milton Friedman published an influential article entitled 'The Social Responsibility of Business is to Increase its Profits'. Friedman argued that the greatest good would be achieved by basing all business decisions on maximizing profits for shareholders.

Friedman's school of thought, known as 'neoliberalism', underpinned the 1980s Reagan/Thatcher era of privatization, deregulation and liberalization that opened up the world's markets for corporations. Social contracts between the state, labor and industry were broken down. 'Free trade' was boosted by the General Agreement on Tariffs and Trade. The debt crisis in 1982 gave the US the opportunity to export the free market model to the Global South, via the IMF and World Bank's 'structural adjustment' programs.

Backlash

By the late 1980s, the painful effects of this global economic restructuring were becoming clear: massive unemployment; economic instability; a growing gap between the very rich and the very poor; corporate misconduct such as the 1984 Bhopal chemical spill by Union Carbide which killed

10,000 people; the *Exxon Valdez* oil disaster in 1989; and Nestlé's ongoing aggressive marketing of breastmilk substitute to Majority World women.

The 1990s saw a backlash against transnational corporations (TNCs). When McDonald's took two environmental activists to court in 1992, the McSpotlight website and campaign did the company's reputation serious damage. In 1995 Shell was implicated in the death of Ogoni activist Ken Saro-Wiwa, executed by the Nigerian Government for protesting against the oil company's operations. An international boycott followed Shell's attempt to sink the Brent Spar oil platform in the North Sea. 1995 was also 'The Year of the Sweatshop' as slave-like conditions in factories supplying Gap, Wal-Mart, Disney and Nike were exposed.

'Corporate Responsibility', sometimes called 'Corporate Social Responsibility', was resurrected by companies whose profits were being damaged by citizens' campaigns. A lucrative industry emerged around enhancing a company's ethical image while avoiding drastic changes to its core business practices. Millions of corporate dollars were simultaneously being devoted behind the scenes to lobbying governments against social and environmental regulation and for further liberalization.

'Anti-globalization'

From the mid-1990s, citizens' campaigns started to look beyond individual corporations to the underlying structures allowing them so much power. In Mexico, the Zapatista movement emerged in direct opposition to NAFTA, a free trade agreement designed to open up Mexico to North American corporations. In 1997-98 an international campaign defeated the Multilateral Agreement on Investment (MAI), a shady deal which sought to remove restrictions on international investment for Western TNCs.

In 1999 the 'anti-globalization' movement arrived on the world stage when 100,000 people converged on the streets of Seattle to shut down a World Trade Organization (WTO) summit. The meeting aimed to launch a round of trade negotiations that would further prise open global markets for TNCs, disadvantaging the Majority World, driving down labor and environmental standards and eroding democracy. From then onwards no major economic summit could take place without anti-corporate protests outside.

The 21st century

Corporations now operate in every sphere of public life: providing water, energy, healthcare and education; running prisons and welfare systems; fighting wars for governments and busting unions for other businesses, all at a profit. The consumer-driven economy continues to boom as corporations scour the earth for more resources to extract and sell.

Many corporations are larger than nation-states, with unrivaled political influence. They have forged strong strategic alliances with bodies that formerly posed a threat to their legitimacy such as NGOs and the UN.

Yet the Corporate Responsibility strategy of voluntary self-regulation has not silenced dissent. Local campaigns against specific corporate abuses have a global audience thanks to the internet. The Enron scandal in 2001 shook faith in the corporate world by exposing fraud and corruption at the heart of one of America's most admired companies.

The specter of climate change is forcing an urgent rethink of the way the global economy operates. The neoliberal project is stumbling, as the WTO's 'Doha Development Round' flounders and regional free trade negotiations are met in the Majority World by mass resistance.

The corporation has grown to dominate the globe, but there is no guarantee that this ruthless moneymaking machine will endure in its current form.

Co-operatives: the Story So Far

People's instinct to co-operate rather than compete has formed human experience everywhere in the world – but it keeps taking different shapes.

First signs

There is evidence of co-operative tenant farming in Babylon and of burial benefit societies in Greece as early as 3,000 BCE. Indigenous cultures in Africa, Asia and Latin America often placed great value on co-operative social structures. Gruyère cheesemakers formed a co-op at Desservilliers, Switzerland, in 1228. Various forms of mutual aid 'guilds' and 'leagues' were common in medieval Europe. 'Friendly societies' were set up to provide help in case of sickness. By 1600 communal granaries – *shaso* – were well established in Japan.

Pioneers

With the growth of industrial capitalism, and its ethos of ruthless competition, a co-operative movement soon emerged to contest it. Industrial capitalism started earliest, and grew fastest, in Britain. In 1821 the Co-operative and Economical Society published *The Economist*, the first newspaper dealing with co-operative ideals (*The Economist* of today, which has rather different ideas, was not founded until 1843). By 1830 there were 300 co-op societies and 12 co-op newspapers. Robert Owen in northern Britain and William King in Brighton experimented with similar ideas. Conditions in industrial towns became so appalling that in 1848 average life expectancy in Rochdale was just 21 years. In 1844 the Rochdale Society of Equitable Pioneers set up a consumers' co-op (followed by a housing co-op) that paid its members a 'dividend' on what they bought and was to become a model for the movement. By 1900 there were 1.7 million members of 1,439 different (mostly consumer) societies around Britain; by the beginning of World War One in 1914 the number had almost doubled.

Variations

Elsewhere co-ops explored different territory. Credit unions were pioneered in Germany and Canada. Often promoted by parish priests, by 1905 there were 13,000 Popular Banks in Germany – one for almost every village. In 1900 Alphonse Desjardins began a mutual savings society in Levis, Quebec. By 1909 the Mouvement des caisses Desjardins had over 100 *caisses populaires* in the Quebec region – many of them, as in Germany, sponsored by parish priests. In Canadian mining districts co-op stores aimed to overcome the 'truck' system, which forced miners to spend their wages in company stores.

Agricultural co-ops developed earliest in North America, Denmark and Japan. By 1867 there were 400 co-op cheese factories and creameries in the US. A Danish delegation visited a co-op creamery in Philadelphia in 1876. In 1882 the first one opened in Hjedding, Denmark. Co-ops of all kinds spread across Scandinavia, while Scandinavian migrants to North America (particularly from Sweden and Finland) stimulated the movement in return. In Japan, four agricultural societies were formed in 1878. By 1920 there were 13,442 – 37 per cent of Japanese farmers belonged to them. Co-ops were important to industrial agriculture in New Zealand/Aotearoa from the outset.

Worker co-ops were pioneered in France, Italy and Russia. In France, Charles Fourier planned self-sustaining communities called *philansteries*. After the Paris Commune in 1871, JBA Godin encouraged workers to buy him out of his stove factory. By 1906 there were three large industrial societies – an iron foundry, a spectacle manufacturer and a cab-drivers' society – as well as 340 smaller ones. In Italy, the Associazione Artistica of glass-makers was set up in Altare in 1856. By 1906 there were 25 societies of bakers, 153 industrial societies and 454 labor and public service societies, mostly around Turin, Genoa and the industrial north. In Russia village communes and artels (labour associations) were common and represented nationally by a powerful federation, the Centrosoyus. As early as the 1820s some of Robert Owen's methods were tried in the Hunter Valley, Australia. The first consumer co-op in Australia was founded in Brisbane in 1859.

Follow the flag

Industrializing countries in Europe had been carving out empires for themselves around the world, taking the co-op idea with them. Co-ops were thought to be a useful way of organizing rural workers to produce for export. The French created the formal structure of the Société Indigène de Prévoyance with this in mind. In Tanzania the first co-operative laws were passed in 1925 and in Zimbabwe in 1926. In India 'registrars' were appointed by the British to regulate co-ops 'from the top down'. During the 1890s Sir Frederick Nicholson made his name as the 'Father of Indian co-operation', mostly by promoting credit co-ops. Indigenous forms of co-operation were inhibited: in 1892 a group that combined credit with land reclamation in Hoshiapur, Punjab, was disbanded. In the Caribbean they were swept away. After the abolition of slavery, ex-slaves in Guyana bought 38 villages on 6,000 hectares of land and ran them co-operatively – but the still-powerful plantation owners broke them up. The huge US-based United Fruit Company encouraged 'co-ops' in the Caribbean because they were more convenient to deal with than individual tropical-fruit growers. In the 1940s the Grenada Co-operative Nutmeg Association had only one representative on its board from its 6,000 growers.

Turbulent times

The International Co-operative Alliance (ICA) was named at a meeting in Britain in August 1893. There was a strong vein of political 'neutrality' within the international co-op movement, but conflict proved impossible to avoid. Socialists in Europe were often critical of consumer co-ops (which wanted lower prices) and supported trade unions (which wanted higher wages). Co-ops became for 'consumers' what trade unions were for 'producers'. Then, following the revolution in Russia in 1917 and the rise of fascism in Europe and Japan, there was turmoil. Co-ops were attacked by fascists in Italy in 1921. Mussolini promoted his own form of 'fascist co-operation'. In Germany the Nazi Party also attacked co-ops, which were eventually taken over by the German Labor Front. There were similar developments in Japan. In Spain, anarcho-syndicalists promoted workers' co-ops vigorously, but they were crushed by General Franco after the end of the civil war in 1939.

Co-ops in fascist 'Axis' countries were generally cut off from the ICA during World War Two. However, the Centrosoyus in Russia had been a member since 1903, and it remained so after 1917, despite the subordination of co-ops to the Soviet system of state enterprises. After the revolution in 1949 enormous numbers of co-ops were formed in China, but they were isolated from the international movement.

Dinosaurs and giants

As Cold War followed World War, the prospects for the international co-op movement began to look bleak. It was questionable whether independent co-ops could exist at all in the Soviet Union or China. In the West they were viewed as 'dinosaurs'. Even so, they began to compete directly – and often very successfully – with conventional businesses, inventing the chain store, among other things.

In Spain the Mondragón workers' co-op became the biggest employer in the Basque region. By the mid-1980s almost 40 per cent of Japanese households had at least one co-op member. In Canada 12 million people now belong to at least one co-op, while 18 giant agri-food 'co-ops' rank among the country's top 500 businesses. Major US brands, like Sunkist and Ocean Spray, are agri-food 'co-ops'. Huge, wealthy co-ops like these became almost indistinguishable from conventional businesses. In 1995 Konsum in Austria was the first major co-op retailer to go bankrupt. The British Co-op network went into sharp decline, from which – after an attempted takeover – it is now recovering well.

Flourishing minnows

In the Global South, however – and particularly in Latin America – co-ops of all kinds began to flourish. There were only 175 in Argentina in 1930, but by 1976 there were 4,800 with seven million members. They grew, too, in Paraguay – promoted by Mennonites from Canada and the US – and in Mexico under the tutelage of the Institutional Revolutionary Party (PRI). In Chile they were active in the Popular Unity movement until it was crushed by a military coup in 1973 – an ugly pattern repeated across the continent. In Africa, co-ops were often promoted by newly independent nation-states. Tanzania developed the *ujamaa* concept of multi-purpose village co-ops. Informal *naam* groups or youth associations became active in Burkina Faso. Farmers in Kenya were required by law to be in a co-op.

In a bizarre twist, the number of co-ops in the Soviet Union rose from 8,000 in 1987 to 220,000 in 1990 – President Mikhail Gorbachev tried to graft them on to his 'opening up' of the Russian economy. Most were promptly privatized or dissolved in scandalous circumstances – within a few years they went from being minnows in the Soviet system to minnows in a privatized one. But here, as elsewhere, the instinct for co-operation persists – to take yet another shape in future.

Taxation and Revolt

It was Mark Twain who claimed that the two certainties of life are 'death and taxes'. But while taxes have always been with us, so too has the struggle against unjust taxation. Time and again throughout history, who should pay how much has been a hotly contested issue – and even a cause of violent revolt.

The Ancient World

In Pharaonic Egypt the all-powerful scribes counted everything from the fish catch to garden produce. Failure to pay could result in a beating or in being sold as a slave. Eventually fleeing tax-payers endangered the revenue base. The Greeks fought a bloody war against the Persians to resist a tribute tax and then had to impose one to pay for the war. It was Jewish tax resisters who held out in the mountain fortress of Masada against Imperial Rome. Rome responded by imposing a special tax on Jews, the 'fiscus judaicus'.

The Poll Tax

Britain has a long history of tax resistance. It was to protest against high taxes, for example, that Lady Godiva took her famous nude ride through the streets of Coventry. But it was the medieval poll tax that provoked most popular indignation. In 1381 Wat Tyler led an armed revolt to oppose King Richard II's levying of a one shilling tax on every person over 14. The tax hit mainly at the peasantry and revolt quickly spread after the execution of three unfortunate clerks sent to investigate poll-tax fraud. Although Tyler and the other leaders of the revolt lost their heads, for centuries to come poll taxes either excluded peasants or taxed them at a nominal rate.

Peasants elsewhere were not so lucky. Britain and other colonial powers used poll taxes on the newly colonized people of Africa not only as a source of revenue but to force them to produce cash crops or to go into paid employment where they could be more readily exploited.

Birth of a nation

If political authority is seen as illegitimate, the taxes it levies are considered particularly odious. Revenue collected by foreigners has been quick to spark popular resentment. William Tell was forced to shoot the apple off his son's head for his refusal to pay the heavy taxes that the Habsburgs were trying to levy on the Swiss. In 1291 Swiss communities joined in a league of mutual assistance to defy the power of both the Austrian military and tax-collectors. It was out of this struggle that Switzerland emerged as an independent nation. To this day, the final decision on tax increases in Switzerland must be made by popular referendum. As a result Swiss taxes are some of the lowest in the world.

The Boston Tea Party

A constant irritant for Britain's American colonies in the 1700s was 'taxation without representation'. Ironically it was the removal of a British tax on tea that provoked Boston merchants dressed as 'Indians' (a favorite US scapegoat) to board ships and pitch the tea overboard. The British had removed the tax to protect their tea monopoly – by cutting prices they hoped to break an American boycott of their tea. But the boycott held and the British responded with more drastic military measures, setting off the six-year-long revolutionary war in 1776. After their victory the fledgling US Government imposed much heavier taxes on their people than the British had ever managed.

War and taxes

Tax politics always seem to heat up during wars. Who is to pay for these huge and wasteful allocations of public funds has always been a bone of contention. It was during the Napoleonic Wars that the first income tax was introduced in Britain. In Canada during World War One the rallying cry of labor and farm organizations in favor of an income tax was 'no conscription of men without conscription of wealth'. By 1917 a reluctant Conservative government was forced to bring in Canada's first income tax.

The first US income tax was imposed during the Civil War. In the 19th century income tax was considered a way to tax the wealthy. In the 1890s a vast populist coalition in the US led by William Jennings Bryant pushed through a renewed income tax in 1894 – only to have it overturned by a conservative Supreme Court. It took a 1913 constitutional amendment to reverse this ruling and make income tax the law of the land.

Revolt of the haves

The late 1970s and the 1980s saw a massive anti-tax movement steered by the political Right into a series of reforms that have lightened the tax load of the well-to-do. The movement was started by a reactionary populist named Harold Jarvis in California, where escalating house prices had pushed property taxes through the roof. The result was a 1978 tax-limitation statute called Proposition 13 which limited taxes but imposed draconian cuts on local services and education. The big winners were corporate properties who saw their tax bills reduced by hundreds of thousands of dollars.

In country after country, the anti-tax theme was picked up by eager right-wing and reluctant social-democratic politicians. Irrationalities in the tax system were used to stoke up public discontent with government. Capital income was handed generous exemptions. Corporate taxes were cut to encourage investment. And some 81 countries slashed their top rates for high-income earners.

Revolt of the have-nots

The pressure from the Right against income tax has tended to push governments into raising money instead by indirect or 'regressive' taxation, which hurts the poor much more than the rich. At the end of the 1980s revolts against unfair taxation began to erupt – there were movements against the modern version of the poll tax in Britain, against the Canadian sales tax (known as the GST) and against US property taxes which are biased towards the wealthy. In Britain, a series of violent demonstrations and the jailing of poll-tax resisters put the tax revolt on the front pages. A reported 14 million people either refused to pay or were in arrears. The poll tax became such a political liability that it had to be dropped, contributing to the fall of the Conservative government in 1997.

Tax justice

Tax cutting had, however, become conventional political wisdom in most liberal democracies. In 2001 President Bush came to power in the US with a commitment to cut taxes on the rich. Massive increases in military spending – particularly after 9/11 – were financed by budget deficits, matched by sharp hikes in repressive state power. The gap between rich and poor grew wider almost everywhere. No longer redistributing wealth from rich to poor, regressive taxation accelerated this trend. Economic globalization made the payment of tax more or less voluntary for both the super-rich and transnational corporations, as governments competed with tax 'havens' to offer the most favorable regimes. By 2008 it was estimated that $160 billion was being lost as a result of companies using false accounting to reduce their tax liability.

The relative decline of government revenues lay behind the repeated failure of rich governments to keep their promises to poor ones, underlined by the lack of funds to mitigate climate change or achieve the UN Millennium Development Goals. However, the banking crisis that began in 2007 proved that huge public funds could readily be found to bail out powerful private banks. Meanwhile, more tax revenues were directed towards corporations by the privatization of public services. The link between taxation and representation weakened as the distinction between public and private dissolved. A new worldwide movement for tax justice started to take shape.

BRIEF HISTORY **35**

Antisemitism: the Longest Hatred

Historical antisemitism peaked with the Nazi genocide, but the nightmare is centuries old.

Anti-monotheism

With its monotheistic theology, Judaism was viewed with deep suspicion by polytheistic societies in the Middle East, particularly in Egypt where nearly a million Jews lived among polytheistic Egyptians, Greeks and the governing Romans. The 'first pogrom' in Alexandria in the year 38 was ordered by the Roman governor Flaccus. Thousands of Jews were beaten, raped, and paraded through the streets to be burned on bonfires.

Bible bashing

That Jesus was Jewish and crucified by the Romans were two major stumbling blocks to the spread of Christianity in the Roman Empire. Many scholars believe that the Gospels were written with the desire to reach out to the Roman emperors in order to preserve the religion and ensure its longevity. To achieve this, the responsibility of the Romans for Jesus' death needed to be minimized and his 'Jewishness' downplayed. This historical revisionism is evidenced by early Christian texts attributing blame to Pontius Pilate and Emperor Tiberius whereas later texts refer to 'the Jews' and also paint the Romans and Pilate in a more sympathetic light. As Christianity spread throughout Europe,

151

further embellishments would be added to Christian doctrine regarding the death of Christ which would set in motion two millennia of anti-Jewish antagonism.

Synagogue of Satan

The Church soon developed a symbolic opposition to all things Jewish. Jews were held up as the demonic other, the 'black and treacherous Judas', and the 'synagogue of Satan'. Christian theologians and emperors would wax poetic in their demonization of the Jews, and churches would be adorned with 'sacred art' depicting the righteous denigration of Judaism. By 534, the Justinian Code would degrade Jews to second-class citizens. Attempting to build a synagogue would be punished by death and forfeiture of all assets. The Toledo Synods of seventh-century Spain forced Jewish children to live with Christian families after the age of seven.

Jews under Islam

As Islam spread, Jews were accepted as 'people of the book' (*dhimmi*) along with Christians and were generally accorded better treatment than in Christian societies. However, they were usually forced to live in separate areas (*mellah*), and were made to wear certain garbs so that they could be easily identifiable. In 807 Caliph Harun al-Rashid ordered all Jews to wear yellow badges. Wooden devils and apes were nailed on the homes of Jews and their places of worship were destroyed under the reign of Caliph al-Mutawakkil from 850. The later period of Moorish Spain (al-Andalus), however, is seen as one of the golden ages of Judaism where persecution was rare and Jewish culture flourished.

'Dark Ages' indeed

European crusaders en route to 'liberate' Jerusalem from Islam, murdered thousands of Jews at the close of the 11th century. The Church forced the remaining Jews to wear distinctive clothing (yellow badges in France, pointy hats in Germany) in order to discourage relations with Christians. Hebrew scriptures were ordered by the Popes to be destroyed in large public book-burning gatherings in local town squares throughout Europe. Passion plays were used to reinforce Jewish responsibility for the death of Christ and other anti-Jewish transmissions and were often followed by pogroms. 'Blood libel' surfaced as part of the demonology of 'the Jew', appearing first in 1144 in England where Jews would be eventually expelled after a series of pogroms. The most famous blood libel accusation involved the allegation of a ritual murder in 1475 of a young boy in Italy, Simon, who was later made a saint (the official Catholic Church account lasted until 1950). The Inquisition established the notion of blood purity – anyone with an eighth of Jewish blood was considered to be impure even if they had converted to Christianity.

Variations on a theme

When the plague ravaged Europe, many blamed the Jews, accusing them of poisoning the wells. This led to spontaneous mob lynchings all over the continent. Increasingly antisemitism took on a more economic and cultural character.

In the Middle Ages it was illegal for Christians to lend money. Money lending, seen as a 'devilish trade', was one of the only professions allowed to Jews, who were forbidden to engage in most other economic activity. This increasingly led to the stereotyping of Jews as 'greedy moneylenders' seeking to ruin Christians. When economies were stressed, Jews would be the first to be blamed by the authorities who found in them useful scapegoats during times of crisis.

The concept of the 'Wandering Jew' (doomed to wander the earth without a home as punishment for killing Christ) appeared in 17th-century popular culture, reinforcing 'otherness' and justifying expulsion from European countries. Jews were increasingly seen as having loyalty only to the 'Jewish nation' (which was then a euphemism for the Jewish community rather than a particular state).

The revolution will not be Judaicized

Despite protestations from the philosopher Voltaire, Jews were eventually given full rights after the French Revolution. They increasingly came to be associated with a number of different leading revolutionary movements and ideologically liberal currents. Demagogues would stir up the population on charges that 'the Jews' were infecting the minds of the populace with egalitarian ideals, socialism and humanism, as well as entrepreneurship, social democracy and internationalism. As such, they were often seen as either enemies of the state, or agents of it.

By the mid-19th century, hatred of Jews was seen through the lens of racialism. The 'Jewish problem' could no longer be solved through conversion since the inherently evil Jewish 'race' was incurable. French philosopher Ernest Renan posited the notion of Aryan racial supremacy over the superficial 'Semitic mind'. His German contemporary, Paul de Lagarde, mobilized such concepts in Prussia where he advocated the complete destruction of European Jewry, whom he saw as 'bacilli and tapeworms'. It was around this time that German journalist Wilhelm Marr founded the League of Antisemites in 1879, which was the first organization committed specifically to combating the alleged threat to

Germany posed by the Jews and advocating their forced removal from the country. Tsarist Russia and neighboring Ukraine also embraced the new politics of racism by encouraging pogroms against Jewish communities and creating and propagating the Protocols of the Elders of Zion to cement popular hysteria about Jews.

L'Affaire Dreyfus

The development of nationalism and the demise of monarchies led to new waves of antisemitism. In France, the infamous Dreyfus Affair of 1894, where a French Jewish army captain was falsely charged with passing military information to Germany, exposed deep antisemitic undercurrents in French society. The alleged actions of one person were blamed on the entire 'race' – represented by the public's hatred of the 'dirty Jew', as outraged novelist Émile Zola would describe it in his famous open letter to the President titled J'accuse...! Jews were attacked and their shops plundered in one of the darkest episodes of French antisemitism.

War of the Worlds

The Russian Revolution of 1917 was quickly seen by counter-revolutionaries as the 'Jewish Revolution' and once again the Protocols were used to incite people to murder Jews in southern Russia. Henry Ford began his lifelong fight against the 'International Jew' who was seen as the human embodiment of the 'evils of socialism'. In parallel, National Socialism in Germany rose on a program of antisemitism as a political movement to eradicate the 'evils of capitalism and international finance'.

Endgames

The Nazis built on millennia of myths and stereotypes to dehumanize the Jews in the public mind, paving the way for the *Endlösung* (final solution). Skilful deployment of the 'methodology' of antisemitism (scapegoating, demonization, Christian animosity, racialism, nationalism, supremacy, fear and superstition) led to the logical conclusion of industrially planned genocide of the Jews. German *Judenhass* (Jew hatred) influenced most 'neutral' and 'allied' countries to reject Jewish asylum seekers, thereby indirectly sentencing millions to their deaths.

When the horrors of the Holocaust began to be revealed, public sympathy encouraged suppression of antisemitic sentiment, particularly in Europe. The devastated Jewish population, however, was not reassured, and the Zionist movement took on vital importance to the vast majority of European Jewry who felt they would never be equal citizens. Mass emigration to Palestine, the biblical homeland, became an imperative for many who dreamed of a Jewish state to protect them from the scourge of antisemitism. This was reinforced by early Holocaust denial and Nazi apologists such as the German Council of the Evangelical Church which published in 1948 a declaration justifying the Shoah: 'The doom of the Jew is silent proof that God will not stand for any nonsense in warning us Christians and admonishing Jews.' Continuing pogroms against Jews in Poland after the War buttressed the notion that Jews were not safe in Europe even after the Shoah. The State of Israel was born. Many Jews in Muslim countries were now targeted by political movements opposed to the Jewish state, leading to massive pogroms in Libya, Syria, Egypt, Yemen and Iraq and eventually mass emigration to Israel.

Atonement

In 1965 the Catholic Church finally repudiated the charge that the Jews were responsible for the death of Christ through a set of reforms known as Vatican II. Many Christian fundamentalists, however, rejected these reforms and their views have been most recently popularized by Mel Gibson's film *The Passion of the Christ*.

Anti-Zionism

After the Six Day War in 1967, which led to the occupation of the West Bank, Sinai, Gaza and the Golan Heights, a significant segment of the Left abandoned its support for Israel. Most communists supported the Soviet anti-Zionist stance. The New Left tended to characterize Israel as an imperialist nation. In 1975 the UN passed a resolution calling Zionism a form of racism. Some Jewish organizations were excluded from anti-racism conferences as a result. The UN resolution was rescinded in 1991.

The Six Day War and resultant occupation led to an explosion of antisemitism in the Arab World and general sympathy towards the plight of the Palestinians. By association with the state of Israel, the 'Jewish state', Jews were now increasingly being seen as oppressors instead of victims. The 1982 Israeli invasion of Lebanon led to a resurgence of attacks in Europe, blurring the lines between legitimate criticism of Israel's policies and antisemitism. This prompted some to describe a 'New Antisemitism' – one which thrived among the radical Left and Muslims.

Right behind

The polarizing politics of the Cold War in the 1980s saw the Far Right's popularity increase. When Austrian presidential candidate (and former UN Secretary-General) Kurt Waldheim was discovered to have fought with the Nazis during the War, it led to intense outbursts of antisemitism. The fall of the Soviet Union led to the increasing popularity of nationalist movements and the revival of feverish Judeophobic sentiment. Openly antisemitic political parties gained mass followings, such as France's Front National, whose leader Jean-Marie Le Pen came alarmingly close to threatening the presidency in France, forcing Left voters to support the conservative Jacques Chirac to stave off the Far Right candidate.

After the Wall

On 28 November 1993, Russian antisemitic newspaper *Pamyat* was embroiled in a libel suit over the validity of the *Protocols of the Elders of Zion*. The court, made up entirely of non-Jews, ruled that the document is indeed a forgery. During this period, hundreds of thousands of Jews were finally allowed to emigrate from the former Soviet Union, many citing antisemitism as the main reason for their flight.

The 1994 bombing of a Jewish community center in Buenos Aires raised fears of a new level of antisemitism – 86 were killed and hundreds wounded. This was followed by a string of horrific attacks against Jews and Jewish institutions in Rome, California, Düsseldorf, France and Tunisia. In the early years of the 21st century there were more extreme events, including stabbings in Antwerp and Paris, the bombing of two synagogues in Istanbul, attacks on French Jewish schools and community centers and the desecration of a mural painted by Jewish children who were being transported to concentration camps from France. In addition, there was the arson of a museum in Indiana, US, dedicated to children who suffered from Nazi medical 'experiments', and a string of cemetery desecrations and death threats across the globe.

Despite its long and dark history, it would be wrong to depict antisemitism as an unbroken continuum. There were periods of relative tolerance and peaceful cohabitation between Jews and non-Jews, particularly in the later period of al-Andalus Spain and 14th-century Poland. The post-War years have been some of the most tolerable for Jews ever. The current resurgence of antisemitism globally, however, is cause for deep concern.

BRIEF HISTORY **36**

A Brief History of Megalomania

Despots claim that they are the only peacemakers, that if order were not imposed people would live in chaos. The historical record suggests otherwise.

Rome

The mother of every imperial pax (the Latin word for peace), the 'Pax Romana' in fact lasted little more than 200 years, from the beginning of the reign of Augustus in 27 BCE to the end of the reign of Marcus Aurelius in 180 CE. The tranquility was only relative to the violence that had preceded it – in 146 BCE the Romans destroyed their rivals in Carthage, killing 200,000 and selling the remaining 50,000 into slavery. Rome imposed brutal penalties, tribute, slavery and military service on subjugated peoples. The eventual result was the collapse of Rome under its own weight, followed by a prolonged 'Dark Age' in Europe.

China

Of all the peoples in the world, perhaps none has been so afflicted by emperors – nor staged so many revolts against them – as the Chinese. From about 1,700 BCE nomadic Shang conquerors set up a feudal system of military tribute that eventually covered 400,000 square kilometers. In the 500 years prior to 221 BCE – when China was unified – there were only 120 years of peace. Imperial dynasties came and went for 2,000 years thereafter. The Great Wall was intended to provide a defense against the Mongols (see 'Central Asia'), but became known as 'the longest cemetery in the world' because its construction claimed so many laborers' lives.

India

An empire was founded by Chandragupta Maurya in 322 BCE – his grandson Asoka converted to Buddhism and renounced warfare altogether. Indians then invented the decimal system and the concept of zero. From 1526 the cultured Muslim Mughal dynasty lived from taxing 150 million Hindu farmers – and collapsed when the ambitious military campaigns of Aurengzeb provoked rebellions by Sikhs and Hindus alike.

Central Asia

The nomadic Mongols, led by the legendary Genghis Khan, ravaged Beijing in 1216 before turning west and conquering Persia, Armenia, northern India and southern Russia. Genghis Khan's successors devastated Poland and the rest of Russia. By the middle of the 13th century they had defeated the Sung empire and become the effective rulers of China. In 1280 Kublai Khan formally assumed the title of emperor. Much like the Romans, the Mongols enslaved anyone who surrendered – and killed everyone else.

Africa
From around the year 1100 the Shona people began to develop small kingdoms in what is now Zimbabwe. Trade increased the wealth of the kings and they built palaces, the largest of which was known as Great Zimbabwe, constructed around 1300. This was abandoned in 1425 by King Mutota, who moved to a new capital and started conquering the people around him, so that he became known as Mwana-Mutapha, or 'lord of ravaged lands'.

Mexico
In 1325 Aztec mercenaries from the arid north of Mexico moved south and founded Tenochtitlán – modern Mexico City. They began to extend their power through a series of treacherous alliances and religious takeovers, as well as military conquest. Tribute was often in the form of captives for blood sacrifice. At the consecration of a new temple in 1487, 20,000 people are said to have had their hearts ripped out. Crop failures and relentless demands for tribute weakened the Aztec empire even before the arrival of the Spanish.

Peru
The Inca kingdom in the High Andes in what is now Peru expanded with extraordinary speed from 1438 until it controlled almost the whole of the Andean region. Recent archeological evidence seems to confirm that children, after making long pilgrimages, were sacrificed on mountain peaks where the gods were believed to reside. Civil war broke out over the succession to the god king in 1525. The Inca, like the Aztec, were seriously weakened by internal conflicts before they encountered the Spanish invaders, who also brought diseases to which they had no resistance.

Turkey
The Muslim Ottoman Empire began at the start of the 14th century and steadily expanded, so that Christians raised a crusading army against it, which was annihilated in 1396. By the 16th century, under Suleiman the Magnificent and after a long sequence of bloody battles, the Ottomans, from their capital in Istanbul, ruled the whole of North Africa, all the

Muslim holy cities and much of eastern Europe. The expansion halted when an army of 200,000 was beaten back from the siege of Vienna in 1683. By the 19th century Turkey had become known as 'the sick man of Europe'.

Russia
The first Russian given the title of Tsar ('Caesar') was the 16-year-old Ivan, a certifiable psychopath called 'The Terrible'. Peter the Great (1685-1725) established the 'Empire of All Russias' by making the army his instrument of power and brutally suppressing all opposition. Catherine the Great (1762-96) expanded the Russian Empire further to the south and east, so that it swallowed a huge number of cultures and 'nationalities'. The degeneration of the Tsarist regime led to revolution in 1917. In many of its practices the Stalinist Soviet Union replicated the tyrannical Tsarist regime.

Spain
In the 16th century, the Spanish Crown used the wealth it extracted from its new 'Latin' American colonies as a means to enhance its own power in Europe. In April 1609 the Spanish King Philip III negotiated an agreement with rebellious Dutch subjects that resulted in a 12-year period sometimes known as the 'Pax Hispanica'. As it turned out, this was 'war by other means' – the Spanish hoped to lull the Dutch into a false sense of security while building up a stockpile of armaments. War resumed thereafter with renewed ferocity.

France
The European obsession with absolute monarchy reached its zenith with the insane 'Sun King', Louis ('I am the state') XIV, who lived in splendor in Versailles, sowing the seeds of eventual revolution in 1789. Though it succeeded in overthrowing the 'old regime' and implanting new political concepts, the revolution itself degenerated into terror. This opened the way in 1799 for a military coup by Napoleon Bonaparte, who went on to become the role model for all subsequent megalomaniacs. Napoleon conquered most of Italy and Spain, defeated Prussia and Austria, spent a decade threatening Europe, crowned himself Emperor, saw the whole thing collapse and was exiled in disgrace – all within 20 years.

Britain
The British Empire reached its fleeting climax with the Diamond Jubilee of Queen Victoria in 1897. By then Britain – using sea power and 'gunboat diplomacy' much as cruise missiles are used today – had placed a quarter of the world's land surface and peoples under a 'Pax Britannica' on which

'the sun never set'. Within two years the vicious Boer War broke out in South Africa, and in 1914 the Great War began. In fact, there were few times when Britain was not directing military campaigns of repression or conquest somewhere in its empire.

Germany

After the collapse of the Roman Empire, the Papacy remained in Western Europe as the only token of superior authority. Particularly in Germany, feudal warlords tried to blend the 'spiritual' authority of the Papacy and the 'temporal' brute force of Rome into a 'Holy Roman Empire'. Centuries later, ancient semi-mystical aspirations and growing economic power propelled the German Kaiser ('Caesar' again) into the Great War of 1914 and humiliation in 1918 – followed by the rise of Hitler and the 'thousand-year Reich'. Around 6 million Jews, 20 million Russians and many millions more around the world (including Germans themselves) were killed.

America

The US is the only former European colony to have created its own 'empire'. In Central America it stages regular military invasions (the Dominican Republic, Grenada, Panama); in Latin America generally it subverts democratic government (Chile) and promotes war (Nicaragua, Guatemala, El Salvador, Colombia). It tries to enforce an embargo on trade with Cuba. With the end of the Cold War, other regions of the world (Iraq, the Balkans, Afghanistan) are finding out what the 'Pax Americana' means – according to the first President Bush: 'Do as we say.' This is the first serious attempt by one nation to police the entire – as opposed to the 'known' – world.

Next stop: outer space

Slavery Through the Ages

Slavery began with civilization – and despite our high-minded international resolutions we have still not outgrown it today.

Origins

Slavery began with civilization. For hunter-gatherers, slaves would have been an unaffordable luxury – there wouldn't have been enough food to go round. With the growth of cultivation, those defeated in warfare could be taken as slaves.

Western slavery goes back 10,000 years to Mesopotamia, today's Iraq, where a male slave was worth an orchard of date palms. Female slaves were called on for sexual services, gaining freedom only when their masters died.

Early abolitionists arose in the form of two Jewish sects, the Essenes and the Therapeutae, who abhorred slave-owning and tried buying slaves in order to free them.

Greece

The ancient Greeks preferred women and children as slaves for domestic work rather than rebellious men, who were simply slaughtered. Any child born to slave women thus had a father who was free – a status that was also conferred upon them. With the growth of the Greek city states and the commercial production of cotton the demand for agricultural slaves grew, leading to an increase in warfare. In the fifth century BCE, Athens had more slaves than free citizens.

Rome

The Roman Empire sprawled across the entire Mediterranean region and slave trading was big business. Slaves were trained for all possible functions, with gladiators fighting to the death for public entertainment at the extreme end. The Roman emperors owned thousands of slaves to indulge their every whim. They acted as clerks, secretaries and even tax agents. Thousands were worked to death mining gold and silver for the Empire. Plantation slavery began in Rome in the second century BCE. Sicily witnessed a series of slave revolts, culminating in the great uprising led by Spartacus. When it was finally crushed, 6,000 slaves were crucified all along the Appian Way from Rome to Capua.

Medieval Europe

In the early Middle Ages the Church condoned slavery – opposing it only when Christians were enslaved by 'infidels'. Vikings raided Britain from 800 and sold their captives to markets in Istanbul and Islamic Spain. Religion was no barrier to the slave trade – Christians, Muslims and Jews all partook. The Black Death – a plague epidemic – made demand for domestic slaves soar in Italy. Slaves were often suspected of poisoning their masters and punishments were dire. One accused had her flesh torn off by hot pincers as she was drawn through the streets of Florence. In the 16th century Pope Paul III tried to stem Protestantism by threatening those who left the Catholic Church with enslavement.

The transatlantic trade

The Portuguese inaugurated the Atlantic slave trade, soon to be joined by the Spanish. Christopher Columbus' conquest of the Caribbean virtually wiped out the indigenous culture. Before long other colonial nations had poured into the Americas to plunder them. Slave labor produced sugar, cotton and tobacco. With the indigenous peoples dying out, African slaves were imported – 900,000 had landed by 1600. The African nations that supplied the slaves had a long history of slavery themselves. European colonists flocked to West Africa trading liquor, tobacco, arms and trinkets for live cargo.

Thus began the notorious Middle Passage where slaves would be loaded lying down in the holds of ships, often on their sides to preserve space. The British were the prime slavers, bringing goods from England to exchange for African slaves whom they then supplied to their own or Spanish and Portuguese colonies in the New World. This triangular trade built Britain's fortune.

Slaves to sugar

Sugar was the mainstay of slavery in Brazil, Cuba and Haiti. In Brazil the Portuguese resisted installing even the most basic machinery to replace human labor; they worked their slaves to death within a span of a few years. Numerous African slaves escaped to the Brazilian interior, forming their own Republic of Palmares in a famous revolt which lasted 70 years. In 1696, when Palmares fell, all the leaders committed suicide rather than be enslaved again. Haiti, then under French dominance and known as Saint-Domingue, was importing 40,000 slaves a year when the fuse for a spectacular revolt was lit. Toussaint L'Ouverture took charge, forcing an abolitionist decree through the French Assembly and becoming the first black man to govern a European colony. Eventually, under Napoleon's despotic reign, Toussaint was toppled by one of his own supporters. But Haiti still gained its independence, in 1804.

Abolitionist moves

The 18th century saw the birth of abolitionist groups in the Western world. In 1804 the Danes made the slave trade illegal; Britain followed in 1807 and the Americans a year later. Anti-Slavery International was founded in 1839, a few years before the complete abolition of the transatlantic slave trade. But slave smuggling and slavery itself continued. The economic climate was changing – Britain's industries, built on the profits of plantation slavery, now sought a labor force closer to home.

The United States

Slaves helped America win freedom from the British during the American War of Independence, without, however, gaining their own. The words 'All men are created equal' had a hollow ring when even Thomas Jefferson, who wrote them, owned slaves. The invention of the cotton gin revolutionized the American South's fortunes – in 1860 a cotton harvest worth $200 million was picked by slaves working under the lash. Slaves did every imaginable job that their masters saw fit, with skilled slaves being hired out for further profit. Fugitives escaped under cover of night, traveling over wild terrain to the Northern states and Canada – their routes became known as the Underground Railroad. The Civil War in 1861 was the death knell of American slavery – over 38,000 black people died fighting in it. The 13th Amendment to the US Constitution abolished slavery.

A global menace

Slavery continued, however, in other parts of the world following emancipation in North America. Indigenous slavery in sub-Saharan Africa, debt bondage and forced labor in European colonies and domestic slavery in Nigeria and the Indian subcontinent thrived. Nine million lost their lives to forced labor and genocide in the Belgian Congo. In China a system of child slavery known as *Mui Tsai*, where children were sold for domestic work, persisted until the second half of the 20th century. In Peru atrocities committed by a British-registered company against indigenous people enslaved to tap rubber led to boycotts. It was estimated that every ton of latex produced by the Peruvian Amazon Company had cost seven lives.

The long shadow

With the formation of the United Nations every member state was obliged to outlaw slavery – at least in principle. But past slavery throws a long shadow, as evidenced by various movements for reparations. In the US reparations for slavery have sparked heated debate. Mary Robinson, the former UN High Commissioner for Human Rights, responded positively to suggestions of compensatory development aid for African countries from which slaves were taken by Europeans. In New Zealand/ Aotearoa an independent tribunal recommended that the Government compensate the descendants of Moriori people who were enslaved by the Maori over 150 years ago.

Slavery today

Millions of people all over the world are still forced to lead lives as slaves in all but name: they are sold, forced to work for little or no pay and find themselves completely at the mercy of their 'employers'. Modern examples include women from eastern Europe or from eastern Asia trafficked and forced into prostitution, forced labor on infrastructure projects under oppressive regimes like that in Burma, and the bonded labor system that still constrains the lives of so many, particularly in South Asia. At least eight million children are estimated to be affected by slavery, trafficking, debt bondage and other forms of forced labor, forced recruitment for armed conflict, prostitution, pornography and other illicit activities. Anti-Slavery International today tries to use the same techniques that led to the abolition of the British slave trade in 1807 to gain support for the eradication of modern-day slavery.

What's in a name?

Aristotle called slaves 'human instruments' signifying their use as tools.

Fifth-century Anglo-Saxons called their slaves 'Welshman', after the people they captured.

The word 'slave' is adapted from Slav, originating from the time when the Germans supplied the slave markets of Europe with captured Slavs.

BRIEF HISTORY **38**

A Short History of Nuclear Weapons

From the Manhattan Project and Hiroshima through the Cold War arms race to today's threats of terrorist 'dirty nukes' and ever wider proliferation.

'The explosive force of nuclear fission has changed everything except our modes of thinking and thus we drift towards unparalleled catastrophe. We shall require an entirely new pattern of thinking if humankind is to survive.'
Albert Einstein, 1946

The Manhattan Project

Scientific breakthroughs in the 1930s made atomic bomb production possible. Fearing the prospect of Hitler developing nuclear weapons, top physicists from around the world joined the secret 'Manhattan Project' to develop them first. Unprecedented funding came from the US. When Germany surrendered in May 1945 the Manhattan Project had not yet developed a working weapon. Many scientists lobbied for their research to be turned to peaceful purposes. But US President Harry Truman saw the advantage of possessing the Bomb ahead of the Soviet Union, and ordered the first test in July, resulting in the mightiest explosion humanity had ever witnessed.

Hiroshima

Truman immediately decided to use this awesome weapon to attack Japan, with which the Allies were still at war. Officially, this was to force the stubborn Japanese leadership to capitulate. In fact, Japan was already seeking a negotiated surrender. It seems likely that the US nuked Japan to show the world that it had a unique and devastating weapon and was prepared to use it.

On 6 August 1945, a bomb known as 'Little Boy' was dropped on Hiroshima. Resident Dr Shuntaro Hida was visiting a patient outside the city at the time: 'My whole heart trembled at what I saw. There was a great fire ring floating over the city. Within a moment, a massive deep white cloud grew out of the center and a long black cloud spread over the entire width of the city, the beginning of an enormous storm created by the blast. I decided I had to return as soon as possible. I looked at the road before me. Denuded, burnt and bloody, numberless survivors were in my path; some crawling on their knees or on all fours, some stood with difficulty or leant on another's shoulder. No-one showed any sign that helped me to recognize him or her as a human being. The cruelest sight was the number of raw bodies that lay one upon the other. Although the road was already packed with victims, the terribly wounded, bloody and burnt kept crawling in. They had become a pile of flesh.'

After shock
'About a week after the bombing, unusual symptoms began to appear in the survivors', remembers Dr Shuntaro Hida. 'When patients raised their hands to their heads while struggling with pain, their hair would fall out. Experiencing severe symptoms of fever, throat pain, bleeding and depilation, the survivors fell into a dangerous condition within an hour of the onset. Very few escaped death. Our patients were dying from a bomb which could kill them long after the blast.' The total number of deaths in the first hours was 75,000, but many more died within a week of acute radiation poisoning. By December 1945, 140,000 were dead, and by the end of 1950, 200,000.

Three days after Hiroshima, the US dropped a second bomb – nicknamed 'Fat Man' – on Nagasaki. Around 40,000 died immediately, rising to 140,000 by the end of 1950. Truman promised to eliminate Japanese cities one by one in a 'rain of ruin'. Japan surrendered on 15 August, on the same conditions it had asked for before the bombings.

The H-bomb
Moscow had obtained information from spies involved with the Manhattan Project. After the War, it took the Soviets only four years to produce their first fission bomb. Truman retaliated with a crash program to develop a weapon thousands of times more powerful again: the 'hydrogen' or thermonuclear bomb. Although many scientists objected, their concerns were ignored. The US tested its first fusion bomb (code-named 'Mike') in 1952. More than 450 times the power of the Nagasaki bomb, it obliterated Elugelab atoll in the Marshall Islands. Not to be outdone, the Soviet Union exploded its first thermonuclear device in August 1953.

Jellyfish babies
The tit-for-tat nuclear escalation of the Cold War had begun. The US conducted a catastrophic H-bomb test at Bikini Atoll, which yielded twice the expected destructive power, producing a fireball five kilometers high. A cloud of radioactive fallout contaminated 11,000 square kilometers. Marshall Islanders fell ill with radiation sickness, their homes rendered permanently uninhabitable. Over time, many suffered horrific after-

effects. In 1996, Lijon Eknilang from Rongelap Atoll told the International Court of Justice how she and other Marshallese women had given birth to 'monster babies': 'One woman on Likiep gave birth to a child with two heads. There is a young girl on Ailuk today with no knees, three toes on each foot and a missing arm. Her mother had not been born by 1954, but she was raised on a contaminated atoll. The most common birth defects have been "jellyfish" babies, born with no bones in their bodies and with transparent skin. We can see their brains and hearts beating. The babies usually live for a day or two before they stop breathing.'

MAD world

Throughout the 1950s the US and USSR competed for nuclear supremacy. By the 1960s both had developed intercontinental ballistic missiles which could be launched far away from their target, and submarine-launched missiles which could sneak up without any radar warning. This situation came to be known as Mutually Assured Destruction (MAD) or 'deterrence'. Never mind who attacked first – both nations would be damaged to the point of collapse. This meant, the theory went, that war would be suicide and so no country would risk it. But far from keeping the arms race under control, MAD provoked the production of thousands of nuclear weapons by both superpowers, each striving to possess enough firepower to launch a nuclear first strike that destroyed the ability of the attacked country to respond.

The climax of diplomatic brinksmanship came in early 1962 when the US discovered that Russia was placing missiles in Fidel Castro's Cuba, allowing for a nuclear attack on the US mainland. The two superpowers came terrifyingly close to a nuclear war, averted by a last-minute compromise.

Join the club

In the meantime, three more countries had joined the nuclear club. The British Government was determined to get its own bomb. As Foreign Secretary Ernest Bevin bluntly put it: `We have got to have this thing over here whatever it costs... and we've got to have the bloody Union Jack on top of it.' Bevin got his wish in October 1952. From 1958, Anglo-American co-operation meant that Britain's nuclear arsenal was dependent on the US for its operation. France launched a civil nuclear research program in the 1950s, a by-product of which was weapons-grade plutonium. Under Charles de Gaulle it successfully tested a nuclear bomb in 1960. China – with help from a subsequently regretful Russia – was able to test an A-bomb in 1964, a nuclear missile in 1966, and an H-bomb in 1967. China is the only state committed to only using its nuclear weapons in retaliation to a nuclear attack.

Resist and control

As the danger grew, public opposition to the bomb snowballed. In 1950, the 'Stockholm Peace Appeal' secured 500 million signatures from 79 countries calling for nuclear weapons to be banned. Shock at the scale of radioactive contamination at Bikini Atoll provoked calls for a ban on nuclear testing. In 1958 the Campaign for Nuclear Disarmament was launched in Britain. Anti-nuclear marches attracted tens of thousands, and dedicated activists engaged in civil disobedience, some undergoing lengthy prison sentences.

The first serious attempts by politicians to reduce tensions and control the spread of nuclear weaponry were prompted by the Cuban Missile Crisis. A military hotline was installed between the US and Soviet leaders, aimed at improving communication and avoiding dangerous misunderstandings. The two superpowers signed the Partial Test Ban Treaty in 1963, agreeing not to test nuclear weapons in the atmosphere, underwater, or outer space. Testing underground continued.

Non-proliferation

To a cultural backdrop of 'make love not war' and 'ban the bomb', the late 1960s was a period of great optimism about disarmament. Several arms-control treaties were signed, culminating in 1968 with the Nuclear Non-proliferation Treaty (NPT). Signed by most countries, it committed the five nuclear weapon states (NWS) – France, China, USSR, Britain, US – not to 'assist, encourage, or induce' a non-nuclear weapon state (NNWS) to acquire nuclear weapons. NNWS agreed in turn not to develop such a capability. This has largely been adhered to. Unfortunately, a commitment within the Treaty to disarm has not been complied with by the NWS. The NPT also enshrines the right of all states to develop nuclear energy, which has proved deeply problematic as the transition from civilian to military capability is relatively simple.

Star Wars and mass protests

Nuclear arsenals continued to grow in the 1970s. In 1979 British and German leaders agreed to allow the US to site 572 US Cruise and Pershing missiles on their territory, with Italy, Belgium and the Netherlands soon signing up as well. In 1981, Ronald Reagan came to power in the US. Treaties were out, and talk of fighting a global thermonuclear war was in. He announced plans for a 'Strategic Defense Initiative' – known as 'Star Wars' – to enable the US to make a nuclear attack on the USSR and protect itself from retaliation.

Fears that the US was planning to fight a nuclear war with the USSR in Europe sparked widespread concern. The first half of the 1980s saw a million people march for nuclear disarmament in New York City.

Hundreds of thousands took to the streets across Europe in the biggest protests since the Second World War. Towns, cities and countries declared themselves 'nuclear-free zones'. New Zealand/Aotearoa was the first country to declare itself a nuclear-free zone in 1984: nuclear-powered or nuclear-armed ships were barred from entering its waters.

The Cold War thaws

When Gorbachev came to power in 1985 it was clear to him that the USSR could no longer afford an arms race with the West. He began to roll back military spending and disarm the Russian nuclear arsenal. He initiated serious negotiations with Reagan who, just before being elected to a second term, had changed his position so as openly to embrace disarmament. A flurry of arms control agreements followed.

As the USSR dramatically disintegrated in the late 1980s, the threat of nuclear apocalypse at last seemed to have receded. In the following decade, the US and Russia both halved their stockpiles of nuclear weapons, from a peak of 65,000 in 1986. But this was by no means the end of world – or nuclear – history.

Nuke kids on the block

By the end of the 20th century the five original nuclear weapons states no longer had a monopoly. Israel has never officially confirmed or denied its possession of the bomb, but in 1986 the existence of nuclear warheads was leaked to the press by technician Mordechai Vanunu. He then spent 18 years in prison for treason. In 1998 India ran tests and declared it had the bomb. National jubilation was quickly dampened when arch-rival Pakistan responded with successful tests, raising the specter of a South Asian nuclear war. In January 2004 it emerged that the revered head of Pakistan's nuclear program, Dr A Q Khan, had been secretly selling nuclear-weapons capability to Libya, Iran and North Korea. Thanks in large part to Khan, North Korea announced in 2003 that it was building a bomb. Its test in October 2006 was more of a 'fizzle', but enough to bring North Korea into the nuclear club. At least 13 nations have the ability to 'go nuclear' in the next decade, including Algeria, Indonesia, Libya, Saudi Arabia and Syria. Many more will soon have the means to join them, as nuclear energy spreads across the world. As if the prospect of a multi-polar nuclear world wasn't disquieting enough, it's conceivable that terrorist groups might get their hands on the necessary technology to build and detonate some kind of nuclear device.

Ending the hypocrisy – and the danger

The 21st century has so far been marked by jaw-dropping hypocrisy, with the existing nuclear states, especially the US and Britain, outraged at the very idea of other countries developing their own nuclear capability, and in the case of Iraq even using non-existent weapons of mass destruction as an excuse to invade and occupy.

The US and Britain are not alone in flouting their disarmament commitments. All the other major nuclear weapons states are busy 'modernizing' their nukes, although both Russia and China have been more than a little provoked by the aggressive US push for a 'Son of Star Wars' ballistic missile defense system that looks suspiciously like it's aimed at them.

The ball is clearly in the court of the US and Britain to start serious negotiations for disarmament, with the ultimate aim of eradicating nukes from the face of the earth. We have perhaps a handful of years before nuclear weapons spread to more countries and are used in anger once again. There are fewer and fewer survivors left to remind us of the horror humans can now unleash upon each other.

We've never been good at learning from history and the signs point towards a whole new generation experiencing a nuclear attack first hand in the not too distant future. But this struggle is too important to leave to the committed few. It's up to all of us to seize the window of opportunity we've been given and ban the bomb, before the shutters slam back down, for good.

BRIEF HISTORY **39**

Africa in Ancient History

Traditional history teaching gave a monopoly of 'greatness' to Western societies. But long before Europeans pillaged Africa the continent produced an imposing array of civilizations. This history is the bedrock upon which Africa must build its future.

The human cradle   *2 million years ago*
Africa was the birthplace of tool-making humans. Two million years ago they ran, hunted, made love, fashioned tools, gathered plants and died in northwestern Tanzania. Among the many implements that they bequeathed us are pointed stones probably used to sharpen the tips of digging implements. A million years later our forebears emerged, whose repertoire of stone tools now included hand-axes. By around 50,000 years ago our ancestors had learned to make fire and were setting up house in caves. And around 15,000 BCE, Africa had begun to be populated by human beings with the same variety of racial characteristics as today.

Promise of the Nile   *4000 BCE*
Out of Africa a new group of people tramped northwards to the land of Egypt. To stay or not to stay? Food was the problem. With pioneering ingenuity they solved the puzzle by becoming the world's first farmers around 4,000 BCE. They split the land into two states

– Upper and Lower Egypt – and after 3,200 BCE one Pharaoh took charge. A stunning civilization sprang up. The élite had a strong central government which lasted for 3,000 years and perfected its techniques of extracting wealth and labor from its subjects. With this they built splendid temples and pyramids stocked with tomb-furniture so that the Pharaohs could live out their after-lives in comfort. There was brilliant development – Aristotle described Egypt as the 'cradle of mathematics', for example – and little disruption until a series of invasions precipitated its decline.

The land of Kush   *500 BCE*

Beyond southern Egypt lay the land of Kush. It was later forgotten because the Greeks, who rarely (if ever) visited it, sweepingly referred to its inhabitants as Ethiopians – meaning all Africans. Herodotus described the place from hearsay: 'Here gold is found in great abundance and huge elephants and ebony, and all sorts of trees growing wild. The men too, are the tallest in the world, the best-looking and the longest lived.' The southern city of Meroe became one of the greatest iron-founding centers of the ancient world after 500 BCE. Its inhabitants – who apparently had a better geographical sense than the Greeks – developed a roaring trade with India and China, while building temples and manufacturing metals. And by 250 BCE the region had a large and powerful empire which lasted until the fourth century of the Common Era.

The Ethiopians   *500 CE*

While Kush was growing, another civilization was flowering in northeastern Ethiopia. This Ethiopian culture borrowed its language and gods from the southern Arabians or Sabeans (the Queen of Sheba's people) with whom they originally traded. The city of Adulis blossomed as a center of world trade and soon after 50 CE, the Ethiopian capital Axum produced a new line of kings. They had the same weakness for self-aggrandizement as some modern heads of state and competed to erect ever-bigger monuments. Finally in 500 and after centuries of trading, King Ezana of Axum decided that he had been provoked beyond endurance and marched his armies into Meroe. Meroe's downfall was complete.

The lords of Ghana   *600*

Ghana – whose markets had supplied the Berbers since ancient times – grew into a big and powerful empire, built on the North African hunger for gold and ivory and the West African hunger for salt. Gradually it began trading in more things: copper, cotton, fine tools and swords from

172

Arabian workshops; horses from Barbary and Egypt; ivory, kola nuts and slaves from the south. The lords of Ghana raked in massive sums by taxing both production and the import-export trade. They behaved like modern-day pop stars, squandering the money on lavish banquets for thousands of guests at a time. Their extravagance became renowned, peaking around 1067. It attracted Berber invaders who stole the wealth and forced many inhabitants to become Muslims. Weakened by these raids, the empire finally fell to an invading people from the north of Senegal, the Tekrur.

Mali and Songhay   *1200*

Ghana split into several states, as oppressed groups freed themselves. Among these groups were the Mandinka, who inhabited the state of Kangaba on the banks of the Upper Niger. They were excellent traders and cultivators whose leaders fought vigorously to build the empire of Mali, which rose in the 13th century and lasted for nearly 200 years. By the end, the empire sprawled from the shores of the Atlantic to the borders of modern Nigeria. Mali's schools of theology and law were famous as far away as Muslim Asia. And its heyday was revered as a golden age – until 1375, when the Songhay rulers of the city-state of Gao rebelled. From 1464 the Songhay set about conquering Mali. They succeeded and set up their own empire, which grew for another century, stretching across the vast region of the Middle Niger.

Kingdom of Great Zimbabwe   *1400*

By 1400 the Iron Age was shaping people's consciousness all across sub-Saharan Africa. States rose and fell. The Swahili peoples had long conducted trade between Africans from the interior and ships from China and India; their buildings expressed the Arab-African influence. Further south was the kingdom between the Limpopo and the Zambezi called Great Zimbabwe. The ambitious Mutota, king of the Karanga, conquered this gold-rich plateau in around 1440 and a new civilization emerged. As well as large buildings the people made beautiful gold objects and fine hand-turned pots. But the empire was torn by internal rivalries, and fell to the Portuguese in the early 17th century.

Military might *1500*

By now Europeans were trading up and down the coast of West Africa. They influenced the coastal people who must have been amazed by their seemingly insatiable desire for gold. But the African states were too strong to be invaded. The Wolof empire in Senegal commanded a cavalry of 10,000 and an army of 100,000. The powerful empire of Benin was growing famous for its ivory and bronze sculptures. Mali was still respected. And inland states continued developing undisturbed. For example, the Yoruba of Oyo became a formidable force after their Alafin or king was exiled by a neighboring state. When the Yoruba returned they organized a cavalry-based army which made them unconquerable in the region for nearly 200 years. But the real African genius lay not in military strength or empires but in its system of decentralized societies run by village chiefs and elders. All across Africa from the Igbo in the west to the Kikuyu in the east and the Xhosa in the south, this was the way societies operated.

Slaves *1650*
Traditionally in Africa, prisoners of war and convicts could be made into slaves, so fortune-seeking African rulers had no qualms about selling a few slaves to the Portuguese in exchange for cotton, woolens or brass. But the discovery of America caused a labor hunger among Europeans that could not be satisfied by a mere human trickle. Africans were kidnapped on a massive scale and transported to the Americas for work on plantations or down mines. African slaves were prized because of their skills in tropical farming and metal working and by 1780 around 100,000 were being shipped across the Atlantic every year. So many died in the process that entire slave populations had to be replaced every few years. And many African communities were decimated. Their industries and fine cities, beautiful temples and skilful works of art, all bled to death as young men and women, the most productive and creative of their citizens, were dragged away.

Conquest and colonialism *1800s*
Europeans began thoroughly exploring Africa after 1795. Invasions followed between 1880 and 1900. The conquering powers divided up their spoils. They imposed colonial boundaries which split some ethnic groups and locked others together. They disrupted traditional systems of government by imposing taxes and appointing subjected chiefs to administrate for them. They flooded Africa with cheap industrial goods like cottons, metalwares and firearms – inhibiting local production and industrial expansion. They traded drink, which brought alcoholism. And they discouraged local food production by promoting cash crops like peanuts, cocoa and bananas, while cultivating markets for imported foods such as sugar. Africa was ensnared in the web of exploitation which still confines it.

BRIEF HISTORY 40

How the Old World Stole the New...

...and how the New World changed the Old. Disease, famine and war wracked 15th-century Europe. The 'discovery' of the Americas offered the possibility of a new beginning – but at the expense of the Native Americans who lived there.

Gold and silver

Columbus hungered for gold but found little. However those who followed him did: Cortes plundered the Aztec temples and Pizarro stole shiploads of Inca wealth. But while Indians worked the Spanish mines of Bolivia and Mexico, most of the wealth eventually wound up in the pockets of Dutch, British and French entrepreneurs.

The old European mercantile economy was shaken by the massive injection of American wealth. In 1500, Europe had $200 million worth of gold and silver: a century later the amount was eight times greater. Inflation sent the value of precious metals plummeting worldwide. (The Ottoman Empire saw the value of its silver hoard fall 50 per cent by 1584, knocking the Islamic power from contention as a major trading bloc.) And as the American booty spread around Europe, a new merchant and capitalist class was launched.

Soon the British and Dutch expanded into North America, India, China and southeast Asia. By 1750 a truly global trading network had been established with Europe in firm control. The catalyst: American gold and silver.

The white death

The impact of the Spanish on the native peoples of Latin America is one of the most terrifying episodes in human history. There were perhaps 21 million Mexicans in 1519 but only 2.5 million in 1565 and just 1 million in 1607. The story in Peru was similar, where only 1.5 million people remained out of 11 million. The vast majority were victims not of the sword but of disease. After thousands of years of separate development, Native Americans had no resistance to diseases of the Old World such as smallpox, measles or influenza. Others died laboring in the mines that produced the gold and silver that the Europeans so coveted.

Profit and slaves

The unimaginable wealth of the Americas soon rendered redundant the old trade routes through Africa – once the main source of new supplies of gold and silver. Africa now had only one thing the Europeans wanted: slaves to work the mines and plantations of the new world. Slavery had existed in Africa for centuries but the demand for cheap labor in the Americas turned the sale of black flesh into a booming and immensely profitable business.

By 1619 a million slaves had been brought to Spanish and Portuguese colonies in South America. The British and French easily dominated the slave trade as Spanish ships were too busy hauling all the new American wealth back home. Like the indigenous peoples, black people throughout the Americas were abused, degraded and murdered in the pursuit of profit. This legacy of racism and intolerance still cripples social relations throughout the Americas – from Argentina to the Arctic.

Banks and business

Opportunities for profit in the Americas also produced the ancestors of today's giant transnational corporations. Pirates like Francis Drake got private financing and royal approval for his plunder of Spanish treasure. Later these pirates also branched out into slavery (forming businesses like the Royal African Company) and eventually plantation agriculture.

In the Caribbean and along the coast of Virginia and the Carolinas, plantations growing sugar, tobacco, rice and cotton were hacked out of the forest and black slaves imported to work them. Later, British traders launched business ventures like The Hudson Bay Company (which was 'granted' by Charles II a chunk of Canada larger than western Europe) and The Virginia Company. The imperial goals of Britain were closely tied to these private business interests. As the corporations prospered (backed by the unrivaled strength of the British Navy) a sophisticated banking system sprang up to handle all the new wealth, followed soon by stock markets to attract new investors.

Cotton catalyst

The Industrial Revolution began in Europe, sparked by raw materials from the colonies – especially American cotton, which was stronger, cheaper and more plentiful than cotton from Asia. As thousands of bales of the new variety poured into Europe, derelict grain mills were quickly converted to process it into cloth.

But the textile industry really took off when Eli Whitney invented the cotton gin in Massachusetts in 1793. This new technology allowed a single worker to process more than 20 kilos of cotton a day. Soon spinning and weaving were also mechanized and the Industrial Revolution was in full gear. From 1790 to 1860, raw cotton production in the US jumped from 3,000 to 4,500,000 bales a year. By 1850, finished cotton cloth accounted for half of all British exports.

The highly mechanized textile business became a model for other newly emerging industries. As this model spread, so did the demand for raw materials. Cotton plantations sprang up right across the US South, scattering the Choctaw, Chickasaw, Creek and Cherokee nations in the process.

Pizza and potatoes

Cotton was not the only American plant with global impact. In the centuries following Columbus, new foods from the Americas changed diets around the world. Imagine India without curry, Russia without vodka, Italy without pizza, Switzerland without chocolate or Africa without maize. Chili peppers, potatoes, tomatoes, cocoa and maize-corn all originated in America. In fact 60 per cent of all crops around the world were first cultivated and eaten by Native Americans.

The potato, in particular, transformed Europe. Although slow to gain acceptance, by the late 1600s the little tuber was widely grown by peasants and soon became a staple. Potatoes were easier to grow than traditional grains like wheat; they also produced more calories per hectare, had limitless uses and were easily stored. As the potato was adopted across northern Europe, famines disappeared, general nutrition improved and populations increased; the Irish population tripled in the century after the potato was introduced. Indeed this vegetable became so crucial to the Irish diet that around a million died after potato blight struck Ireland in 1845.

Cornucopia

Indian corn had a similar impact. It was carried by returning slave ships to Africa where thick maize porridge quickly became an essential part of the diet – especially in southern Africa. In Europe maize was mainly used to feed livestock and poultry, producing healthier animals and increasing the supply of protein-rich milk, eggs, cheese and meat. By the late 1700s maize was widely cultivated in Italy and Spain; more abundant protein led to improved health, lower infant mortality and larger populations. The number of people in Italy grew from 11 million to 18 million in less than a century after maize was introduced.

Guano-ecology

Native Americans also practised farming techniques which were eagerly adopted by the colonizers. They planted mixed crops like corn, beans and squash in small mounds, not neat rows of one plant variety. The method was copied by early white settlers, since it was ideally suited to newly cleared land studded with tree stumps. Recent Mexican studies have shown that this kind of mixed cropping can increase maize yields by as much as half.

In Peru, Inca farmers collected guano – the nitrogen-rich droppings of sea birds along the Pacific coast. The fertilizer was so valuable that Inca law forbade the killing of sea birds. In the 19th century millions of tons of guano were exported to Europe, reinvigorating depleted soils and improving yields in an ecologically sound way. From 1840 to 1880 Peru exported 11 million tons of guano worth $600 million. More importantly, the guano trade prompted research into other fertilizers and was an important step in the development of modern agriculture.

Native democracy

The political structures of Native North Americans did more than classical Greece to spread ideas of freedom and democracy around the globe. From the time of Columbus, Europeans were astounded by the lack of hierarchy in Native American society. In general, there were no kings, no social classes and community respect was based on good works, not wealth or property. Life was ruled by ceremony, tradition and kinship, although there were wide variations between peoples and many undemocratic tendencies. (The Maya and the Aztecs practised blood sacrifice, and slavery was common.)

Native American democracy inspired both Europeans and the emerging United States. (The eagle design on the US insignia was stolen from the Iroquois; the six arrows in the bird's talons represent the six Iroquois nations.) The Iroquois League was studied by Tom Paine (whose writing influenced both the American and French Revolutions) and Ben Franklin, one of the fathers of the US Constitution. The Iroquois system, which underlies US democracy today, is a true 'federal' democracy, blending several sovereign nations into one government. The French and British could never accept such nations were run collectively rather than by supreme rulers. They insisted on dealing with a 'chief', even though political power was vested in a group. This fundamental conflict in political values continues to poison relations between indigenous peoples and national governments throughout the Americas.

South Pacific – an Environmental History

The South Pacific was the last habitable region on earth to be settled by human beings. It is now becoming the first to be made uninhabitable.

Gondwanaland

About 160 million years ago Antarctica, Australia, South America, India and part of Southeast Asia formed the single supercontinent Gondwanaland. It gradually broke into 'tectonic plates' which are still moving today. Where they pull apart, molten magma sometimes breaks the surface to form ridges. Where they come together, one plate plunges beneath the other, throwing up mountainous ridges to one side and deep oceanic trenches to the other. Most of the islands of the South Pacific are formed by one of these two forces. The Pacific remains the most volatile geological region on earth.

Freeze and flood

During the past two million years there have been at least 20 occasions when the earth's climate was colder than it is now. At such times, because water cooled and contracted, sea levels fell. The islands of the South Pacific were then larger and fewer. At the height of the last ice age, 18,000 years ago, the sea level in Fiji was between 120 and 150 meters below the current level. By the end of the Ice Age most of the older island ecosystems became stabilized with grassland, woodland and tropical rainforest. This made them suitable for human settlement.

Miraculous migrations

People probably first moved from Indonesia to New Guinea and Australia around 40,000 years ago, when sea levels were low. With the end of the Ice Age sea levels rose and longer-distance migrations in dug-out canoes began. By the time of the 'Little Climate Optimum', between 1200 BCE and 650 BCE, temperatures were higher than they are now, with persistent trade winds, clear skies and few storms. These were favorable conditions for oceanic migrations: among the greatest feats of navigation ever

179

accomplished. People finally reached the Marquesas Islands to the east about 2,000 years ago. From there they went on to form the 'Polynesian Triangle', with Hawai'i to the north and New Zealand/Aotearoa to the south, by about 750 – though evidence of earlier settlement is now being examined.

Human impact

Migration brought great changes to island ecosystems. New crops and animals were introduced and forests were cleared for cultivation. Combined with the effect of tropical storms, these increased soil erosion. The sediment from erosion, in turn, smothered coral reefs. Reefs protect many islands from the ocean and are rich in fish. Most island ecosystems were badly degraded within 1,000 years of human settlement. Pollen records show that forests on Rapa Nui (Easter Island) were completely destroyed. On Aneityum, southern Vanuatu, early settlement and forest clearance on the uplands led to soil erosion and forced a shift of population to the lowlands – similar shifts had to be made on other islands, too.

European intrusion

The initial effect of European intrusion during the 17th century was to reduce human impact on the environment. Indigenous peoples, as elsewhere around the world, had no immunity to European diseases and many died, so cultivation and land degradation slowed. But the burning of vegetation increased as commercial farming commenced; repeated burning weakened the soil and led to landslides. Bad management of commercial croplands – such as sugar cane in Fiji – also degraded soils. Native plant and animal species began to disappear and extractive industries ruined entire islands. Phosphate mining rendered much of the islands of Banaba and Nauru uninhabitable.

Wars of the worlds

Occupation by Allied and Japanese troops during World War Two, and the vast scale of the conflict that followed, totally disfigured many of the islands of Melanesia and Micronesia. 'Strategic' military bases proliferated. After the war the US, Britain and France (with the 'loss' of Algeria in 1962) conducted nuclear tests in the Pacific atmosphere. The great lagoon of Kwajalein in the Marshall Islands became the target zone for missile tests launched from Vandenberg Space and Missile Center in California. Entire populations were removed from Bikini, Enewetak, Rongelap and Wotho atolls, and from Kwajalein and Noi Namur islands. The long-term effects of nuclear testing on ecosystems and human health remain. Since 1977 'burnships' have been incinerating chemical weapons off Johnston Atoll.

Greenhouse growth
For the first time the South Pacific has become vulnerable to global 'anthropogenic' (created by humans) climate change. Already, tropical  storms have increased in frequency as sea-surface temperatures rise beyond the critical 28°C. Degradation by extractive industries has risen sharply with the application of large-scale industrial techniques. Local pollution from combustion engines, power stations, pesticides, fertilizers, plastics and domestic waste has also increased. The construction of roads, airports, causeways and hotels, together with the clearance of mangrove swamps, have all interfered with the fragile ecology of coastal strips and reefs.

The photograph on this page shows Daydream Island, Fiji.

Within the next 20 years it will disappear due to sea-level rise and global warming.

The Amazon's Hidden History

The people of the Amazon have left few historical records. This is because most of their artifacts were made from organic matter which rotted or disappeared. But attempts are now being made to reveal the history of the forest and its people.

Changing forest
Recent scientific discoveries show that, far from being 'ageless', the Amazon rainforest has undergone dramatic natural transformations. The most notable were during the last Ice Age. At this time the world's tropical regions became cooler and drier. The forest shrank and broke up, the savanna grasslands expanded. The small patches of forest or 'refugia' that remained did not all evolve in the same way, with the same vegetation or animal life. So, when the forest eventually came together again there was great genetic variety within it.

Arrival of humans

Humans are only recent arrivals in the forest. They first crossed the frozen Bering Straits into North America about 40,000 years ago – reaching the lowlands and forests of South America between 15,000 and 20,000 years ago. People first started farming and settling on the Amazonian floodplains some 5,000 years ago. Few settlements were static: groups would migrate long distances through the forest, little of which was left completely untouched. Conflicts between groups were regular occurrences. The more archeologists discover about the forest the clearer it becomes that estimates of how many people were living in the Amazon before the arrival of Europeans will have to be revised upwards – to perhaps as many as 15 million.

European 'discovery'

Soon after Columbus first set foot on American soil, Pope Alexander VI divided the uncharted lands of the 'new world' between Spain on the Pacific coast and Portugal on the Atlantic coast. This happened at the Treaty of Tordesillas in 1494. Quite coincidentally, most of the Amazon Basin fell within the area designated for Portuguese colonization. Initial contacts between Portuguese explorers and the indigenous peoples were fairly friendly. They focused on the extraction of brazilwood – used to produce dye – after which the Portuguese 'colony' was named. The people were, of course, named 'Indians' by Europeans because of their mistaken belief that they had landed in India. Why the river was named the Amazon remains uncertain, but it seems likely that it was because women warriors resembling those in Greek mythology were thought to live there.

Red gold rush

The first European to navigate the Amazon was actually Spanish. Francisco de Orellana traveled downstream from Peru in 1542. For the next 150 years Portuguese interest in the Amazon was largely limited to unsuccessful attempts to recruit Indian labor ('red gold') for sugar plantations on the coast. But the indigenous peoples were not interested in working as wage laborers and violent conflicts ensued. The only Europeans actually to explore the rainforest were Christian missionaries – particularly the Jesuits. But in 1777 the first systematic attempt to develop the region was devised by the Portuguese Marquis of Pombal, mostly out of fear of encroachment by the Spanish, Dutch and British. He created the Companhía Grão Pará e Maranhão in imitation of the British East India Company as a state-backed entity to stimulate and monitor trade in the eastern Amazon region.

Rubber barons

A small trade in rubber began during the 18th century; by 1800 Belém was exporting 450,000 pairs of rubber shoes to England. But it was only after Charles Goodyear accidentally discovered 'vulcanization' in 1842, and the Industrial Revolution increased demand for rubber products, that the Brazilian 'boom' got under way. Rubber
trees existed nowhere else in the world. Commercial houses, initially financed by the British, extended credit to laborers who penetrated the furthest reaches of the Amazon in search of rubber trees. Once there, the *seringueiros* (rubber tappers) were ensnared in debt bondage to the estate owners, the *seringalistas*, who sold basic necessities to them at grossly inflated prices. The wealth of the trade reverted mostly to Manaus and Belém, and there was no attempt to establish rubber-based industry in the Amazon itself. The trade collapsed during the First World War with the development of rubber plantations in Asia from plants smuggled out of the Amazon.

Land of dreams

The great naturalists Alexander von Humboldt and Aimé Bonpland traveled to the Amazon in 1799. This was to inspire botanists and explorers throughout the 19th century to roam the forest – to the displeasure of the Portuguese prior to Independence in 1821. These explorers returned with fantastic tales. The Amazon became the focus of 19th-century romantic interest in the notion of the 'natural state' and 'the noble savage'. Mark Twain wrote: 'I was fired with a longing to ascend the Amazon. Also with a longing to open up a trade in coca with all the world. During months I dreamed that dream.'

Empire of schemes

The US Navy conducted the first survey of the navigability of the Amazon in 1849. The first steamboats – which made it easier to ascend the river against the current – began operating in 1853. Growing US interest in the Amazon found one expression in US involvement in the revolution in the rubber-rich region of Acre, which in 1899 declared independence from Bolivia and finally became part of Brazil. The first of many US entrepreneurs to devise grandiose schemes in the Amazon, Percival Farquhar, managed to raise $70 million in Europe for a variety of projects, including the completion of the Madeira-Mamoré railway in the middle of the jungle. It cost 6,000 lives to construct. Farquhar was ruined by the collapse of the rubber boom.

Military maneuvers

Since the 1930s – and the 'New State' established by the military Brazilian President Getúlio Vargas – the modern invasion of the Amazon has progressed along largely 'strategic' and 'geopolitical' lines. Particularly since the military coup in 1964, the 'incorporation' of the Amazon into Brazilian territory has been the main motive behind Government policies encouraging the colonization and deforestation of the area. Thus much of the initial deforestation in Rondônia and Pará took place around 'Development Poles' constructed by the Government from 1966 onwards. These were combined with a preference for 'big projects', building roads, dams and other debt-inducing industrial enterprises largely with the backing of multinational lending agencies like the World Bank.

Cause célèbre

In the 1980s two major forces overtook the Amazon. One was the rapid development of industrial agriculture in southern Brazil, which displaced many thousands of rural workers northwards towards the 'empty' Amazon Basin. This accelerated the pace of 'slash and burn' deforestation, particularly in the south and east of the region. The second was satellite technology, which revealed the extent of the devastation to a wider world.

For a while the Amazon became an international cause célèbre, especially after the murder of Chico Mendes in 1988. He had been leading the remaining rubber tappers, sometimes in alliance with indigenous peoples and non-governmental organizations, in defending the relatively pristine western region of primary forest. Powerful logging, drug-running and bio-prospecting interests were moving in. Partially successful attempts were made to establish 'extractive reserves' that would exclude those interests.

High expectations accompanied the election of 'Lula' da Silva of the Workers' Party as President of Brazil in 2002. This promised an end to the dominance of the wealthy oligarchy, which had been the chief beneficiaries of the destruction. However, the pressures of corporate globalization began to encroach from the western region of primary rainforest in Colombia, Ecuador and Peru, with the discovery of significant oil reserves. In the first decade of the 21st century, what remains of this vital ecosystem and its indigenous inhabitants is under greater threat than ever before – and a new phase of resistance is under way.

BRIEF HISTORY **43**

A Brief History of Persia and Iran

From Cyrus the Great, Omar Khayyam and the Shahs to Ayatollah Khomeini and Mahmoud Ahmadinejad.

Origins 3500–600 BCE

Iran's rich history stretches back to the dawn of civilization in the fourth millennium BCE. The Elamite civilization, eventually focused on the city of Susa in what is now eastern Iran, rivaled its near neighbors first in Akkad and Sumer, then in Babylon and Assyria, for more than 2,000 years. Elamite cultural influences survived even once other peoples had come to dominate the region. The Medes, a people from the mountainous north of the region thought to have been among the ancestors of today's Kurds, were the first to build a significant empire, from the seventh century BCE. Mede king Cyaxares destroyed the Assyrian capital Nineveh in 612 BCE; Babylon's king Nebuchadnezzar held off the Mede threat by marrying Cyaxares' daughter, for whom he built the Hanging Gardens.

Cyrus the Great 550 BCE

The Medes were overcome in 550 BCE by the Persians, whose king Cyrus II merited the accolade 'the Great'. Cyrus was a conqueror, extending the Persian Empire to absorb Lydia (now western Turkey) and Babylon. But his 'greatness' derives more from his reputation for benevolence. When he took control of Babylon – apparently without excessive violence – he issued a decree (recorded in cuneiform script on a cylinder) which has been called the world's first human rights charter. In recent years extra modern-sounding text has been falsely attributed to Cyrus and may derive from propaganda by the last Shah, who was fond of stressing the greatness of the Persian monarchy. But Cyrus does seem to have respected local religions and was responsible for freeing the Jews from their slavery in Babylon, winning him reverence in the Old Testament Book of Ezra.

Zoroastrianism

Cyrus may have come under the influence of Zoroastrianism; his successors Darius and Xerxes certainly did. The dates of Zoroaster (or Zarathustra) are disputed but linguistic analysis of his holy poems, the Ga-tha-s, suggest that they date from, give or take a century, around 1000 BCE – well before the Buddha or before the Jews first recorded their oral history, both in the sixth century BCE. Zoroaster saw the universe as a battle between good (represented by the supreme deity Ahura-Mazda) and evil (in the shape of Ahriman). He believed in the notion of 'free will' and that if humans did not live well they would be damned at a final judgment. The Magi in the Christian nativity story may well have been Zoroastrian priests. The Parsee people in northwest India still practise the Zoroastrian religion, while Baha'is accord Zoroaster prophetic status.

Imperial efficiency 330 BCE-226 CE

The Persian or Achaemenid Empire was one of the greatest civilizations in the ancient world, efficiently governed by 23 local authorities and connected by thousands of kilometers of paved roads, as well as by the world's first postal service. Its original capital, Susa, was one of the world's foremost cities, but Darius I erected a new ceremonial capital, Persepolis or Parsa, which was built in a range of different styles by artists and craftspeople from all over the empire. Its size and beauty dazzled visitors. Persepolis was destroyed by the Greek troops of Alexander the Great in 330 BCE. One of Alexander's generals then established the Seleucid dynasty, with its Greek orientation. After 200 years this was overcome by Parthian nomads from the Caspian.

Golden age 226-637
Neither the Seleucids nor the Parthians had full control of Persia, but their successors the Sassanids came from the Persian heartland of Fars, and their rule from 226 to 651 is seen as the second great phase of the Persian Empire. The Sassanid empire encompassed not only modern Iran but stretched from Arabia to Central Asia. It was acknowledged by Rome as a second superpower. The Sassanid period is revered in Persian literature – embodied particularly in the reign of the fifth-century king, Bahram V. Among the many contributions of ancient Persia to world culture are wine, peaches, windmills, backgammon, polo and ice cream.

Coming of Islam 637
When Islamic forces erupted from the Arabian peninsula following the death of Muhammad in 632, Persia was an inevitable early target. The new religion won its converts as much through its fervent simplicity as its naked force. It offered a readily accessible faith in one true God, unmediated by a priestly élite. Yet this was no simple colonization, since Persian culture was strong enough to influence Islam profoundly – especially during the Golden Age of the Abbasid caliphs between the 8th and 11th centuries. The great geniuses of this period – Al-Khwarizmi, who invented modern numbers and algebra, the medical pioneer Ibn Sins (Avicenna) and the poet and mathematician Omar Khayyam – were all Persians. And it was an obscure Persian library in the Fars region – the only one that survived the Muslim onslaught on 'idolatry' – that kept intact the great works of Greco-Roman antiquity. They were later translated into Arabic and stored in Baghdad, whence they eventually percolated back into the Western world and fed the Renaissance.

From Mongol disaster to poetic genius 1219-1400s
Iran was ravaged by a series of invasions in the 13th and 14th centuries. Genghis Khan's Mongol invasion not only resulted in mass slaughter but also many years of starvation due to the destruction of irrigation systems. The Mongols returned under Hulegu Khan in 1256 and so many millions died in the ensuing years that the Iranian population did not again reach its pre-Mongol level until the late 20th century. A century later there was yet another slaughter, at the hands of the forces of Timur, said to have left a pile of 70,000 heads in the square of Isfahan in 1384. Ironically, this dreadful period also saw an astonishing flowering of Persian poetry – the works of Rumi and Hafez in particular remain among the great works of world literature.

187

Shi'as & Safavids 1400s-1600s

The great split in Islam between Sunni and Shi'a took place early on, in the lifetimes of Muhammad's son-in-law Ali and his grandson Hussein, whose valuing of social justice over tradition is among the core principles of Shi'ism. Hussein married the last Sassanid princess before his death at Karbala in 680 and thus linked Persia to Shi'ism, yet the Shi'a faith did not take hold in Iran until much later. In the 15th century a mystic order called the Safavids, from present-day Azerbaijan, started to gain a following, embracing Shi'ism even as they formed their own army. From 1493 onwards they spread south in a holy war. As in the earlier Muslim invasion, mass conversion followed due to the potent combination of military force and the promise of social justice. The greatest Safavid ruler, Shah Abbas, came to the throne in 1588 and not only made Shi'ism the state religion but connected it to ancient ideas of Persian kingship. He secured Iran's borders and presided over another great flowering of art and architecture, including the magical mosques of Isfahan.

Stagnation and the Shahs 1700s-1800s

Previously always at the hub of world events, Iran drifted into stagnation during the age of the Western industrial revolutions. Afghan invaders who deposed the Safavids were expelled by a megalomaniac ruler with the appropriate name of Nadir. His excesses plunged the country into civil war, which was followed by the Turkish Qajar shahs, who presided over the massively corrupt, casually repressive and politically frozen period of the 19th century. In 1872 Nasir ed-Din Shah sold off all Iran's industries, mineral resources and even its national bank to a British entrepreneur, Baron Julius de Reuter. Iranians were so outraged that he canceled the deal, at huge cost. Again in 1891, to fund a European jaunt for him and his harem, the Shah sold the entire tobacco industry to British Imperial Tobacco. There was universal consternation: farmers would have to sell their whole crop to the British and smokers would be forced to buy from British shops. Mosques also benefited from tobacco sales, and the leading cleric of the day proclaimed a fatwa (religious injunction) against the sell-off. The Shah was again forced to renege on the deal and was assassinated five years later.

Constitutional Revolution 1905-1911

In 1905 the arrest and torture of merchants protesting sugar prices sparked mass opposition. Intellectuals, clerics and traders demanded a constitution that would limit the power of the Shah. Shah Mozzafar al-Din was eventually forced to concede, signing the new constitution on his deathbed, and the first *Majlis* (parliament) was opened on 7 October 1906. A free press began to operate. The new assembly was dogged by difficulty, not least as differences emerged between liberal intellectuals and Shi'a clerics. But support for the new constitution was passionate and when the new Shah bombarded the Majlis with artillery and arrested key constitutionalists in 1908, civil war ensued. After a year of resistance, rebels took control of Tehran and forced the Shah into Russian exile. The Constitutional Revolution was ultimately derailed by foreign powers. In a bold attempt to confront the country's economic crisis, the Majlis appointed an American financial adviser who urged it to collect revenue countrywide. This angered the Russians and British, who had by now divided Iran into 'spheres of influence'. An ultimatum demanded the adviser's dismissal and, as Russian troops advanced toward Tehran, the new Shah's regent dissolved the Majlis in December 1911.

Reza Shah 1920s to 1940s

A middle-ranking army officer, Reza Khan, seized control of Shah Soltan Ahmad's bodyguard in 1921, marched into Tehran and arrested the entire Cabinet. In the ensuing years he put down a Bolshevik rebellion and reasserted central control of wayward provinces, winning the status of a savior. When the clinically obese Shah went abroad for medical treatment, the clerical establishment in Qom encouraged Reza to take the throne; he duly became Shah in 1925. He was a ferocious modernizer, building a vast railway from the Persian Gulf to the Caspian Sea, constructing roads and factories, making education compulsory for girls as well as boys. He even made it illegal for women to wear the veil in public. The mullahs were simply overridden – and in 1936 Reza's soldiers machine-gunned a crowd protesting his attacks on Shi'ism, killing at least a hundred. His ruthless authoritarianism had much in common with fascism and his overt support of Hitler led British and Soviet forces not only to occupy Iran during the Second World War but also to oust him, placing his son Muhammad Reza Pahlavi on the Peacock Throne.

Mossadegh and the CIA 1950s

Iranian oil rights had been given away to the Anglo-Iranian Oil Company (later BP) in 1901. By the 1950s, resentment over British control of this vast resource was seething. The hitherto dormant Majlis sprang back to life, led by a brilliant politician, Muhammad Mossadegh. As the campaign for a better deal hotted up, the British pressurized the Shah to bring the Majlis to heel. His clampdown, together with a blatantly rigged election, provoked urban riots. Mossadegh led a protest to the palace gates and refused to move until free and fair elections were promised. The Shah gave way. Mossadegh became head of Iran's first major political party, the National Front. He told the Majlis he would only take the job of prime minister if it agreed to the nationalization of the Anglo-Iranian Oil Company. Britain reacted by blockading Iranian oil exports, sabotaging equipment and withdrawing all its technical staff. When US President Eisenhower took over at the start of 1953, he was receptive to British allegations that Mossadegh – by now ruling under emergency powers – favored communism. The CIA was given orders to oust Mossadegh – Operation Ajax. A few months and millions of dollars' worth of covert activity later, the CIA team, led by Kermit Roosevelt (grandson of President Theodore), achieved their goal. Mossadegh remained under house arrest until his death, but remains the great hero of many Iranians.

Shah of Shahs 1960s and 1970s

Restored to power, the Shah embarked on a new modernization program dubbed the White Revolution, which included land reform and the enfranchisement of women. The land reform was badly managed, leading to the collapse of ancient irrigation networks, and by the 1970s Iran was no longer self-sufficient in food. The Shah vaingloriously crowned himself King of Kings in 1967. But he maintained control only by savage repression, embodied in his Savak secret police. The Shah's most prominent opponent now was Ayatollah Ruhollah Khomeini. A dedicated Islamic scholar for decades, in 1962 he denounced the seizure of the clergy's lands; the Shah sent troops to the theological center at Qom who killed two Islamic students. At their funeral Khomeini condemned the Shah so roundly that he was arrested, prompting mass rioting in which 86 people died. In 1964 Khomeini was exiled to Iraq but continued to lambast the Shah and lay out his vision of a country led by Shi'a jurists.

The Islamic Revolution 1979

When oil prices fell in the late 1970s, Iran's economy was hit hard – and discontent mushroomed. Democrats, human-rights campaigners and clerics made common cause, united in their opposition to the Shah, who in turn responded with greater repression. Thousands of demonstrators were shot dead in street battles in Tehran, Qom and Tabriz, and in August 1978 Savak police burned down a cinema in Abadan containing 400 women and children. The wave of opposition became a tsunami, bringing in crowds of ordinary people and leading to mass desertions from the army. In January 1979 the Shah fled the country and on 1 February Khomeini returned from exile to a tumultuous welcome.

Clerical rule 1980s

In March 1979 the world's first Islamic Republic was proclaimed. Mullahs appointed Khomeini Supreme Leader, supposed to have special access to Allah's wisdom. Khomeini's vision was of a society constructed entirely according to his own rigid rules and religious prejudices. Many were inspired by the concept of a Muslim state but many others were crushed by it. Vigilantes started patrolling streets and invading homes in search of 'unIslamic' Western elements; revolutionary tribunals condemned and executed 'enemies of Islam'; women were forced to wear the chador. In November 1979 students, hearing that the Shah had been allowed into New York, occupied the US embassy – and held staff there hostage for more than a year, despite a bungled US rescue attempt. Khomeini denounced the US as the Great Satan and stepped up his Islamicization drive. When, in 1981, the Mujahedin-e Khalq, a movement describing itself as Islamic Marxists, began a bombing campaign, the repression became even more intense and at one stage 50 people were being executed by firing squad every day.

War with Iraq 1980-88

By now, however, there was an external enemy against which to rally the people: Saddam Hussein's Iraq, which had invaded in September 1980. The fervor and sheer numbers of Iranian volunteer soldiers drove back the Iraqis but the war eventually lapsed into years of bitter trench warfare in which chemical weapons were widely used. The war was sustained by ruthless leaders on either side who placed no value on human life. Thousands of Iranian children enlisted as Basij (volunteers who went to the front in school holidays) and died walking through minefields clearing them for soldiers. But the war was also prolonged by direct US support for Saddam Hussein, which kept the two sides in a hellish balance. By the time the war finally collapsed in 1988, it had taken the lives of three-quarters of a million Iranians and maimed hundreds of thousands more.

Pragmatism ascendant 1988-97

When Khomeini was finally persuaded to accept peace with Iraq – a decision he described as like 'drinking hemlock', it was Majlis speaker Ali Rafsanjani who did the persuading. After Khomeini's death in 1989, Rafsanjani's more pragmatic approach came to the fore. Khomeini was replaced as Supreme Leader by Ali Khamenei; Rafsanjani became President. Rafsanjani enforced Islamic law ruthlessly. But he abandoned Khomeini's aim of exporting the revolution to other Muslim countries and concentrated on addressing the economic ruin at home. He tended to do so, however, via measures that hit the poor hard – slashing subsidies, for example – rather than by tackling the corruption of clerics who had creamed off the great houses of the Shah's élite.

Reform 1997-2005

In 1997 the presidential election produced a major surprise, as the token moderate, Muhammad Khatami, won a landslide victory. People relished both his modest demeanor and his talk of reform: his supporters soon won control of the Majlis and he secured an even bigger majority in the presidential election of 2001. Encircled by the clerical establishment, however, even President and Majlis combined had little impact. Hundreds of reforms were introduced, only to be vetoed or hamstrung by the Council of Guardians. Khatami affected social atmosphere rather than political substance – there was greater freedom of speech, more room for women to maneuver, the educated young felt at last that they could breathe. But his impotence on the economy – and perhaps also the US refusal to encourage reform by relaxing its embargo – fatally undermined him.

Reaction 2005-
Many reformists were banned by the Council of Guardians from standing in the 2004 Majlis elections, with the result that hardliners took control. And in the 2005 presidential election, faced with the establishment choice of Rafsanjani or the maverick outsider Mahmoud Ahmadinejad, people overwhelmingly opted for the latter, without a clear sense of the abrasive, ultra-conservative package he was to present. Ahmadinejad clamped down at home and was confrontational abroad, showing particular defiance about maintaining Iran's nuclear-power program in the teeth of UN sanctions imposed in December 2006 and overt threats from Washington.

The underlying trend in Iran remains towards reform and greater democratic health. The great danger is that this will be undermined by military confrontation, which serves to strengthen the position of hardliners.

BRIEF HISTORY **44**

A Short History of Free Speech in China
From Confucius through the Cultural Revolution to Tian'anmen Square and beyond.

200 BCE The legacy of Confucius
From 200 BCE to the beginning of the 20th century, Chinese statecraft was based on the ideas of Kung Fu-tzu (known in the West as Confucius), a political thinker who lived in the fifth century BCE. Confucian thinking stressed ethics. It regarded order and stability as essential to enable people to behave in a moral way. Despising violence and force, it also

looked down upon profit and commerce. China did not develop an idea of rights that were inherent and natural to the individual as had arisen in western Europe. However, the ideally organized Confucian society was supposed to provide social welfare and just treatment. People were expected to know their place – kings ruled over subjects, fathers over children, husbands over wives. The powerful were expected to behave with benevolence and failure to do so could result in forfeiture of power. Of course, the reality was often different. Nevertheless, for much of the last two millennia, this system allowed a civilization to flourish and a variety of thinkers of many persuasions to debate ideas.

1842 Imperialism and new thinking

China's relations with the outside world changed profoundly in the 19th century as European empires expanded. Britain and China clashed in the Opium War, culminating in the Treaty of Nanjing in 1842 – a humiliating agreement forcing China to open up territory and trading rights to the West. These 'unequal treaties' have not been forgotten even today, and shape debates about free trade and globalization. For most of the next century, portions of Chinese territory were under foreign control. It was often in the imperialist-controlled areas where China's dissidents hid from their own governments and published their radical thoughts.

Imperialism had a profound effect on political thinkers in late 19th and early 20th century China as they encountered liberalism, social Darwinism and Christianity. Yan Fu drew on ideas of evolution to argue that China was a nation struggling against others for survival. Thinkers argued for a greater role for individual rights than in pre-modern China, but also valued collective action. The Qing (pronounced 'ching') dynasty – initially ambivalent about these reforms – swiftly changed tack after various military defeats between 1895 and 1900, and tried to carve out a new role for China as one sovereign state among many. Popular discontent was too great to save the dynasty, and it was swept away in the revolution of 1911. China was officially reconstituted as a modern republic at the start of 1912.

1919 The May Fourth Movement

On 4 May 1919, 3,000 students demonstrated at the Tian'anmen, the gate at the front of the Forbidden City in Beijing (the palace complex of the Ming and Qing dynasties). Incensed at the news that the Treaty of Versailles was not going to hand back former German colonies on Chinese soil, but award them to Japan instead, they burned down the house of a pro-Japanese government minister. This one demonstration, lasting only a few hours, remains legendary. Called the 'May Fourth Movement', it became shorthand for perhaps the most liberal and fruitful period in modern Chinese history.

Between 1915 and the early 1930s reform-minded Chinese looked in every possible direction for solutions to the twin problems of militarism and imperialism that they felt needed to be overcome to 'save the nation'. The most radical – including members of the fledgling Chinese Communist Party (CCP) – argued that Confucianism was at the root of China's problems and must be utterly rejected. Overall, the era was shaped by a shared agenda among reformers for 'science and democracy'. But the promise of the May Fourth era was dealt a crushing blow by the horrifying Japanese war against China (1937-45), which killed more than 20 million Chinese and hardened political attitudes against pluralism.

1949 Mao Zedong and 'democratic dictatorship'

Mao Zedong – who would rule all of China for more than a quarter-century – left his southern rural home as a young man and became involved in the May Fourth Movement while working in the Beijing University library. He was a founding member of the CCP in 1921 and followed it through its persecution by the Nationalist Government (founded by Chiang Kaishek in 1927), the Long March northwards (1934-35), the war with Japan (1937-45), and then the civil war with the Nationalists (1946-49).

The CCP's adoption of the Bolshevik ideas of 'democratic dictatorship' meant that open dialogue within the Party became restricted. After the CCP's victory in 1949, the tentative moves toward freedom of speech – already restricted by the war with Japan – were mostly cut off. There were short windows of opportunity, such as the Hundred Flowers Movement in May 1957, when the public were encouraged by Mao to speak out about problems. But when the criticisms turned out to be more savage than expected, the Movement was ended and millions of critics were sent into internal exile. The Cultural Revolution (1966-76) sought to encourage the young and re-energize Mao's revolutionary vision. In the process it fueled a near-theological cult of Mao's personality and created an atmosphere of paranoia that led to denunciations, murders and suicides across China. Schools and universities were shut down, thereby robbing a generation of its chance of education.

1976 Deng Xiaoping: China opens for business

The death of Mao in 1976 was followed swiftly by the arrest of the 'Gang of Four', the ultra-radical supporters of Cultural Revolution policies. People who had been persecuted were rehabilitated, and a genre of writing known as 'scar' literature allowed people to express their sufferings. Deng Xiaoping – one of the longest survivors in the CCP – eased himself into paramount power by 1978, and until the early 1990s was the prime force behind China's economic reforms.

Deng believed that the nation's progress was dependent on a well-educated population. As part of the reform process, official sanction was given to more open debate and discussion. Throughout the 1980s, students demonstrated publicly, newspapers and radio shows began to discuss social problems openly, and it became possible once again to travel and study abroad. The daring documentary 'River Elegy' (Heshang) was broadcast on national Chinese television in 1988, arguing that China had been led astray by Mao, the false 'peasant emperor', and that the country needed to return to the message of the May Fourth Movement – 'science and democracy'.

1989 Tian'anmen Square and beyond

By 1989, Deng's economic reforms had contributed to massive growth, but had also led to spiraling inflation and discontent. Demonstrations of workers and students demanding more democracy appeared in many cities in the spring of 1989. While most were dispelled peacefully, Tian'anmen Square in Beijing proved the exception. With up to a million protesters at its height, this demonstration was co-ordinated to start on the 70th anniversary of the original May Fourth demonstration so as to point out that the CCP's founders (some of whose contemporaries were now China's leaders) had once been angry radicals standing in the same spot seven decades before. Despite attempts to negotiate, the demonstrations were ended with bloodshed when tanks rolled into the Square on the night of 4 June.

Tian'anmen Square now shapes popular understanding of the Chinese Government in the West. However, it was not the end of openness in China (though the period from 1989 to 1992 was highly repressive). China is slowly opening up a space for discussion in a way that was difficult to imagine in 1989. Criticism of one-party rule is still impossible but there is increasingly wide discussion about policy. Indigenous NGOs have mushroomed: between 1965 and 1996 national social associations grew from 100 to 1,800 while local groups ballooned from 6,000 to 200,000. Environmentalists and activists for HIV and AIDS awareness are among those who are opening up political campaigning space.

The Divided States of Latin America

History, culture and poverty unite as well as divide the peoples of Latin America. But their diversity has been exploited to promote division rather than solidarity, uniformity rather than unity.

Origins

The two great empires, Aztec in Mexico and Inca in Peru, controlled a relatively small number of the 25 million people thought to be living on the continent when Columbus bumped into it in 1492. Prior to the Aztecs, sophisticated cultures had been developed by the Maya to the south and by the Olmecs along the coast of the Gulf of Mexico. Before the Inca in the Andean highlands, the Nasca and Chimu peoples organized complex systems of irrigation along the lowland coastal strips of Ecuador and Peru. Some estimates suggest that in the Amazon basin there were 2,000 different groups and seven million people. Evidence is only now emerging of the many groups inhabiting the grasslands of southern Brazil, Uruguay and Argentina. The ancestry of the majority of Latin Americans today derives from all of these peoples.

Colonies

European colonizers exploited the diversity of indigenous groups, even persuading them to fight on the side of the invaders. In 1493 the Papal edict Inter Caetera pronounced that 'barbarous nations be overthrown'. The Treaty of Tordesilles was signed by the Spanish and Portuguese crowns in 1494 and divided the continent between them – roughly along the current borders of Brazil. A genocide of indigenous peoples followed, to the point where slave labor had to be brought in from Africa, not just to Brazil and the Caribbean but right across the continent. The feudal structures of Europe were replicated in colonies designed to extract their natural wealth – particularly silver and sugar – thereby enriching both the imperial rulers and their local agents.

Independence

Following the US Declaration of Independence in 1776, independence movements proliferated in Latin America. They were for the most part controlled by the local European – 'Creole' – élites, which cultivated populist nationalism to strengthen their own position. They wanted to preserve the administrative subdivisions and vast landed estates of the old feudal order, and thus their own wealth and privilege. However, when the most prominent 'liberator', Simon Bolivar, became the first President of Colombia in 1819, it included present-day Ecuador, Panama and Venezuela. Bolivar went on to control Peru – Upper Peru was named Bolivia in his honor in 1825 – in pursuit of his vision of a single Andean republic, which never materialized. The vast territory of the former Portuguese colony became the state of Brazil.

Dependence

In 1823 President James Monroe told the US Congress that 'the American continents... are henceforth not to be considered as subjects for future colonization by any European powers'. The US declared itself protector of the Americas, thereby discouraging independent alliances between Latin American nations. The 'Monroe Doctrine' has informed US foreign policy ever since, justifying repeated interventions into its own 'back yard'. In 1948 the Organization of American States (OAS) was founded, dominated by the US and the politics of the Cold War – although Latin American states have far more in common with each other than with the US. Only with the Cuban Revolution in 1959 was there a concerted effort to link Latin American countries independently from the US. Failure was symbolized by the death of Che Guevara, an Argentinean, while trying to promote revolution in Bolivia in 1967.

Liberation

Since the end of the Cold War the official emphasis in Latin America, as elsewhere, has been on trade. The US aim is to create a single Free Trade Area of the Americas (FTAA), dominated by US business interests, supported by Mexico, Colombia and Chile but excluding Cuba.

Counterposed to this is the Bolivarian Alternative for the People of Our America (ALBA), which was initially proposed by Venezuelan leader Hugo Chávez and advocates social, political and economic integration between the countries of Latin America and the Caribbean; Venezuela, Cuba, Nicaragua, Bolivia, Dominica, Antigua & Barbuda and St Vincent & the Grenadines have so far signed up. The willingness of the Venezuelans to offer their oil bounty at discount prices to Latin American allies is proving a major counterweight to the traditional hulking hegemony of the US in the region. The election of Leftist regimes (of varying hues of radicalism) in Brazil, Argentina, Uruguay, Chile, Ecuador, Nicaragua and Bolivia has finally put the 'Bolivarian' project onto Latin America's 21st-century agenda.

A Brief History of Britain's 'Adventures' in Ireland...

... and how more than eight centuries of resistance finally arrived at peace.

Beyond the Pale

Gaelic Ireland's relatively egalitarian social system holds land in common, elects its kings – and its culture produces the oldest vernacular epic in west European literature, the Tain Bo Cuaihge. From 1169 Ireland is invaded for the first time by the Normans under King Henry II of England, who has already been 'given' the country by Pope Adrian IV (an Englishman). Dublin is captured and colonized, but English control over the next three centuries seldom extends further than the small strip of land around Dublin called the Pale. Henry VIII makes more headway, forcing local kings to trade in their native titles for anglicized ones – so Conn Bacach O'Neill of Tir Eoghain becomes the first Earl of Tyrone.

Still, Ireland is hard to subdue. The colonizing of Ulster, first disastrously attempted by the Elizabethans, takes off in 1607 – the same year as the first boats of colonists leave for the New World. Colonizers, who include everyone from fugitive criminals to City of London financiers, are required to clear their estates completely of native Irish but in practice find they need them as laborers.

The judgment of God

All colonists have to take an oath of allegiance to Protestantism as a condition of getting their land. The dispossessed native Irish are Catholic, which gives them a double reason for resentment. In 1641 this turns to rebellion – 12,000 settlers are killed, most from exposure and hunger as they straggle towards safer territory. The Catholic rebellion is put down the following year but real revenge comes after the English Civil War when Oliver Cromwell's army puts all but 30 people of the town of Drogheda to the sword – 2,600 of them. 'I am persuaded,' he says, 'that this is the righteous judgment of God upon those barbarous wretches...' He swiftly follows it with another massacre at Wexford. Between 1641 and 1651 the Irish population is halved – 616,000 die as a result of conflict, hunger and disease, while 100,000 are transported, mostly to the West Indies. All Catholics in Ulster have their land confiscated. By the 1680s the plantation of Ulster has succeeded.

In 1685 James II embarks on a vigorous program to recatholicize his kingdoms. His blundering leads the English aristocracy to invite the Dutch Prince of Orange to become King William III. The showdown between James and William takes place in the north of Ireland. The Protestant towns of Derry and Enniskillen hold out bravely against siege by a Catholic army. Then King William himself leads his army to victory at the Battle of the Boyne in 1691. Victory is consolidated the following year at the even bloodier battle of Aughrim whose anniversary, 12 July, is still the most important celebration in the Ulster Protestant calendar.

Fury and famine

From 1691 onwards, penal laws dispossess Catholics and dissenting Protestants of their land and deny them religious freedom, voting rights and access to education. Ireland becomes a colonial economy, run by a small Protestant landowning caste who extract rent from the peasants in the form of foodstuffs and export it to England.

The first idealistic rebellion is staged in 1798 by the United Irishmen, whose leading lights are Presbyterians passionate about winning political rights for Catholics. They pursue legal reforms until the Government decides against Catholic emancipation but then take up arms. Despite initial success, the insurrection is savagely crushed and 30,000 die. Two years later the Act of Union of Britain and Ireland is passed and the Irish Parliament abolished – though Catholic emancipation is finally won in 1829. The revolutions that sweep Europe in 1848 produce a tiny echo in the Young Irelander movement. But their call to arms has no chance of success in a country gripped by an appalling famine. The potato crop, on which the rural Irish depend, fails through blight from 1846 onwards. The Great Famine is not purely a natural disaster, though: peasants produce enough food but must sell it to pay their rent; throughout the Famine ships leave Ireland for England laden with grain and cattle. More than a million people die and at least as many emigrate to the US.

Fenians and home rulers

By the 1860s half of Ireland is owned by just 750 people, nearly all of them Protestants. Tenant farmers are regularly evicted to benefit the landowners. It is against this backdrop that the Fenian and Land League rebellions take place. The Fenians originate in New York but spread as a secret oath-bound movement in Ireland during the 1860s. In 1867 a group of American Civil War veterans travel to Ireland and inspire the declaration of an Irish Republic. The rebellion is easily put down but the movement achieves greater notoriety later by violent attempts to free its members from English prisons. 'Fenian' remains a common term of abuse applied by Protestants to nationalist Catholics to the present day.

The Irish Land League, formed in 1879, secures its goal of fair rent and fixed tenure for farmers largely by nonviolent direct action. Protestants are prominently involved in the land campaign but from the 1880s onwards the religious divide widens as the campaign for 'home rule' gains momentum. In 1884 voting rights are extended to most adult men in the UK and from then on Irish nationalists regularly win 80 per cent of Irish parliamentary seats. Because they often hold the balance of power at Westminster they are promised home rule – devolution of some powers to an Irish Assembly.

The Easter Rising and the Free State

The first two Home Rule bills are voted down – the British Conservative Party has now taken on the name Unionist and made continued rule over Ireland a fundamental part of its identity. But in 1912, as Irish Nationalists again hold the balance of power, the Liberal Government introduces a Home Rule bill which seems certain to become law in 1914. Outraged Irish loyalists launch the Ulster Volunteer Force (UVF) and recruit a 100,000-strong paramilitary force pledged to seize control of Ulster if home rule becomes reality. The Government concedes that special arrangements will be made for Ulster once the First World War is over. Now it is nationalists' turn to despair. Convinced that constitutional methods are doomed to failure, a small group of republicans stage the Easter Rising in 1916, seizing key buildings in Dublin and holding them for a week. The execution of 15 of its leaders (together with conscription for the killing fields of France) rallies Irish public opinion behind the rebels: the republican party, Sinn Féin, wins the first post-war election in 1918 by a landslide. Its members refuse to go to Westminster and form their own parliament, Dail Eireann. A guerrilla war ensues between the Irish Republican Army and British forces, with the IRA controlling much of the country.

Britain's political response is the Better Government of Ireland Act of 1920, which divides Ireland in two (the three most Catholic counties in Ulster are left out of the new statelet to ensure a Protestant majority). A year later Sinn Féin representatives negotiate a treaty under which Britain withdraws from the new Irish Free State. The IRA leader Michael Collins also signs up but a year-long civil war follows between pro-treaty and anti-treaty forces. Collins is assassinated but his side wins the day.

Civil rights in the Orange state

Northern Ireland is now a province of the UK but is ruled by its own parliament, Stormont, which is dominated by Protestants not just because the border was designed to leave them in a two-to-one majority but also because they use every means to entrench and expand their power at Catholics' expense. Catholics suffer systematic discrimination in employment and housing. Stormont gives itself draconian security powers, enforced by an overwhelmingly Protestant police and judiciary.

In the 1960s, the Northern Ireland Civil Rights Association – organized on non-sectarian lines – is formed, inspired by Martin Luther King and the black battle for civil rights in the US. Its demands for one person one vote and freedom from discrimination meet with widespread support but also with violence from extreme loyalists, who attack civil-rights marches and relaunch the paramilitary UVF.

Pro-civil-rights feeling in working-class Catholic areas runs ever higher and when rioting breaks out in Derry and Belfast the British Government sends in troops as a temporary measure to restore order.

Bloody Sunday

The British start trying to end discrimination in housing and local elections but the rioting increases during 1970 and 1971, not least because loyalist pogroms against Catholics lead to the re-emergence of the IRA. Catholics' initial welcome for British troops soon dissipates as the Army cracks down hard on civil-rights protest. When internment without trial is introduced in 1971 nearly all those imprisoned are Catholic and even the few Protestants interned are civil-rights activists. Internment sparks further protests and at a march in Derry in January 1972 13 civilians are shot dead by British soldiers from the Parachute Regiment – the incident infamous as Bloody Sunday. Two months later Stormont is suspended and direct rule from Westminster is imposed. This is seen as a short-term measure but Northern Ireland will be governed in this way through to the 1990s.

Hunger strikes and handshakes

Britain's first attempt to restore local rule – shared between Protestants and Catholics – is brought down by a loyalist workers' strike in 1974. For the next decade Britain sees the problem as one of law and order rather than politics: local security forces are strengthened and IRA and loyalist paramilitaries are treated as common criminals. The latter policy backfires in 1981 when republican prisoners go on hunger strike to demand 'political' status. As ten men starve to death without the Thatcher Government giving ground, the republican cause wins significant support worldwide; two of the hunger strikers are elected to the Irish Parliament and one, Bobby Sands, to the British Parliament. The IRA's political wing, Sinn Féin, takes renewed interest in democratic politics, supplementing the 'bullet' with the 'ballot box'. Partly to counter this new republican threat Britain sets up another elected assembly in 1982 – but this time nationalist members refuse to take their seats.

In 1985 the Anglo-Irish Agreement sees the British Government for the first time conceding a special role for the Irish Republic while the Irish Government agrees that the country can be reunited only with the consent of the majority in the North. The Agreement is reached without consulting unionists: their sense of betrayal increases, as does loyalist paramilitary violence.

The Good Friday Agreement

Talks between the constitutional parties founder and Northern Ireland seems stalemated – until talks between moderate nationalist leader John Hume and Sinn Féin leader Gerry Adams, followed by the Downing Street Declaration at the end of 1993, reawaken hopes that the conflict can be resolved. A new Ulster Unionist leader, David Trimble, despite hardline initial rhetoric, participates in all-party negotiations that eventually produce the historic Belfast or Good Friday Agreement of 1998. The Agreement is wide-ranging, committing all parties to using 'exclusively peaceful and democratic means', establishing a Northern Ireland legislative Assembly and recognizing the birthright of all the people of Northern Ireland to identify themselves and be accepted as Irish or British, or both. The Agreement is approved in separate referenda in the Irish Republic and Northern Ireland a few weeks later.

Peace at last

In the ensuing years there are still many thorny issues to work through – in particular the decommissioning of paramilitary weapons and the initially implacable opposition of Ian Paisley's Democratic Unionist Party (DUP). But essentially the war is over. The Irish Republic's territorial claim to Northern Ireland is dropped from its constitution in 1999. Assembly elections in 2003 see the most extreme parties on either side – Sinn Féin and the DUP emerge as victors. Paradoxically this clear mandate seems to make progress on agreeing to share power more possible over the next few years. The IRA formally announces an end to its armed campaign in 2005. On 8 May 2007 home rule finally returns to Northern Ireland; DUP leader Ian Paisley becomes First Minister and Sinn Féin's Martin McGuinness Deputy First Minister.

Global Institutions 47-50

BRIEF HISTORY **47**

A Brief History of the United Nations...

...from the first stirrings of international co-operation to the Millennium Development Goals.

Early signs

In the 16th century the 'known' world came to be dominated by violent, seagoing and increasingly nationalist European empires: Spain, Portugal, France, Britain and the Netherlands in particular. They attempted to carve up the planet into colonies that would replicate the rivalries and fuel the wealth of European rulers. The idea of a supranational 'plurality' of sovereign (European) nation-states that might prevent constant wars between them was first set out at the Peace of Westphalia in 1648. It was developed by a 'Holy Alliance' following the final demise of Napoleon's imperial ambitions in 1815.

First steps

The lethal results of industrialized weaponry led to the foundation of the Red Cross at a conference of 16 countries in Geneva in 1863 – the first Geneva Convention of 1864 sought to protect the sick and wounded in time of war. As international trade and communications grew, commercial interests led to the foundation of the International Telegraph Union in 1865 and the Universal Postal Union in 1874 (both survive today as 'specialized agencies' of the UN). In 1899 an International Peace Conference was held in The Hague. It adopted a Convention

UN PHOTO

The opening session of the League of
Nations in Geneva, 15 November 1920.

for the Pacific Settlement of International Disputes and established the
Permanent Court of Arbitration, which began work in 1902.

War means peace

Nonetheless, in 1914 the Great War – 'to end all wars' – began in
Europe. Once the carnage was complete in 1918, the Treaty of Versailles
was imposed on Germany by the victors, including Britain, France and
the US. The Treaty brought the League of Nations into being on 10
January 1920 'to promote international co-operation and to achieve
peace and security'. Though US President Woodrow Wilson had been
an architect of the Treaty, Congress refused to ratify it, on the grounds
that it would intrude on its own power, and as a result the US did not join
the League. Defeated Germany was excluded and so was revolutionary
Russia. Britain and France, still with their colonies in tow, were the
only 'Great Powers' left.

Rogue states

In 1921 the League successfully brokered an accord – which is still
in force today – between Finland and Sweden on the disputed Åland
Islands. But in 1923 it failed to prevent France from invading the Ruhr
region of Germany in search of unpaid war reparations. Work had begun
on the vast Palais des Nations in Geneva (now occupied by the UN) in
1929 when the economic Great Depression struck worldwide and was
exacerbated by 'beggar-thy-neighbor' national trading policies. A long-

delayed World Disarmament Conference failed almost as soon as it began in 1932. The League again proved impotent when Japan invaded Chinese Manchuria in 1931, and when Italy invaded Abyssinia (Ethiopia) in 1935. In 1933 Hitler came to power in Germany and in 1938 invaded Czechoslovakia. The League's doctrine of 'collective security' between sovereign nation-states translated into the appeasement of expansionist fascism in Italy, Germany and Japan. No concerted attempt was made to forestall the impending Nazi genocide of the Jews in Europe.

Peace means war

A Second World War began in Europe in 1939 when Germany went on to invade Poland. As early as August 1941 – even before the US had joined the war – US President Roosevelt and British Prime Minister Churchill met on a warship 'somewhere at sea' to sign the Atlantic Charter. It proposed a set of principles that became the basis for all future discussions. On 1 January 1942, 26 nations – in fact, the Allies – met in Washington DC to sign the 'Declaration by United Nations'. The first blueprint of the UN was prepared at a conference organized by the US at the Dumbarton Oaks mansion in Washington DC in 1944. It was attended by Britain, the Soviet Union (which had lost upwards of 20 million people in the war) and China – the 'four horsemen' who would later be joined by liberated France in declaring themselves the Permanent Five members of the Security Council.

We, the rulers

Delegates of the 50 nations that had declared war on the fascist Axis were invited to San Francisco on 25 April 1945. The UN logo incorporated a map of the world reputedly designed to obscure Argentina, which had not declared war on the Axis but was invited nonetheless. On 28 April Mussolini was shot while attempting to flee Italy, and on 30 April Hitler shot himself in Berlin. The UN Charter, substantially unchanged from Dumbarton Oaks, was adopted on 25 June in the San Francisco Opera House. On 6 August the US detonated one atomic bomb over Hiroshima and on 9 August another over Nagasaki, Japan, bringing the war in the Pacific to a devastating end. The UN was officially founded on 24 October, when its Charter was ratified by the five permanent members of the Security Council and the majority of other signatories. The document – which began: 'We the Peoples of the United Nations...' – was flown to Washington DC in a fireproof strongbox with its own parachute.

Control

The League of Nations finally expired at a requiem Assembly on 18 April 1946. Unlike the League, the UN would be controlled by the

Permanent Five of the Security Council. The Soviet Union conceded US pre-eminence – and the location of UN headquarters in New York – in exchange for Soviet dominance over Eastern Europe and veto rights for the Permanent Five. However, after the revolutionary People's Republic of China was declared in 1949, the Republic of China (Taiwan today) continued to occupy the 'China' seat until 1971 – so one of the Permanent Five was effectively absent. Another, the Soviet Union, was 'diplomatically' absent in 1950 when the Security Council endorsed the invasion of Korea by US troops – at least two million people died in the three-year 'forgotten conflict' that followed.

Cold War
An undeclared Cold War had already broken out between the two post-war 'superpowers', the US and the Soviet Union. It was to cripple the UN for the next 40 years, even though many UN members, mostly in the South, formed a 'Non Aligned' group. The superpowers pursued the Cold War primarily through a nuclear arms race and by proxy in a plethora of conflicts elsewhere in the world. Only on rare occasions, such as the Berlin airlift in 1948 and the Cuban missile crisis in 1962, were they in any real danger of direct military confrontation with each other.

Impotent assembly
Although every UN member had an equal vote at the General Assembly, that body was left powerless. It adopted its first resolution on 24 January 1946, focusing on the elimination of weapons of mass destruction. But, unlike the Security Council, its resolutions were not binding on all UN members and had no legal force. It had limited membership and scope. Japan did not join until 1956; the two halves of divided Germany until 1973. Large parts of Africa and Asia (and thus of the world's population) were still colonies. The economic and financial institutions thought necessary for post-war reconstruction, and to prevent a recurrence of the Depression, were hived off to the World Bank, the International Monetary Fund (IMF) and the General Agreement on Tariffs and Trade (GATT). Here the US held an exclusive financial veto of its own – the Soviet Union and China did not participate. These institutions became economic weapons in the Cold War.

A third world
In 1947 India became independent from Britain – and at the end of 1948 the General Assembly adopted the Universal Declaration of Human Rights. These two events helped to reshape the dynamics of the UN. Decolonization became a priority. Newly independent countries eventually formed a 'third world' majority at the General Assembly.

Hopes were high that a 'new world economic order' would bring prosperity and respect to impoverished former colonies. In 1964 the UN Conference on Trade and Development (UNCTAD) was set up, largely at the behest of these countries. UNICEF (children), UNESCO (education), UNHCR (refugees) and the World Health Organization (WHO) became more active – though they were reliant on voluntary contributions for funds. Concerted action prompted by the UN began to prove effective, such as in the fight against smallpox which the WHO eventually declared eradicated in 1980.

What peace to keep?

The first UN 'observer mission' was established in Palestine in June 1948. In 1956 the first UN peacekeeping force was formed following a disastrous attempt by Britain, France and Israel to occupy the Suez Canal. In 1961 UN Secretary-General Dag Hammarskjöld was killed in an airplane crash while on a peacekeeping mission to the Congo. In 1964 a peacekeeping force was dispatched to Cyprus. Without troops of its own, the UN was required to 'keep' rather than 'make' peace; a distinction that proved difficult to draw on the ground. The superpowers accelerated their nuclear arms race. A lucrative trade in conventional weapons was promoted by the Permanent Five themselves. No sustained attempt was made to act on Article 11 of the Charter, which gives the General Assembly powers to consider 'the principles governing disarmament and the regulation of armaments'.

Lost decades

The emphasis shifted towards conferences and declarations. The first UN Environment Conference was held in Stockholm in 1972; the first conference on women in Mexico City in 1975. The late 1970s and early 1980s can be seen as the worst period in UN history. The Heritage Foundation, advisors to the Reagan Administration, published a study in 1982 concluding: 'A world without the UN would be a better world' and significant antipathy towards UN institutions from the Reagan and Thatcher governments culminated in the withdrawal of the US and Britain from the UN Educational, Science and Cultural Organization in 1984.

Some practical advances were made, like the Treaty on the Protection of the Ozone Layer – the 'Montreal Protocol' – in 1987 and the Comprehensive Nuclear Test Ban Treaty in 1996. The UN became a skilful facilitator of elections, as in Cambodia in 1993 and South Africa in 1994. But hopes for greater parity between people and nations evaporated in a cloud of debt and economic orthodoxy. The 'peace dividend' anticipated with the end of the Cold War in 1989 was quickly spent by the US-led (and UN-endorsed) war against Iraq in 1991, followed by savage UN sanctions. Although the membership of the Security Council had been increased from 11 to 15 in 1965, any further attempt at significant reform foundered on the veto of the Permanent Five.

Humanitarian heyday

The zenith of UN humanitarian intervention was reached in the early 1990s. There was a historical high of 29 in the number of wars in 1992-93. Although most were in developing countries, war had also returned to Europe – in former Yugoslavia – for the first time since the 1940s.

An important precedent was set following the first Gulf War. This had led to the flight of 1.5 million Kurdish refugees into the mountains on Iraq's border with Turkey. In April 1991, the Security Council passed a landmark resolution (No 688) linking the violation of human rights to threats to international peace and security. This demanded that immediate access be allowed to those in need of assistance 'in all parts of Iraq', ignoring the principle of national sovereignty that had always taken precedence before.

Some terrible cases from the mid-1990s showed the limits of UN intervention. In Somalia massive US military involvement helped save victims of a famine in 1992 caused by the country's devastation by warlords – the first occasion on which an internal humanitarian crisis was defined by the UN Security Council as a threat to international peace. A smaller peacekeeping operation took over in mid-1993 but UN forces became embroiled in fighting one of the Somali leaders, General Mohamed Farah Aideed, thereby forfeiting any claim to impartiality. US marines were killed in a high-profile incident and the US unilaterally withdrew its troops, leaving the UN with egg on its face and Somalia with a civil war that has never been resolved. Then came arguably the worst Security Council and UN failure in its history: the appalling spectacle in April 1994 of UN peacekeepers in Rwanda powerless to stop the extremist Hutu genocide. If Rwanda were not enough of an indictment, in 1995, Bosnian-Serbs massacred 8,000 people at Srebrenica with UN peacekeepers standing helplessly by. The UN as a force for intervention had both over-reached and under-reached itself.

The Millennium Development Goals

In 2000 the UN held a Millennium Summit in New York in what was the biggest gathering of world leaders in history to that point. Inevitably there was plenty of optimistic rhetoric about creating a better world. More substantially, there was also commitment to a series of Millennium Development Goals (MDGs) to be achieved by

2015 – and not just the broad aims (among them eradicating extreme poverty and hunger, achieving universal primary education, and promoting gender equality) but specific ambitious targets by which they were to be measured. The drive towards the MDGs continues and remains a vital priority for the UN, and could yet save and improve the lives of millions, though almost none of the targets will be completely met.

But the broader hopes of greater cohesion and peace largely evaporated with the 9/11 attacks on the US. The (UN-endorsed) invasion of Afghanistan was followed

UN HQ lit up for the 50th anniversary in 1995.

by the illegal invasion of Iraq in 2003 (on which the Security Council could not agree). The damage to the UN was incalculable and it is yet to be seen how the international organization will function effectively in a world in which the US is currently the only hyperpower.

Reform and the future

The world in which the UN now operates is radically different from the one in which it was created. The system has evolved and adapted to new circumstances, but many believe that it is in need of major repair. A significant attempt at structural reform was made by UN Secretary-General Kofi Annan in the 60th anniversary year, 2005 – which would have included the expansion of the Security Council to include new permanent (though non-veto-holding) members. The reform package made serious headway but was ultimately smashed on to the rocks by the hostile appointee of the Bush Administration, John Bolton.

Those who want system replacement or radical overhaul, and have no patience with incremental change via diplomacy, will probably have to wait for the kind of global conflagration that sunk the League in 1939.

BRIEF HISTORY **48**

UN Secretaries-General

The UN is only as effective as national governments allow it to be. But it still needs good leadership. A look at the eight men who have held the job of World's Top Civil Servant, from the Visionary to the Sheep, the Campaigner to the Crook.

UN PHOTO

Trygve Lie (Norway) 1946-52

The first Secretary-General (SG) was by far the most outspoken. His strength reflected the high hopes for the new organization in the aftermath of a devastating war. But Lie's readiness to wade in with his own opinions on any and every world issue had mixed results. In supporting (in vain) Communist China's right to take its seat at the UN after the 1949 Revolution he was admirably clear-sighted and prepared to stand up to the US. But he cravenly propitiated the McCarthyist witch-hunt by allowing the FBI to vet the UN's American employees. And ultimately his passionate advocacy of the US/UN position in the Korean War won him the enmity of the Soviet Union, which refused to take part in UN activities when he was present, forcing him to resign. Lie greeted his successor with the words: 'You are about to enter the most impossible job on this earth.'

UN PHOTO / JO

Dag Hammarskjöld (Sweden) 1953-61

Hammarskjöld was the finest of the UN's early leaders. More carefully diplomatic than Lie, he was just as prepared to take independent initiatives and not simply serve the major powers. He behaved with credit during the Suez Crisis when Britain and France were clearly at fault. And he was largely responsible for the whole idea of peacekeeping, which is not provided for in the UN Charter. The first UN peacekeeping force was deployed in Egypt in 1956. The perils of peacekeeping were soon evident during his intervention in the civil war following the Belgian Congo's independence in 1960. The UN soon found itself 'taking sides' and imposing 'peace' through military force. The intervention also cost Hammarskjöld his life – he died in a suspicious plane crash in Northern Rhodesia while on his way to meet secessionist rebels. His Congo policy incurred the wrath of the Soviet Union. Hammarskjöld's idealistic response was that he was there to serve the interests not of the great powers but of the small states.

U Thant (Burma) 1961-71

The major powers now informally agreed that no future SG should have the power and presence of Hammarskjöld. U Thant was the first fruit of that change of policy, being quiet and bureaucratically inclined, almost never speaking at Security Council meetings. He presided over 10 further years of Cold War in which the UN was frozen into immobility on the peace-and-security front. But these were also the years in which newly independent developing countries joined the organization in droves, full of hope that they could harness it in the cause of global

UN PHOTO / YUTAKA NAGATA

justice and equality. The presence of a leader from the South symbolized that new phase for the UN, as did U Thant's own most daring initiative – his repeated and passionate criticism of the US war in Vietnam, which drew the scathing comment from US Secretary of State Dean Rush: 'Who do you think you are, a country?'

UN PHOTO / MILTON GRANT

Kurt Waldheim (Austria) 1972-81

Waldheim will be remembered less for his work at the UN than for the accusations of involvement in Nazi war crimes which dogged his later career as President of Austria. He was arguably the least distinguished of all the UN's leaders. Publicly diplomatic, even obsequious to the major powers – he was described as behaving 'like a head waiter in a restaurant' – in private he was vain, with a violent temper. During his term the UN Secretariat lapsed in standards as the quality of senior staff was continually diluted by backscratching 'political' appointments and hints of corruption – staff morale in New York sank ever lower.

Javier Pérez de Cuéllar (Peru) 1982-91

Pérez de Cuéllar, a sensitive, soft-spoken aesthete, was bored stiff by budget discussions, which notoriously sent him to sleep. The perilous financial basis of the UN, forever dependent on an increasingly hostile US, was never likely to be turned around in his term of office. And it may also be no coincidence that during his decade the World Bank and the IMF – UN organizations both – started to set the global economic agenda, effectively undermining the UN's humanitarian development work. Pérez de Cuéllar concentrated instead on the 'good offices' function of the SG – the power to act as an independent mediator in international disputes – and achieved some success in later years in this role, most notably in El Salvador. The sudden shift from confrontation to co-operation between the US and the Soviet Union unlocked things during Pérez de Cuéllar's term of office: in the new circumstances of détente, the US suddenly saw that a UN-brokered peace in Central America might be in its interest, while the Soviet Union could seek a UN figleaf to cover its withdrawal from Afghanistan. Pérez de Cuéllar instituted informal meetings of key ambassadors in the Security Council to help it run smoothly.

Boutros Boutros-Ghali (Egypt) 1992-1996

Boutros-Ghali had no patience at all with such informal meetings, seeing them as a waste of his time. He was the most forceful UN leader since Hammarskjöld, as 'hands on' as Pérez de Cuéllar was 'hands off'. But he was unable or unwilling to accept that his only real power was over the international civil service; he felt he should have independent clout in relation to world leaders. This was partly because he was more intellectually gifted than many or most of those world leaders and partly because he was the most experienced diplomat ever to become SG. One of his first tasks was to prepare An Agenda for Peace, laying out the UN's new role in the post-Cold War era – already a more active one than in the past, particularly in Central America. The UN's peacekeeping role certainly took off in the early 1990s. Between 1987 and 1994 the number of peacekeeping operations it was involved in grew from 5 to 17, and the number of troops at its disposal from 9,570 to 73,400. Two major disasters, however, destroyed much of the optimism about the UN's potential role. In Somalia UN forces intervened in an internal humanitarian crisis on the grounds that it was a threat to global security; and in 1993 Boutros-Ghali himself directed an operation aimed at disarming the militias. Things went badly wrong, not least because UN forces ended up fighting a particular warlord and became sucked into the chaos; US soldiers were unilaterally withdrawn and from that point on US confidence in Boutros-Ghali drained away. Worse was to come: in Rwanda in 1994 the world watched UN peacekeepers stand by while genocide was committed. Boutros-Ghali had over-reached himself and the US set itself against his being granted a second five-year term.

Kofi Annan (Ghana) 1997-2006

Kofi Annan was the only Secretary-General appointed from within the UN system – ironically he had been Boutros-Ghali's head of peacekeeping, bearing much of the responsibility for the failure in Rwanda. He was a self-effacing civil servant, quite unlike his predecessor, and yet paradoxically he became the biggest star as SG since Hammarskjöld. In 1998 he staved off an attack on Iraq by flying to meet Saddam Hussein; in 2000 he convened the biggest summit in UN history and oversaw the setting of the Millennium Development Goals; in 2001 he won the Nobel Peace Prize. He also developed the new policy of humanitarian intervention to protect people in serious distress, which became enshrined in 2005 as the 'responsibility to protect'. Nor did he neglect the need for reform within the system, overseeing negotiation of a plausible package, including the expansion of the Security Council, only to see it torpedoed by the US Administration of George W Bush. Annan's problem was also the UN's as a whole – how to deal with the aftermath of 9/11 and in particular the US-led 'War on Terror'. Eventually this led to the crisis over Iraq, and the intense pressure from the US and Britain for a UN resolution approving an attack.

Annan, to his eternal credit, held the line and said overtly in 2004 that the attack was not a legitimate act of 'peace enforcement' under the Charter. The US never forgave him – and did all it could to besmirch him with allegations of corruption that were unjustified.

Ban Ki Moon (South Korea) 2007-

If the US had known how independent-minded Boutros-Ghali and Annan were to prove to be, there is no way they would have been appointed

213

– which speaks volumes about the relationship between the World's One Hyperpower and the World's Top Civil Servant. One of the main concerns in choosing a successor will have been to find someone suitably emollient. The jury is still out on the career diplomat Ban Ki Moon, though he did show leadership in making a dramatic eleventh-hour appearance at the Bali Conference on Climate Change at the end of 2007 to persuade delegates to set aside their differences in the interests of future generations.

BRIEF HISTORY **49**

A Short History of Corporations

A whirlwind ride from the East India Company to ExxonMobil, replete with monopolies, 19th-century bun fights and revolutions.

The first corporations
Prior to the 17th century, the first corporations were created in Europe as not-for-profit entities to build institutions, such as hospitals and universities, for the public good. They had constitutions detailing their duties overseen by the Government. Straying outside these was punishable by law.

Colonial companies
Only in the 17th century did making money become a major focus for corporations. Their wealth was used to finance European colonial expansion. Companies were used by the imperial powers to maintain draconian control of trade, resources and territory in Asia, Africa and the Americas. First in an ignoble line was the East India Company, set up by British merchant adventurers and granted the Royal Charter of Queen Elizabeth I in 1600. Partners combined their personal stock, turning it into company stock to create the world's first commercial corporation. It shipped out gold and silver to Asia in return for spices, textiles and luxury goods. The East India Company expanded into a vast enterprise, conquering India with a total monopoly on trade and all the territorial powers of a government. At its height, it ruled over a fifth of the world's population with a private army of a quarter of a million.

The American Revolution

In America, resentment was brewing against British rule, including corporations that ran American colonies with ruthless monopoly powers. Royal charters decreed that raw material was shipped from the colonies to Britain for manufacture, with the colonies forced to purchase the finished goods. The American Revolutionary War began in 1776 with a determination to rout the British. Adam Smith, the father of free-trade theories, who published *Wealth of Nations* in the same year as the Declaration of Independence (1776), argued that large business associations limit competition: 'The pretence that corporations are necessary to the better government of the trade is without foundation.'

Ending colonial monopoly

After Independence, US corporations, like the British companies before them, were chartered to perform specific public functions – digging canals, building bridges. Their charters lasted between 10 and 40 years, often requiring the termination of the corporation on completion of a specific task, setting limits on commercial interests and prohibiting any corporate participation in the political process. Britain had fiercely protected its own textile industry and forced the Indian market open. In the words of Governor-General William Bendick: 'The bones of the cotton weavers are bleaching the plains of India'. Conditions under the colonial capitalists led to the Rebellion ('Mutiny') of 1857. In 1858 Britain reined in the East India Company, dissolving its territorial power and making India the responsibility of the British Crown. The Company continued trading opium to China, which led to the Opium Wars of the 19th century.

Corporate 'personhood'

Corporations as we know them came to being in Britain with an 1844 Act allowing them to define their own purpose. The power to control them thus passed from the government to the courts. In 1855, shareholders were awarded limited liability: their personal assets were protected from the consequences of their corporate behavior. In 1886 a landmark decision by a US court recognized the corporation as a 'natural person' under law. The 14th amendment to the Constitution: 'no state shall deprive any person of life, liberty or property' – adopted to protect emancipated slaves in the hostile South – was used to defend corporations and strike down regulations.

Free trade

Unchecked capitalism ran rampant, and by the end of the 19th century railroad tycoons and robber barons were in charge of monopolies and

215

cartels. So much so that the health of capitalism itself was threatened. Massive labor unrest was brewing. In the US, antitrust laws to break monopolies were brought in. Taxation and tariffs were raised and state regulation crept in once more. However, one railroad executive observed that regulation was good only 'in order to impress the popular mind with the idea that a great deal is being done, when in reality, very little is intended to be done'.

State intervention

The labor movement; the depression of the 1930s; World War Two; the creation of welfare states in Europe: all of these brought about a resurgence of state intervention. However, European and US corporations controlled land, military forces, ports and railroads in poorer countries. The term 'banana republics' was applied to countries such as Guatemala, where United Fruit backed a right-wing coup in 1953.

Newly independent former European colonies such as India recognized the necessity for controls on corporate activity – they were concerned to protect their domestic industries in the name of development, and to restrict foreign investment.

In the US, social activism in the 1960s pushed forward demands for environmental and labor standards, as well as some break-ups of monopolies. Overall, between 1950 and 1980 social welfare provision and state intervention to regulate economic activity were widely accepted as economic orthodoxy.

The neoliberal era

In the 1970s Milton Friedman and his 'Chicago School' economists developed ultra free-market ideas based on deregulation and privatization that harked back to the laissez-faire capitalism of the 19th century (hence the term 'neoliberalism'). This was to become the economic orthodoxy of globalization. In the early 1980s, the full political resources of corporate America mobilized to regain control of the political agenda and the court system. US President Ronald Reagan and British Prime Minister Margaret Thatcher did their utmost to make the world safe for corporations. They dismantled the social contract through tax cuts, ignoring unemployment, rolling back social welfare and increasing privatization. The debt crisis of 1982 gave the US its chance to dominate the world economy and for the rich nations to re-subordinate the global South. This was managed by proxy through the 'structural adjustment' programs of the World Bank and the International Monetary Fund, which offered loans on condition that economies were opened up to foreign investment and that measures such as food subsidies to help the poor were removed.

Globalization

The power of transnational corporations is greater than that of many nation-states. The most important battles over deregulation take place at the global level with free-trade agreements such as NAFTA and those of the World Trade Organization (WTO). The level of mergers and monopolies are reminiscent of the end of the 19th century. However, now as then, social movements and resistance to unrestrained global capitalism are also growing, questioning the legitimacy of corporate rule.

BRIEF HISTORY **50**

How Bretton Woods Reordered the World...

...and how the IMF and the World Bank have ruled the roost ever since.

The Bretton Woods Conference

In July 1944, as World War Two was drawing to a close, the world's leading politicians – mostly from Northern countries – gathered to set forth notions of how to reorganize the world economy. For the first time in human history almost universal institutions – the International Monetary Fund (IMF), the World Bank and the General Agreement on Tariffs and Trade (GATT) – were established to solve global economic problems. The common view at the Conference was that the depression of the 1930s and the rise of fascism could be traced to the collapse of international trade and isolationist economic policies.

The Conference rejected proposals by the eminent British economist John Maynard Keynes that would have established a world reserve currency administered by a central bank and created a more stable and fair world economy by automatically recycling trade surpluses to finance trade deficits. Keynes' notion did not fit the interests of a US eager to take on the role of the world's economic powerhouse. Instead the Conference opted for a system based on the free movement of capital and goods with the US dollar as the international currency. The Fund and the Bank were limited to managing problems related to deficits and to currency and capital shortages.

Rebuilding Europe

One of the first tasks assigned to these new institutions was to provide the capital to help put the war-ravaged European economies back on their feet. Not only did they lack the resources for such a massive undertaking, but European finance ministries balked at the harsh 'conditionalities' that accompanied support from the IMF as too great an infringement of their sovereign right to shape their domestic economies. So the much looser Marshall Plan was set up to provide US finance to rebuild Europe largely through grants rather than loans. Developing countries now emerging into independence did not fare so well – from the very beginning any loan was accompanied by pressure to keep their economies completely 'open' to foreign goods and capital. In the late 1950s the World Bank was pressured into setting up the International Development Association (IDA) – this would provide 'soft loans' and so head off attempts by the new countries of the Third World to set up an independent funding agency under UN auspices.

New International Economic Order

By the early 1960s the Global South had started demanding a better deal. But political sovereignty did not bring economic independence. Even Latin America (which achieved independence more than a century earlier) was caught in a global economic system established over centuries of colonial pillage. Raw materials were exported at cut-rate prices while manufactured goods were imported from ex-colonial powers. Rallying in such organizations as the Non-Aligned Movement and the Group of 77, they created the United Nations Conference on Trade and Development (UNCTAD) where they argued for fairer terms of trade and more liberal terms for financing development. The North responded with pious declarations of its good intentions – but also with a hard-nosed insistence that the proper forum for any economic changes continued to be the Bretton Woods institutions where they held the balance of power.

By the late 1960s, however, the Bretton Woods dream of a stable monetary system of fixed exchange rates with the US dollar as the only international currency was collapsing under the strain of US trade and budgetary deficits. A guarded optimism took hold in the South, fueled by moderately high growth rates and a boom in the price of Third World-produced primary commodities, particularly oil. This came to

a head in 1974 with the declaration of principles for a New International Economic Order. The response to these sweeping demands for change was a few tinkering, inconsequential reforms.

The Debt Crisis

The windfall surpluses accruing to the oil-producing countries of OPEC during the 1970s – $310 billion for the period of 1972-1977 alone – created a massive recycling problem. Much of this money went into Northern commercial banks who turned around and loaned it to non-oil producing Third World governments desperate to pay escalating fuel bills and fund their development goals. The debt of the non-oil producing Third World increased five-fold between 1973 and 1982, reaching a staggering $612 billion, and the high interest rates of the mid-1980s further exacerbated the problem. Much of this loan money was squandered on ill-considered projects or simply siphoned off by Third World élites into personal accounts in the same Northern banks that had made the original loans.

Money was needed to cushion the blow of high oil prices and pay for grandiose mega-projects, whether a nuclear reactor in the Philippines or Mirage jets in Peru. Commercial bank loans to the Third World increased by 550 per cent from 1973 to 1980. Cash-strapped countries like Peru and Mexico were unable even to pay the interest due on their debts. Northern politicians and bankers began to get nervous that the sheer volume of unpayable loans would undermine the world financial system. They turned to the World Bank and the IMF, who were to restructure developing countries' economies so they could meet their debt obligations. External debt ballooned throughout the 1990s, with Africa's external debt increasing 400 per cent since the IMF and World Bank began managing their economies.

Rollback

The Bank and the Fund have made full use of the new leverage over Third World economies that accrued to them during the debt crisis. The right-wing economic views made popular by the Reagan and Thatcher governments in the US and Britain became the reigning economic

orthodoxy at the Bank and the IMF. They pursued the 'structural adjustment' of the Third World by deflating economies and demanding a withdrawal of government not only from public enterprise but also from basic health and welfare support for the most vulnerable. Exports to earn foreign exchange were privileged over almost all production of food and other goods for domestic use. There is little proof these policies do anything more than help bankers collect interest. In fact competition for scarce export markets holds down prices and depresses wages. The main winners have been Western consumers and transnational corporations who benefit from both low commodity prices and low wages in the Third World. This restructuring was highly successful from the point of view of the private banks who squeezed $178 billion out of the South between 1984 and 1990 alone.

Yet Third World debt continued to grow, reaching $1,300 billion by 1992. Much of this debt had shifted – particularly in the case of Africa – from private banks to the IMF and the World Bank themselves. The level of debt in developing countries continued to grow, totaling $2,500 billion by 2002. Throughout the 1990s, these nations paid off far more debt than they received in new loans. The IMF and World Bank somewhat acknowledged the failure of structural adjustment, when they set up the Heavily Indebted Poor Countries (HIPC) initiative in 1996, meant to make loan payments more 'sustainable.' By 2003, 27 countries were receiving HIPC assistance, but most still spent more on debt repayment than on the welfare of their citizens. A push toward Foreign Direct Investment by these Bretton Woods institutions has done little to decrease debt and poverty. In 1999, investment in developing nations hit $649 billion, but this enormous free flow of capital has left many economies hostage to market forces – which was exactly what Keynes warned world leaders about at Bretton Woods.

The Resistance
The stark fact that the Fund and the Bank now operate with reverse capital flows – in other words they take more money out of the Global South than they put back in – is sobering for those who believed these institutions were there to help. Peoples of what we now call the Majority

World are resisting structural adjustment either through street riots or through less confrontational politics. The collapse of the Argentine economy in 2001 was a direct result of the IMF knocking down trade barriers and privatizing state enterprises. When the export market dried up and they were refused more loans, the economy slid into recession. Millions of Argentineans lost their jobs and savings. At the peak of the crisis, more than half of them lived in poverty. Massive unrest in towns and cities caused riots that toppled successive governments.

Similar protest is coming from the four million people uprooted or to be uprooted by World Bank mega-projects, particularly the building of large dams. Rejection of all things Western is on the rise. Fundamentalism and the politics of ethnic exclusion (from Somalia to India) are turning political costs into military ones. And the Bretton Woods institutions themselves are coming under direct pressure from community activists and environmentalists calling for either reform or outright abolition.

Six decades on, the decisions reached at Bretton Woods need some fundamental rethinking. Even stalwart IMF and World Bank economists are admitting their mistakes. Jeffrey Sachs, mastermind of neoliberal policies in Russia and Latin America, wrote: 'Governments have long since gone bankrupt under the weight of past credits from foreign governments, banks and the World Bank and IMF. These countries have become desperate wards of the IMF... Their debts should be canceled outright and the IMF sent home.'

Opposition to Free Trade throughout the Americas is also on the rise, and governments opposed to the Washington Consensus have been elected in Venezuela, Brazil, Chile and Bolivia. Large demonstrations have become a regular occurrence at meetings of the Bretton Woods institutions since the infamous 1999 Seattle protests against the World Trade Organization (which replaced GATT in 1995). Everywhere they meet, they encounter similar resistance.

About the *New Internationalist*

The *New Internationalist* is an independent not-for-profit publishing co-operative. Our mission is to report on issues of world poverty and inequality; to focus attention on the unjust relationship between the powerful and the powerless worldwide; to debate and campaign for the radical changes necessary if the needs of all are to be met.

We publish informative current affairs titles and popular reference, like the *No-Nonsense Guides* series, complemented by world food, fiction, photography and alternative gift books, as well as calendars and diaries, maps and posters – all with a global justice world view.

We also publish the monthly *New Internationalist* magazine. Each month tackles a different subject such as State of the World's Ocean, Ethical Travel or Indigenous Peoples, exploring each issue in a concise way which is easy to understand. The main articles are packed full of photos, charts and graphs and each magazine also contains music, film and book reviews, country profiles, interviews and news.

To find out more about the *New Internationalist*, subscribe to the magazine or buy any of our books take a look at: **www.newint.org**